Integrated Electronic Health Records:
A Worktext for
Greenway Medical Technologies'
PrimeSUITE®

Second Edition

M. Beth Shanholtzer, MAEd, RHIA

Director, HIM Program
Lord Fairfax Community College, Middletown, VA.

Danielle M. Mbadu, MA, MAEd

INTEGRATED ELECTRONIC HEALTH RECORDS: A WORKTEXT FOR GREENWAY MEDICAL TECHNOLOGIES' PRIMESUITE®, SECOND EDITION

1 2 3 4 5 6 7 8 9 0 RMN/RMN 1 0 9 8 7 6 5 4

ISBN   978-0-07-783484-5
MHID   0-07-783484-4

Senior Vice President, Products & Markets: *Kurt L. Strand*
Vice President, General Manager, Products & Markets: *Martin J. Lange*
Vice President, Content Production & Technology Services: *Kimberly Meriwether David*
Director: *Chad Grall*
Executive Brand Manager: *Natalie J. Ruffatto*
Director of Development: *Rose Koos*
Managing Development Editor: *Michelle L. Flomenhoft*
Digital Product Analyst: *Katherine Ward*
Executive Marketing Manager: *Roxan Kinsey*
Director, Content Production: *Terri Schiesl*
Content Project Manager: *Rick Hecker*
Senior Buyer: *Michael R. McCormick*
Design: *Srdjan Savanovic*
Cover Image: © *Yagi Studio/Getty Images*
Senior Content Licensing Specialist: *Jeremy Cheshareck*
Typeface: *11/13.5 Palatino Roman*
Compositor: *Laserwords Private Limited*
Printer: *R. R. Donnelley*

Library of Congress Control Number: 2013953805

www.mhhe.com

brief contents

contents

preface

Welcome to the second edition of Integrated Electronic Health Records: An Online Course and Worktext for Greenway Medical Technologies' PrimeSUITE®!

Electronic Health Records implementation in the United States is creating great opportunities for people who want to work in the health professions. From front office staff to nurses, doctors, and every worker in between, understanding how health information is transferred and how that information can improve the quality of healthcare is a valuable skill. Everyone working in a healthcare setting will be impacted by Electronic Health Records as they complete their daily tasks.

Developed as a comprehensive learning resource, this hands-on course for *Integrated Electronic Health Records* is offered through McGraw-Hill's *Connect Plus. Connect Plus* uses the latest technology and learning techniques to better connect professors to their students, and students to the information and customized resources they need to master a subject.

Integrated Electronic Health Records: A Worktext for Greenway Medical Technologies' PrimeSUITE complements the online *Connect Plus* course, and is written by an author with an extensive Health Information Management/Health Information Technology background—Beth Shanholtzer, MAEd, RHIA. New coauthor Danielle Mbadu brings a wealth of experience in the learning and assessment fields with her background in instructional design.

Both the worktext and online course include coverage of Greenway Medical Technologies' PrimeSUITE, an ONC-ATCB-Certified, fully integrated, online Electronic Health Records, Practice Management, and interoperable physician-based solution. The book is not meant to be an extensive user manual for PrimeSUITE, but rather it covers the key topics for Electronic Health Records, with PrimeSUITE as the vehicle to demonstrate those topics. Attention is paid to providing the "why" behind each task so that the reader can accumulate transferable skills. The coverage is focused on using an EHR program in a doctor's office, while providing additional information on how tasks might also be completed in a hospital setting.

Electronic Health Records impact a variety of programs in the health professions; as such, this content will be relevant to Health Information Management, Health Information Technology, Medical Insurance, Billing & Coding, and Medical Assisting programs! To help you determine which exercises would most benefit your students, all exercises are designated with PM (Practice Management), EHR (Electronic Health Records), HIM (Health Information Management) tags, or some combination of those three.

GREENWAY

PrimeSUITE

Instructors can access a correlation of the worktext's Learning Outcomes to key accrediting bodies such as CAHIIM, ABHES, and CAAHEP both in the Instructor Resources under the Library tab in *Connect* and at the book's website, **www.mhhe.com/greenway2e**.

Here are the advantages you will gain using this Online Course and Worktext:

- The opportunity to work hands-on with simulated content of real software—PrimeSUITE is a commercially available program used in physician practices across the country by more than 13,000 providers, impacting more than 30 million patient charts. The course contains 55 simulated PrimeSUITE exercises in the areas of Practice Management, Electronic Health Records, and Health Information Management.
- Having the same content for each mode of an exercise (Demo, Practice, Test, and Assessment) gives the student an opportunity to master the tasks.
- Simulating the software means the students' work can be assessed and the activities can be auto-graded by *Connect Plus*.
- *Connect Plus* is completely online—no software to install!
- Easy implementation of this product into online, onground, and hybrid programs.

New to the Second Edition

In this second edition of IEHR, ICD-10-CM is the coding system used in exercises. ICD-9-CM is referenced as a legacy coding system. To enhance learning, the definitions of key terms are now found in the margin as well as in a glossary. New key terms have been added to several of the chapters. Each chapter ends with a new feature, Applying Your Skills, to give yet another opportunity for students to use what they have learned in each chapter. Ten additional PrimeSUITE exercises have been added as well.

While content updates have been made to all of the chapters, here are the highlights:

Chapter 2

In keeping with the expanding roles of health information professionals, new titles and certifications have been added to the listing of medical professions within healthcare in the second edition. Also, the Nationwide Health Information Network and National eHealth Collaborative are addressed. The end of chapter assessments have been expanded.

Chapter 3

The second edition goes into more detail about integration of practice management and electronic health records systems including Clinical Documentation Architecture (CDA), Continuity of Care Documents (CCD), and Quality Reporting Document Architecture (QRDA). Accountable Care Organizations (ACOs) are introduced in this chapter. An additional PrimeSUITE exercise has been added to this chapter as well.

Chapter 4

The Applying Your Skills exercises for this chapter are additional PrimeSUITE exercises, which give students the opportunity to practice tasks they previously completed with different data.

Chapter 5

In the second edition, the use of scribes for documentation has been expanded upon, and a new exercise related to maintenance of files has been added.

Chapter 6

The second edition includes exercises based on ICD-10-CM with reference back to ICD-9-CM and includes two new exercises using PrimeSUITE.

Chapter 9

The second edition includes the addition of Stage 2 Meaningful Use requirements. A PrimeSUITE exercise related to running a report that is used for internal purposes has been added.

Integrated EHR Preparation in the Digital World: Supplementary Materials for the Instructor and Student

Instructors, McGraw-Hill knows how much effort it takes to prepare for a new course. Through focus groups, symposia, reviews, and conversations with instructors like you, we have gathered information about what materials you need in order to facilitate successful courses. We are committed to providing you with high-quality, accurate instructor support. Knowing the importance of flexibility and digital learning, McGraw-Hill has created multiple assets to enhance the learning experience no matter what the class format: traditional, online, or hybrid. This product is designed to help instructors and students be successful, with digital solutions proven to drive student success.

A one-stop spot to present, deliver, and assess digital assets available from McGraw-Hill: McGraw-Hill Connect Integrated EHR

McGraw-Hill *Connect* Integrated EHR provides online presentation, assignment, and assessment solutions. It connects your students with the tools and resources they'll need to achieve success. With *Connect* you can deliver assignments, quizzes, and tests online. A robust set of questions and activities, including the Check Your Understanding questions in Chapters 1, 2, and 10; all of the end-of-chapter questions; PrimeSUITE exercises; and interactives (new for the second edition!) are presented and aligned with the textbook's learning outcomes. As an instructor, you can edit existing questions and author entirely new questions. *Connect* enables you to track individual student performance—by question, by assignment, or in relation to the class overall—with detailed grade reports. You can integrate grade reports easily with Learning Management Systems (LMSs), such as Blackboard, Desire2Learn, or eCollege—and much more. **Connect Plus Integrated EHR** provides students with all the advantages of *Connect Integrated EHR plus* 24/7 online access to an eBook. This media-rich version of the textbook is available through the McGraw-Hill *Connect* platform and allows seamless integration of text, media, and assessments. To learn more, visit **http://connect .mcgraw-hill.com**.

Fifty-Five Hands-On Simulated PrimeSUITE Exercises are available through *Connect* and *Connect Plus*:

- PrimeSUITE Exercises appear in Chapters 3 through 9. All are correlated to Learning Outcomes.
- PrimeSUITE Exercises include the following modes:
  - *Demo Mode—watch a demonstration of the exercise (includes optional audio of the steps).*
  - *Practice Mode—try the exercise yourself with guidance (includes optional audio of the steps).*
  - *Test Mode—complete the exercise on your own.*
  - *Assessment Mode—answer three to four conceptual questions about the exercise you just completed.*
- Students receive a score from *Connect Plus* after completing each mode. They receive 100% for completing all steps in Demo Mode and again in Practice Mode. They receive a percentage based on how many steps they execute correctly in Test Mode or how many questions they answer correctly in Assessment Mode.
- For each PrimeSUITE Exercise, the same data is used for all of the modes in order to reinforce the skill being taught in that exercise.
- Each PrimeSUITE Exercise is labeled with: **HIM** **PM** **EHR**
  - *HIM (Health Information Management)*
  - *PM (Practice Management)*
  - *EHR (Electronic Health Records)*
  - *Or some combination of the above three.*

Much more information on how to complete the exercises in *Connect* or *Connect Plus,* can be found both in the Library tab in *Connect* and at **www.mhhe.com/greenway2e!**

A single sign-on with Connect *and your* Blackboard *course:* McGraw-Hill Higher Education and Blackboard

Blackboard, the web-based course management system, has partnered with McGraw-Hill to better allow students and faculty to use online materials and activities to complement face-to-face teaching. Blackboard features exciting social learning and teaching tools that foster active learning opportunities for students. You'll transform your closed-door classroom into communities where students remain connected to their educational experience 24 hours a day. This partnership allows you and your students access to McGraw-Hill's *Connect* and *Create* right from within your Blackboard course—all with a single sign-on. Not only do you get single sign-on with *Connect* and *Create,* but you also get deep integration of McGraw-Hill content and content engines right in Blackboard. Whether you're choosing a book for your course or building *Connect* assignments, all the tools you need are right where you want them—inside Blackboard. Gradebooks are now seamless. When a student completes an integrated *Connect* assignment, the grade for that assignment automatically (and instantly) feeds into your Blackboard grade center. McGraw-Hill and Blackboard can now offer you easy access to industry leading technology and content, whether your campus hosts it or we do. Be sure to ask your local McGraw-Hill representative for details, including if you use a different learning management system as McGraw-Hill likely has options for those as well.

Create a textbook organized the way you teach: McGraw-Hill Create

With **McGraw-Hill *Create*,** you can easily rearrange chapters, combine material from other content sources, and quickly upload content you have written, such as your course syllabus or teaching notes. Find the content you need in *Create* by searching through thousands of leading McGraw-Hill textbooks. Arrange your book to fit your teaching style. *Create* even allows you to personalize your book's appearance by selecting the cover and adding your name, school, and course information. Order a *Create* book and you'll receive a complimentary print review copy in 3 to 5 business days or a complimentary electronic review copy (eComp) via e-mail in minutes. Go to **www.mcgrawhillcreate.com** today and register to experience how McGraw-Hill *Create* empowers you to teach *your* students *your* way.

Record and distribute your lectures for multiple viewing: My Lectures—Tegrity

McGraw-Hill Tegrity records and distributes your class lecture with just a click of a button. Students can view it anytime and anywhere via computer, iPod, or mobile device. It indexes as it records your PowerPoint presentations and anything shown on your computer, so students can use keywords to find exactly what they want to study. Tegrity is available as an integrated feature of **McGraw-Hill *Connect* Integrated EHR** and as a stand-alone product.

Instructor Resources

You can rely on the following materials to help you and your students work through the material in this book. All of the resources in the following table are available on the book's website, **www.mhhe .com/greenway2e** (instructors can request a password through their sales representative). *Instructors can access these same resources through the Library tab in Connect or Connect Plus Integrated EHR.*

Supplement	Features
Instructor's Manual (organized by Learning Outcomes)	Each chapter has: • Lesson Plans and Teaching Tips • Outline of PowerPoint Presentations • Answer Keys for Check Your Understanding Questions, End-of-Chapter Questions, and PrimeSUITE Exercises
PowerPoint Presentations (organized by Learning Outcomes)	• Key Terms • Key Concepts • Teaching Notes
Electronic Test Bank	• EZ Test Online (computerized) and *Connect Plus* • Word Version • Questions are tagged with learning outcomes, level of difficulty, level of Bloom's taxonomy, feedback, ABHES, CAAHEP, and CAHIIM competencies
Tools to Plan Course	• Transition Guide, by chapter, from Shanholtzer, 1e to Shanholtzer, 2e • Correlations by learning outcomes to ABHES, CAAHEP, CAHIIM, and NHA • Sample Syllabi and Lesson Plans • Certificate of Completion • Asset Map—a recap of the key instructor resources, tied to the learning outcomes, as well as information on the content available through *Connect* or *Connect Plus*
Tips for PrimeSUITE Exercises	• Multiple documents to help you and your students implement the PrimeSUITE exercises in your course through *Connect* or *Connect Plus*

Need help? Contact McGraw-Hill's Customer Experience Group (CXG). Visit the CXG **website at www.mhhe.com/support**. Browse our FAQs (frequently asked questions) and product documentation and/or contact a CXG representative. CXG is available Sunday through Friday.

Want to learn more about this product? Attend one of our online webinars. To learn more about the webinars, please contact your McGraw-Hill sales representative. To find your McGraw-Hill representative, go to **www.mhhe.com** and click "Find My Sales Rep."

Best-in-Class Digital Support

Based on feedback from our users, McGraw-Hill Education has developed Digital Success Programs that will provide you and your students the help you need, when you need it.

• One-to-One Training for Instructors: Get ready to drive classroom results with our Digital Success Team—ready to provide in person, remote, or on-demand training as needed.

- Peer Support and Training: No one understands your needs like your peers. Get easy access to knowledgeable digital users by joining our Connect Community, or speak directly with one of our Digital Faculty Consultants, who are instructors using McGraw-Hill digital products.
- Online Training Tools: Get immediate anytime, anywhere access to modular tutorials on key features through our Connect Success Academy.

Get started today. Learn more about McGraw-Hill Education's Digital Success Programs by contacting your local sales representative or visit http://connect.customer.mcgraw-hill.com/start.

about the Authors

M. Beth Shanholtzer, MAEd, RHIA has been in the Health Information Management field for 34 years. Her experience has included HIM department management positions within hospitals in New Jersey, Pennsylvania, West Virginia, and Maryland. She has been in academics for nearly 20 years, and is currently the program director for an HIM associate degree program at Lord Fairfax Community College in Middletown, Virginia. She previously held positions as program director and instructor of associate degree programs at Kaplan University.

She is active in AHIMA as a member the Faculty Development Workgroup of the Center for Excellence in Education and the Envisioning Collaborative. On the state level, Beth has served as president, education chair, and legislative chair of the West Virginia Health Information Management Association.

Beth lives in Martinsburg, West Virginia, with her husband; they have three children.

M. Beth Shanholtzer, MAEd, RHIA

Danielle M. Mbadu has been an educator all of her professional life. She currently works as a freelance learning and assessment specialist. Previously, Danielle has coached and taught at the high school level, worked in the special education department of a middle school, and managed curriculum development at Knowledge Universe and Kaplan Higher Education. It was at Kaplan where she began her entry into the healthcare professions, working on Medical Assisting, Dental Assisting, and Health Information Technology programs. Danielle has served on a number of accreditation and curriculum committees, and is a passionate college basketball fan in her spare time. She holds an MA in Curriculum & Instruction and a CAS/MEd in K-12 Educational Administration. Danielle lives in Glen Ellyn, Illinois, with her husband and two children.

Danielle M. Mbadu

Walkthrough of Integrated EHR
Connect Plus

EHR Matters . . . Be Prepared!

Complete 55 simulated PrimeSUITE exercises, organized into the following modes:

DEMO: Watch a demonstration of the exercise. Note the Step Window on the right of the screen, which includes a Printer icon that allows you to print the steps when clicked. Audio is available with this mode (no plug-in required!).

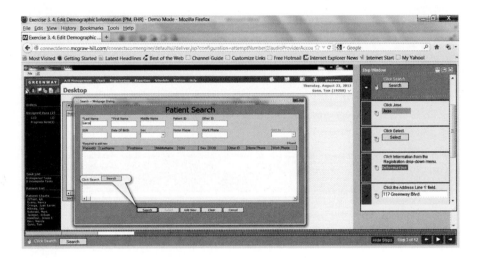

PRACTICE: Try the same exercise yourself with guidance. The Step Window and Audio are also available with this mode.

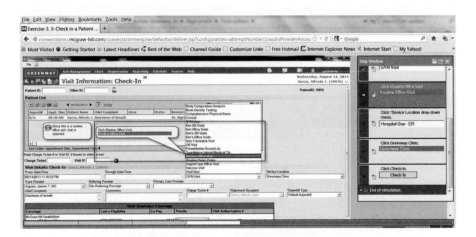

TEST: Complete the same exercise on your own, with a point given for each correct step.

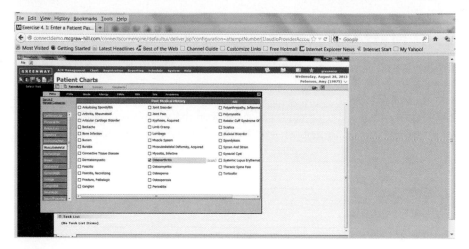

ASSESSMENT: Answer conceptual questions about the exercise you just completed.

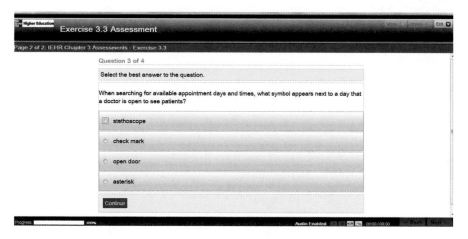

FOR INSTRUCTORS:

LIBRARY TAB: This includes access to the eBook and the Instructor Resources.

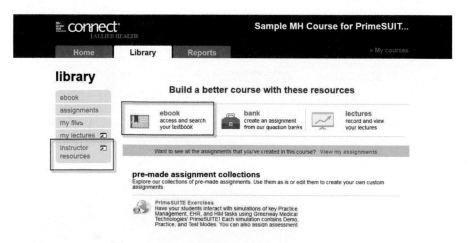

Acknowledgments

Suggestions have been received from faculty and students throughout the country. This vital feedback is important for product development. Each person who has offered comments and suggestions has our thanks. The efforts of many people are needed to develop and improve a product. Among these people are the reviewers and consultants who point out areas of concern, cite areas of strength, and make recommendations for change. In this regard, the following instructors provided feedback that was enormously helpful in preparing the manuscript.

Manuscript Reviewers

Multiple instructors reviewed the manuscript while it was in development, providing valuable feedback that directly impacted the book.

Annette Baer, CMA
Ridley-Lowell Business and Technical Institute

Rhoda Cooper, BS, NCICS, CPC, RMC
Piedmont Virginia Community College

Lois Fluker
Virginia College

Savanna Garrity, MPA
Madisonville Community College

Deborah Gilbert, RHIA, CMA
Dalton State College

Jacquelyn Harris, MEd, CMA
Bryan University

Patricia Jones, MBA, CPC, CMAA, CBCS
Ultimate Medical Academy

Gregory Latterell, CCS-P
Alexandria Technical College

Jorell Lawrence, MSA
Stratford University

Barbara Westrick, CMA, CPC, CBCS
Ross Education

Colleen Zagoreos, CBCS, CEHRS
Ridley-Lowell Business and Technical Institute

Mary Margaret Zulaybar, MHA
ASA College

Technical Editing/Accuracy Panel

A panel of instructors completed a technical edit and review of the content in the book page proofs to verify its accuracy.

Carolyn Eberly, RHIT, MSHCM
Coppin State University

Amy Jewell, BBA
Baker College

Angela M.B. Oliva, BSHA, CMRS
Heald College Stockton, Boston Reed College

Lauri L. Perry, MJ, RHIA
Indiana University Purdue University Indianapolis (IUPUI)

Christina Thomas, MHA/Ed, MS, CPC, CMAA, CCMA, CBCS
Florida Career College

Deborah Ann Zenzal, RN, BSN, MS, CCS-P, CPC, RMA
Penn Foster

Symposia

An enthusiastic group of trusted faculty members active in this course area attended symposia to provide crucial feedback.

Sandra Brightwell, RHIA
Central Arizona College

Linda Buchanan-Anderson, RN, BSN, RMA (AMT)
Central Arizona College

William Travis Butler, RMA, MHA
ECPI University

Mohammed Y. Chowdhury, MBBS, MPH, CCA(AHIMA), CBCS(NHA), CAHI(AMT)
Lincoln Technical Institute

Kristy Comeaux, CMA, CPT, EKG
Delta College

Amanda Davis-Smith, NCMA, AHI, CPC
Jefferson Community & Technical College

Marylou de Roma-Ragaza, BSN, MSN, RN
Lincoln Educational Services

Kathy Gaeng, RMA, CAHI
Vatterott College

Karlene Jaggan, PN, NRCAHA, BIT
Centura College

Jennifer B. Kubetin, CEHR
Branford Hall Career Institute

Cheryl A. Kuck, BS, CMA (AAMA)
Rhodes State College

Lynnae Lockett, RN, RMA, MSN
Bryant & Stratton College

Marta Lopez, MD, LM, CPM, RMA, BMO
Miami Dade College-Medical Campus

Carrie A. Mack, CMA (AAMA)
Branford Hall Career Institute

Nanci Milbrath, AAS, CMA (AAMA)
Pine Technical College

Corina Miranda, CMPC-I, CPC
Kaplan College

Angela M.B. Oliva, BS, CMRS
Heald College and Boston Reed College

Debra J. Paul, BA, CMA-AAMA
Ivy Tech Community College

Denise Pruitt, Ed.D.
Middlesex Community College

Wendy Schmerse, CMRS
Charter College

LaShawn D. Sullivan, BSHIM, CPC
Medtech

Gina F. Umstetter, BA, MSIT (ABT)
Delta College of Arts & Technology

Lisa Wright, CMA (AAMA), MT, SH
Bristol Community College

Deborah Ann Zenzal, RN, BSN, MS, CCS-P, CPC, RMA
Penn Foster

Special thanks to the instructors who helped with the development of *Connect* and the PrimeSUITE Exercises. These include:

Antonio Calviño MIS, MCSE
T.C. Network Management. Inc.

Kimberly Christensen MHA/ED, CPC, CPC-I
Ultimate Medical Academy

Kristin L. Hawthorne, CCA, CMOM, CMIS
CCI Training Center

Jennifer Kubetin, CEHR
Branford Hall Career Institute

Gina F. Umstetter, BA, MSIT (ABT)
Delta College of Arts & Technology

Acknowledgments from the Authors

From Beth Shanholtzer: This text is dedicated to my family, friends, colleagues, and students who encourage and enlighten me every day.

From Danielle Mbadu: I want to thank the McGraw-Hill Health Professions Team, especially Natalie Ruffatto, Michelle Flomenhoft, and Katie Ward, who gave me this opportunity and have been a continual source of support and encouragement (not to mention a fantastic team to work with!).

I also need to thank my entire family, especially Adanya and Jaden, who lost some "Mommy Time" as I worked on this project, and Bavin, who is the best teammate one could ask for. I love you **all,** and you make my life full.

From Both: Much appreciation goes to the McGraw-Hill staff for bringing this product to life: Chad Grall, Director for Health Professions; Natalie Ruffatto, Executive Brand Manager for Health Professions; Roxan Kinsey, Executive Marketing Manager for Health Professions; Harper Christopher, Market Development Manager for Health Professions; Katie Ward, Digital Product Analyst for Health Professions; Michelle Flomenhoft, Managing Developmental Editor for Health Professions; Rick Hecker, Content Project Manager; Michael McCormick, Buyer; Srdj Savanovic, Designer; and Jeremy Cheshareck, Content Licensing Specialist. Additional thanks go to Amber Bettcher and Karen Jozefowicz for the support on the digital end as well as to Melinda Bilecki, who lent her copyediting and reviewing skills to the project.

We would also like to thank our partners at Greenway Medical Technologies, Inc. for their continued support of this project, especially Matt Pierce and Diane Nivens.

An Overview of

PrimeSUITE's Practice Management and Electronic Health Record Software

Learning Outcomes

At the end of this chapter, the student should be able to:

1.1 Describe Practice Management applications.

1.2 List the advantages and disadvantages of an electronic health record.

1.3 Describe EHR applications.

1.4 Chart the flow of information from registration through processing of the claim.

1.5 Use the help feature in PrimeSUITE.

Key Terms

Application
Care provider
Clearinghouse
Current Procedural Terminology (CPT)
Demographic information
Electronic claims submission
Electronic Health Record (EHR)
Electronic Medical Record (EMR)
Encounter form (Superbill)

International Classification of Diseases-10th revision, Clinical Modification/Procedure Coding System (ICD-10-CM/PCS)
Interoperability
Master Patient (Person) Index
Patient list
Point of care
Practice Management (PM)
Speech recognition

What You Need to Know and Why You Need to Know It

The purpose of this worktext is to introduce students to software used to gather, track, and store the clinical and administrative information of patients seen in the medical facility. This information is used for patient care; to file claims for reimbursement; for reporting practice information to insurance carriers, government, and non-government agencies; and to gather statistics about the types of patients treated at the facility. We will be using Greenway Medical Technologies' PrimeSUITE Practice Management (PM) and electronic health record (EHR) software throughout the text. This worktext is not meant to teach all of the functionality of PrimeSUITE; instead it is meant to demonstrate the most common electronic functions carried out in a medical office, hospital, or other healthcare facility.

This first chapter is an introduction and overview. The concepts in this chapter will be further explained throughout the text.

Practice Management (PM) Software used in physicians' offices to gather data on every patient and perform administrative functions from the time an appointment is made through the time the bill for each visit is paid.

Electronic health record (EHR) Comprehensive record of all health documentation for a patient, which can be shared electronically with other healthcare providers as necessary.

Electronic medical record (EMR) The legal patient record that is created within any healthcare facility (hospital, nursing home, ambulatory surgery facility, physician's office, etc.). The EMR is the data source for the electronic health record (EHR).

Master Patient Index (MPI)/ Patient List A permanent listing of all patients who have received care in a hospital (inpatient or outpatient). In physicians' offices, more often referred to as Master Patient List or Patient List.

for your information fyi

A healthcare facility includes a hospital, physician's office, dental office, outpatient diagnostic center, outpatient rehabilitation, outpatient psychological services, hospice, home health care, long-term care, or ambulatory surgery center.

1.1 Practice Management Applications

Typically, software (computer programs that carry out functions or operations) used in a medical office is known as **Practice Management (PM)** software. Filing an insurance claim for a patient is an example of an administrative function. Through the use of PM software, data is gathered on every patient from the time an appointment is made through the time the bill for each visit is paid. **electronic health (medical) record (EHR/EMR)** software includes the clinical documentation of patient care. The patient's chief complaint, record of vital signs, results of physical examination, and past medical history are all examples of clinical data.

Greenway Medical Technologies' PrimeSUITE is both a PM and EHR solution using a single database. The use of this single database to document the administrative and clinical aspects of patient care allows the provider to concentrate on the care of the patient, improve quality of the documentation collected, and share that documentation with other healthcare providers as appropriate, with the result of better coordination of the patient's overall care.

We will first look at the applications typically found in Practice Management software, including PrimeSUITE. Practice Management is a term used in physicians' offices. In other healthcare facilities, including hospitals, these functions will also be computerized, but are referred to as Admission, Discharge, Transfer (ADT), and billing systems.

The main applications include:

Entering Each Patient Seen into a Master List

Each patient seen, whether in a physician's office or a hospital, is only entered once into what is known as the **Patient List** or **Master Patient (Person) Index** (listings of all patients seen in an office or hospital). These will be further discussed in a future chapter.

Scheduling Appointments

To maintain efficiency in an office, it is important that appointments be accurate. Think of it this way—if a patient were told to come to the office for an appointment at a particular date and time, but the appointment book showed another date and time for that patient to be seen, the end result would be disorganization as well as unhappy patients and staff. Computerizing this function allows sufficient time to be allotted to that patient based on the reason for his or her visit, and also allows for more efficient scheduling of the provider's time.

Assign ICD-10-CM/PCS Diagnosis and CPT Procedure Codes

You may have noticed on your own visits to your physician's office that you are given a piece of paper when you leave the examining room. This is referred to as an **Encounter form** or **Superbill**. There are many numbers or codes found on this paper. Every diagnosis made by a care provider is written in narrative form on a patient's chart and then carried over to the Superbill. These narrative diagnoses are converted into numeric form with a coding system known as **International Classification of Diseases, 10th revision, Clinical Modification Procedure Coding System (ICD-10-CM/PCS)**. The same occurs for each procedure performed, but the coding system used is **Current Procedural Terminology (CPT)**. The Superbill and coding functions will be covered in detail later in this text. Most likely, you will have a separate course or courses in billing and coding as well.

Complete a Billing Claim Form for Each Visit

In order to submit bills to health insurance carriers, a claim form must be generated for each visit. This is done by compiling the patient's identifying information, insurance information, and the ICD-10-CM/PCS and CPT codes into a form called the CMS-1500, which is used by physicians' offices, or the UB-04, which is used to bill hospital claims.

Send the Insurance Claims to Insurance Carriers

Once the claim form is generated, it is submitted to the insurance carrier for payment. Some hard-copy claim forms are still mailed to the insurance carrier, but the majority of forms are sent by **electronic claims submission**. Filing a claim electronically means that the information is sent by wire to a **clearinghouse** or directly to the insurance carrier. Filing claims electronically cuts down on billing errors and cuts down on processing time, which results in faster payment. A clearinghouse is a service that processes data into a standardized billing format and checks for inconsistencies or other errors in the data.

The information collected as explained is considered administrative information. The patient's **demographic** (identifying) **information** is collected as part of the administrative information, as well as information needed for the business processes that take place in a healthcare facility, for instance gathering of insurance information, completing a claim form, submitting a claim, and so on.

---

for your information fyi

The length of an office visit is based on the reason for the patient's visit. A follow-up appointment for an earache would be assigned 10 minutes, whereas a physical exam would be allotted 30 minutes or more.

for your information fyi

Throughout the text, the term insurance will be used generically to refer to any type of commercial insurance, Medicare, Medicaid, TRICARE, CHAMPVA, or Workers' Compensation.

Encounter form Also known as a Superbill. A document (paper or electronic) that is used in medical offices to capture the diagnoses and services or procedures performed and from which the CMS-1500 billing form is completed.

International Classification of Diseases-10th revision, Clinical Modification/Procedure Coding System (ICD-10-CM/PCS) The classification system used to convert narrative diagnoses and procedures into numeric codes. Effective October 1, 2014, replaces ICD-9-CM.

Current Procedural Terminology (CPT) Coding system used to convert narrative procedures and services into numeric form. CPT is used to code procedures and services in a physician's office; in a hospital setting, it is used for outpatient coding (emergency room, outpatient diagnostic testing, or ambulatory surgery, for example).

Electronic claims submission Submitting insurance claims via wire to a clearinghouse or directly to the insurance carrier.

Clearinghouse A service that processes data into a standardized billing format and checks for inconsistencies or other errors in the data.

Demographic information Administrative data that identifies the patient. Consists of name, date of birth, sex, and social security number (may vary by facility policy).

Copyright © 2015 McGraw-Hill Education

Administrative information includes the insurance information, authorization to bill the insurance company, correspondence related to billing matters, etc. Demographic information identifies the patient—name, address, phone numbers, etc. The demographic information is specific administrative information that helps differentiate one patient from another with the same name.

Check Your Understanding

1. Is PrimeSUITE a Practice Management tool or an electronic health record? Support your answer.
2. List the types of information that insurance companies need to be provided with on a billing claim form.

1.2 Why Adopt Electronic Health Record Applications?

The widespread acceptance of an electronic health record has been slow compared to other industries such as banking or retail. Healthcare administrators and care providers have long been leery of electronic health records. Security concerns, the lengthy implementation process, and the high cost of implementing an EHR headline the reasons for a culture of uncertainty and a "let's wait and see" attitude. The perception has been that paper records are more secure and are not as susceptible to loss, theft, or tampering since there is a tangible object that can be seen or carried from place to place by a human being. In reality, paper records are potentially more susceptible to loss or tampering than an electronic record. A paper record cannot be "followed," whereas every entry, change, or view of an electronic record can be tracked and reported. With proper backup procedures, EHRs cannot be lost or misfiled, which is not the case with a paper record. Of course, if a patient's name is misspelled or if a patient used a different name on a previous registration, then yes, location will be difficult, but there are other ways to search for the record such as by social security number or date of birth, which is not possible with a paper record. Security will be discussed in more detail in the chapter on privacy and security.

The initial purchase and implementation costs are high—much higher than the cost of file folders and filing equipment in a paper system. The research and development of an electronic system by service providers (software companies), the allocation of human resources to planning and training, and the cost of hardware and additional software all contribute to this cost. There is an ongoing cost of maintaining any system, paper or electronic. The return on investment of an electronic system is in patient safety, enhanced quality of care, less duplication of effort, a more efficiently run office, instant access to patient health records, and the data needed for reporting purposes. Also, the costs of filing supplies, physical space needed for paper records, and long-term storage (archiving) will eventually lessen once the electronic system is in place.

For care providers, there is a high learning curve, and they must be willing to devote time to the new system before it is second nature to them. Though care providers are often resistant to putting in that investment of time, in the end they will find their time is used more for patient care than "charting." The productivity of healthcare professionals such as nurses, laboratory technicians, or medical assistants will be negatively impacted in the beginning until they too learn the electronic system.

As for administrative staff, learning an EHR system is more time consuming and has a higher learning curve than the manual processes associated with paper records. After all, filing, whether alphabetic or numeric, is more intuitive than searching a computer database or knowing which screen a particular piece of data resides on; and again, a piece of paper or a folder full of papers is tangible, an electronic system is not.

Sharing information has also been a sticking point. Though patients have had access to their records for many years, they were not well informed about how to go about it, and many did not know that they could even request an amendment to their health records. Healthcare providers have been fearful of releasing patients' health records to others, including other healthcare providers, because there is a sense of loss of control over the information and lack of confidentiality.

This sharing of health information with other healthcare providers or entities is possible because of **interoperability**. It means that through a single database, many different functions can take place and information can be shared, which is not possible with a manual or paper record system. For instance, in her physician's office, Alicia Matthews's medical information is readily accessible and just a couple of clicks away regardless of whether a list of her allergies is needed before refilling a prescription, or her policy number is needed by the billing staff. Also, let's say Alicia is a patient of Dr. Ingram. She has been seen for repeated bouts of strep throat. Dr. Ingram has referred her to Dr. Johnson, an otorhinolaryngologist (ear, nose, and throat specialist). Her appointment with Dr. Johnson is set up for July 2. When she arrives for her appointment, Dr. Johnson already has her records from Dr. Ingram, and rather than having to take all of Alicia's information over again, the doctor can spend the time examining Alicia and determining a plan of care. Because the computer systems at the two offices are interoperable, the information can be shared seamlessly.

In recent years, this "wait and see" culture has been subsiding. As research shows that there has been a decrease in medical errors and an increase in timeliness of diagnosis and treatment due in large part to timely access to information—for instance a patient's allergy to penicillin, or the fact that a patient has already had her gallbladder removed—care providers and administrators are more open-minded and are pushing for totally paperless systems within their facilities. Increasingly, healthcare providers are accepting that an informed patient is a more compliant patient, and that patients should have a say in their medical care.

Assuring regulatory compliance is also made easier and more efficient through use of an electronic health record. Report-writing capabilities available in electronic systems allow for fast, reliable data submission and retrieval.

Interoperability Through a single database, many different functions can take place and information can be shared.

TABLE 1.1	Comparison of Paper to Electronic Health Records
Paper Health Records	**Electronic Health Records**
Security concerns of theft or tampering with documentation	Security concerns of loss of data or computer hackers
Individual records are easily lost or misfiled	Misfiling is not an issue as long as the name is spelled correctly
Startup costs are relatively inexpensive	Startup costs are relatively high
Operating costs are relatively inexpensive as the system does not change drastically from year to year	Operating costs are dependent on level of support from software vendor, maintenance costs, and cost of upgrades
Records take up a great deal of space	Does not take up physical space other than the desktop computers
Archiving costs are high	Archiving costs are for disk or server space
Training staff is a relatively short and inexpensive process	Staff and physician training is time consuming
Physicians' perception that writing or dictating is easier than typing into a computer	Once learned, documentation is easily done by point and click or voice recognition systems
Documentation by care providers tends to be less detailed	Documentation by care providers tends to be more detailed
Sharing health information with other care providers or health-care facilities is a time-consuming process and may delay diagnosis or treatment	Sharing health information with other care providers or health-care facilities is done in a timely manner and may assist in timely diagnosis and treatment

From a more global perspective, the use of electronic medical records will allow for the collection and use of incredible amounts of clinical data for use in medical research and epidemiology, which will have a profound effect on healthcare worldwide (Table 1.1).

Check Your Understanding

1. Is a paper-based system of records more secure than an electronic one? Explain your answer.
2. Why are startup costs significantly higher with EHRs versus paper-based records?

1.3 Electronic Health Record Applications

Applications Software that has a special purpose, such as word processing, spreadsheet, or for a particular industry such as practice management or electronic health record software.

Care provider Term used to refer to physicians, physicians' assistants, dentists, psychologists, nurse practitioner, or midwife.

Now, let us take a look at the electronic record using PrimeSUITE.

It is through the EHR functionality that clinical information is collected and includes the patient's medical history, current condition(s), treatment rendered, results of treatment, prognosis, plan of care, diagnosis, and any instructions given by the provider.

PrimeSUITE's EHR **applications** (functionality) include:

- Clinical documentation of a patient's visit (the progress note) by the **care provider**

- Prescribing medications electronically to the patient's pharmacy of choice through use of the ePrescribing solution.
- Exchange of clinical information between medical providers or other entities with a need to know, through the PrimeEX-CHANGE solution.
- The ability to access clinical trials, evidence-based medicine, and pharmaceutical research to improve patient care, and access to clinical and financial benchmarking services to enhance financial management by using the PrimeRESEARCH solution.
- Mobile EHR applications available on personal digital assistants (PDAs) or smartphones to allow providers instant access anytime and anywhere through PrimeMOBILE.
- **Point of care** dictation of progress notes by the provider through PrimeSPEECH, which is a form of **speech recognition** technology. Speech recognition technology allows documentation to occur on the computer screen as the care provider dictates notes. Point of care refers to the dictation occurring at the very time the patient is being seen.

Point of care Documentation, dictation, ordering of tests and procedures that occur at the same time the patient is being seen.

Speech (voice) recognition Software that recognizes the words being said by the person dictating, and converts the speech to text.

Check Your Understanding

1. What does PrimeSUITE's PrimeEXCHANGE function do?
2. What is PrimeSPEECH?
3. Take a look at all of the functionality of PrimeSUITE. Open your Internet browser and access the following link, and then answer the following questions:

   http://www.greenwaymedical.com/specialties/family-practice/

   a. Where would you look to determine if a patient has had a polio vaccine?

   b. Where would you go to write a letter to a specialist to whom a patient is being referred?

   c. Where would you go to send tasks or make requests of physicians or other practice staff?

4. Take a look at the functionality and a demonstration of Greenway Medical Technologies' PrimeSUITE. Pay particular attention to the Web demonstration of PrimeSUITE applications to become familiar with it. Then answer the following questions:

   http://www.greenwaymedical.com/web-demo/

   a. PrimeSUITE uses a _____ database, allowing for interoperability.

   b. The electronic Superbill is automatically generated from the _____.

   c. The Superbill includes charges, diagnosis, and _____ for the patient.

   d. PrimeSUITE is _____ in meaningful use standards.

1.4 The Flow of Information from Registration through Processing of the Claim

If you think about your past experiences visiting a physician's office, you will recognize many of these steps and how similar they are to your experience. Of course, not every step is exactly the same in every office, but the basic premise is the same.

Step one (Figure 1.1) is that an appointment is made. Of course, if you are going to an urgent care center or an emergency room, this step would be skipped. Once the appointment is made, you go to the office on the day and time of the appointment and you are "checked in." This is known as registration, i.e., the patient's administrative information is taken either on the phone or when the patient appears for the appointment. It is during this time that any incorrect or missing information is captured. Also, if new authorization forms or other administrative forms need to be signed, that is done at this point.

After you are checked in, you wait to be seen by the care providers (Figure 1.2). First, you are called back to the exam room by a healthcare professional (Figure 1.3), your height, weight, and vital signs (temperature, pulse, blood pressure) are taken, and you are asked questions about why you are being seen today as well as questions about your medical history. Once those are complete, the care provider steps in for the actual exam (Figure 1.4).

Once the care provider has completed the exam, assessed the patient's condition, and given the patient a plan of care including instructions, the business functions begin (Figure 1.5 and Figure 1.6). These include the check-out and billing procedures. Some of these procedures are repeated or continue for several weeks or months until the claim is paid and the patient's account is at a zero balance.

In cases where the care provider ordered diagnostic procedures such as x-rays or laboratory tests, then the clinical documentation steps would be repeated (Figure 1.7).

for your information fyi

The term *care provider* will be used to refer to any physician, physician's assistant, dentist, psychologist, nurse practitioner, or midwife.

for your information fyi

The medical assistant, nurse, receptionist, health information technician, medical biller/coder, and office administrative personnel will be referred to as *healthcare professional* throughout the text.

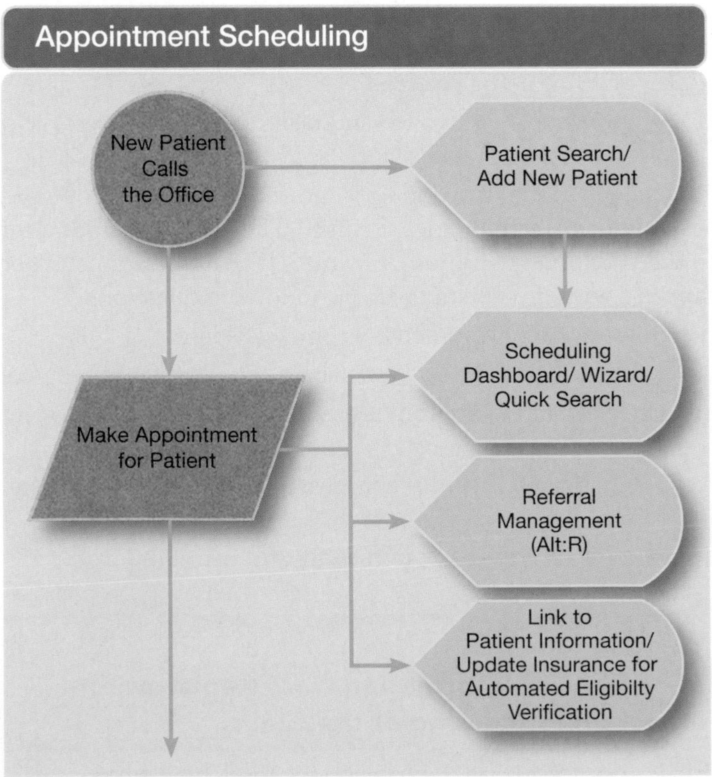

Figure 1.1 **Appointment scheduling flowchart**

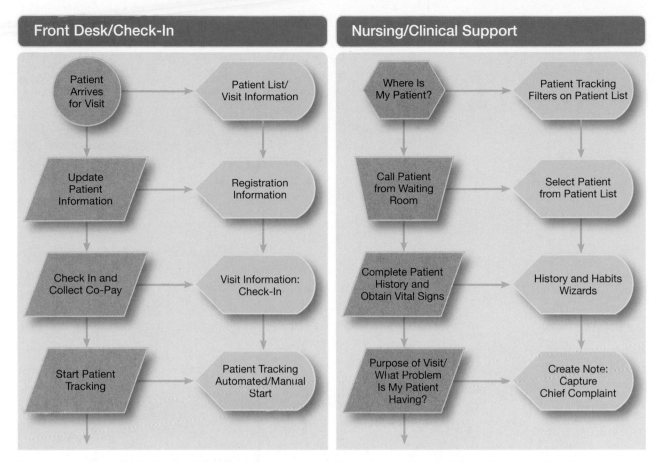

Figure 1.2   Front desk check-in flowchart

Figure 1.3   Nursing/clinical support flowchart

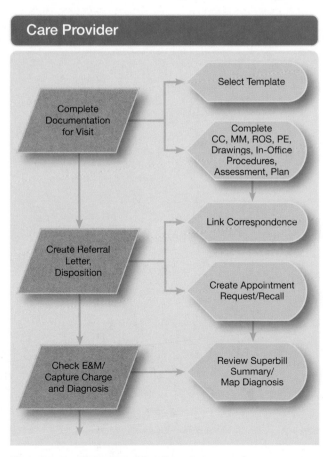

Figure 1.4   Care provider flowchart

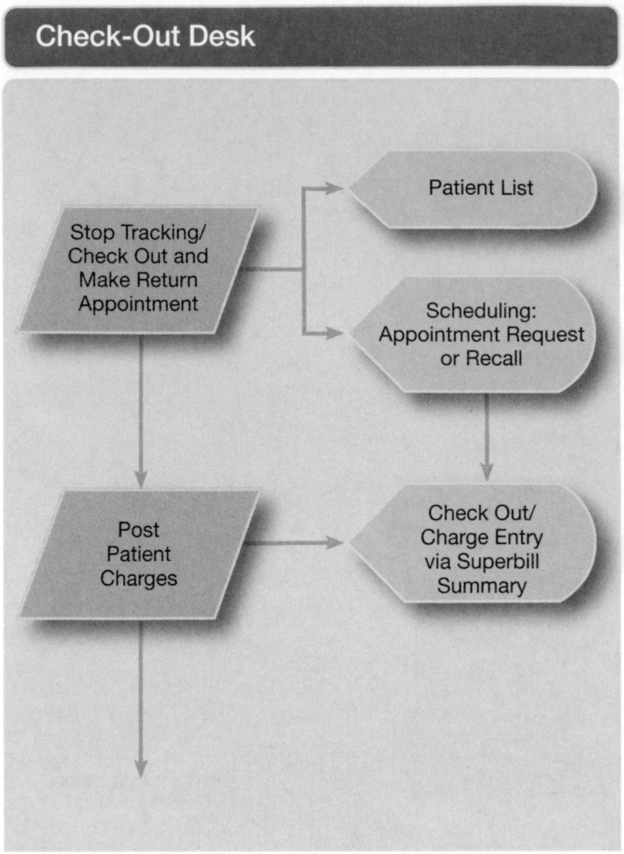

Check-Out Desk

Stop Tracking/Check Out and Make Return Appointment → Patient List

Stop Tracking/Check Out and Make Return Appointment → Scheduling: Appointment Request or Recall

Post Patient Charges → Check Out/Charge Entry via Superbill Summary

Figure 1.5   Check-out desk flowchart

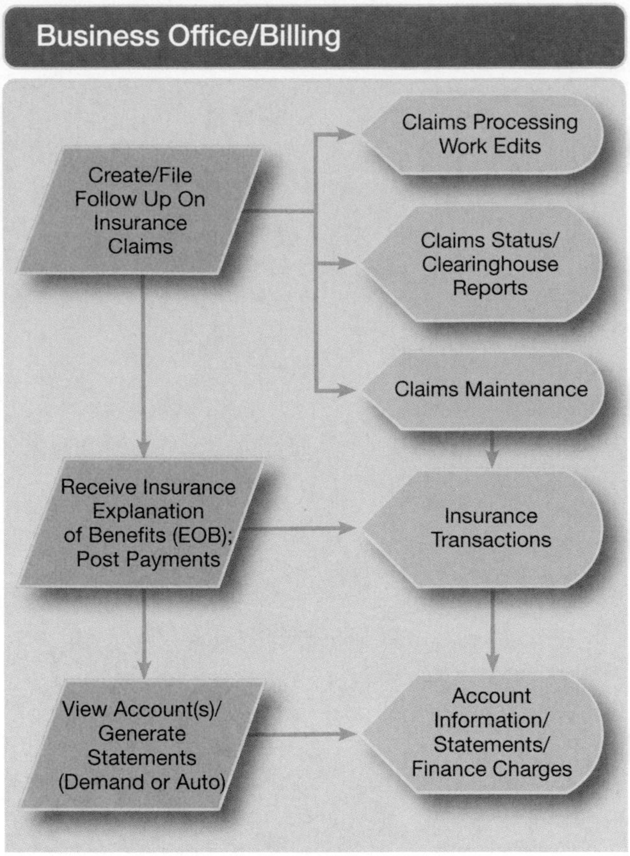

Business Office/Billing

Create/File Follow Up On Insurance Claims → Claims Processing Work Edits

→ Claims Status/Clearinghouse Reports

→ Claims Maintenance

Receive Insurance Explanation of Benefits (EOB); Post Payments → Insurance Transactions

View Account(s)/Generate Statements (Demand or Auto) → Account Information/Statements/Finance Charges

Figure 1.6   Business office/billing flowchart

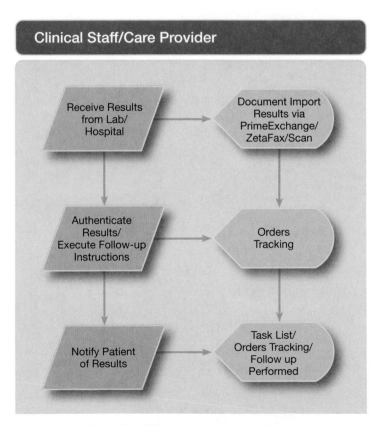

Clinical Staff/Care Provider

Receive Results from Lab/Hospital → Document Import Results via PrimeExchange/ZetaFax/Scan

Authenticate Results/Execute Follow-up Instructions → Orders Tracking

Notify Patient of Results → Task List/Orders Tracking/Follow up Performed

Figure 1.7   Clinical staff/care provider flowchart

Check Your Understanding

1. Put the following steps in the flow of information into the correct order: Care Provider; Front Desk/Check-In; Business Office/Billing; Check-Out Desk; Appointment Scheduling; Nursing/Clinical Support; Clinical Staff/Care Provider.

2. Under what circumstances would clinical documentation steps need to be repeated?

1.5   Use of the Help Feature

The use of help text or of a help function is standard in most software applications. You have no doubt used it from time to time when preparing word processing or spreadsheet applications. PrimeSUITE is no different.

PrimeSUITE help text can be accessed through any screen, as you see in Figure 1.8.

By clicking on Help, you will gain access to the entire user's guide (Figure 1.9). The guide can be searched by topic, or by using the index or glossary. For instance, if you wanted to know more about vocabulary reconciliation, clicking on index allows the user to access a keyword search, where the system begins to predict what

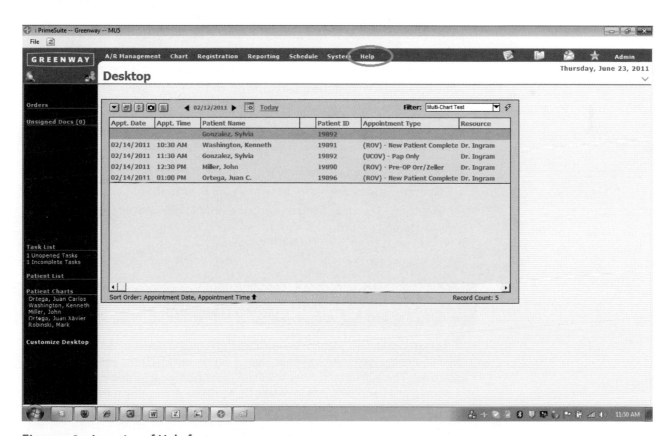

Figure 1.8   Location of Help feature on any screen

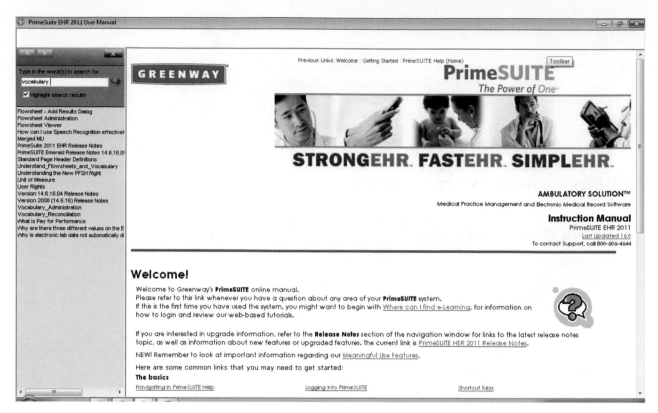

Type in the word(s) to search for:
vocabulary
☑ Highlight search results

Flowsheet - Add Results Dialog
Flowsheet Administration
Flowsheet Viewer
How can I use Speech Recognition effectivel
Merged MU
PrimeSuite 2011 EHR Release Notes
PrimeSUITE Emerald Release Notes 14.6.16.0
Standard Page Header Definitions
Understand_Flowsheets_and_Vocabulary
Understanding the New PFSH Right
Unit of Measure
User Rights
Version 14.6.16.04 Release Notes
Version 2008 (14.6.16) Release Notes
Vocabulary_Administration
Vocabulary_Reconciliation
What is Pay for Performance
Why are there three different values on the E
Why is electronic lab data not automatically di

Previous Links: Welcome : Getting Started : PrimeSUITE Help (Home)   Toolbar

GREENWAY

PrimeSUITE
The Power of One™

STRONGEHR. FASTEHR. SIMPLEHR.

AMBULATORY SOLUTION™
Medical Practice Management and Electronic Medical Record Software

Instruction Manual
PrimeSUITE EHR 2011
Last Updated 16.0
To contact Support, call 800-606-4644

Welcome!

Welcome to Greenway's **PrimeSUITE** online manual.
Please refer to this link whenever you have a question about any area of your **PrimeSUITE** system.
If this is the first time you have used the system, you might want to begin with Where can I find e-Learning, for information on how to login and review our web-based tutorials.

If you are interested in upgrade information, refer to the **Release Notes** section of the navigation window for links to the latest release notes topic, as well as information about new features or upgraded features. The current link is PrimeSUITE HER 2011 Release Notes.

NEW! Remember to look at important information regarding our Meaningful Use Features.

Here are some common links that you may need to get started:
The basics
Navigating in PrimeSUITE Help   Logging Into PrimeSUITE   Shortcut Keys

Figure 1.9   PrimeSUITE EHR 2011 user manual

the user is searching for based on the first few characters typed or by typing the entire word in the search field (Figure 1.9).

The important thing about Help is that it is there for just that—to help you learn PrimeSUITE, assist you when you are unsure of the steps you need to complete, and to help you keep up to date with changes or new functionality added to the software.

Check Your Understanding

1. How do you access the Help feature in PrimeSUITE?
2. How many ways are there to locate information?
3. Using the Help feature, describe how to add a new allergy to a patient's chart.

APPLYING YOUR SKILLS

This textbook covers electronic health records and to some extent Practice Management functionality through use of Greenway Medical's PrimeSUITE software. There are many other software systems available; searching out other software and becoming aware of what is available is something that a health-care professional (and provider) should do periodically. Take some time now to do an Internet search of PM software and EHR software. Write a brief summary of three or four types of each software.

chapter 1 **summary**

LEARNING OUTCOME	CONCEPTS FOR REVIEW

1.1 Describe Practice Management applications. Pages 2–4	- What is Practice Management?
	- Practice Management applications
	  • Master Patient Index/Patient List
	  • Scheduling appointments
	  • Assign ICD-10-CM/PCS and CPT codes
	  • Complete billing claim form
	  • Send insurance claims to carriers

1.2 List the advantages and disadvantages of an electronic health record. Pages 4–6	- Disadvantages
	  • Increased security functions
	  • High cost of implementation
	  • Training requirements
	- Advantages
	  • Possibly more secure than paper records
	  • Return on investment is high
	  • All information in one place
	  • Interoperability
	  • Assures regulatory compliance
	  • Exchange of information with those who have a need to know

1.3 Describe EHR applications. Pages 6–7	- Clinical documentation - Electronic prescribing - Exchange of clinical information - Research evidence-based medicine, pharmaceutical research, clinical and financial benchmarking studies - Speech recognition

1.4 Chart the flow of information from registration through processing of the claim. Pages 7–11	- Appointment scheduling
	- Front desk check-in
	  • Verify demographic information
	  • Sign authorization/administrative forms, if necessary
	- Patient taken to examining room
	  • Height, weight, vital signs are taken
	  • Patient states the reason for today's visit (chief complaint)

(continued)

	- Care provider meets with the patient
	  • Provider verifies reason for visit; updates history
	  • Provider examines patient
	  • Provider makes referrals, if necessary
	  • Prescriptions are electronically sent to pharmacy, if necessary
	  • Provider completes the chart, which then starts the coding and claims process
	  • Provider completes the visit and provides patient with a Superbill or encounter form
	- Patient stops at the check-out desk
	  • Superbill is given to staff member at the check-out desk
	  • Patient pays co-pay, if not paid during check-in process
	  • Patient leaves the office
	- Business office/billing
	  • Insurance claim form is completed electronically
	  • Insurance claim is submitted electronically
	  • Insurance payment (or notice of denial) is received
	  • Payment is entered in the system
	  • Patient's account is updated
	  • Statement is sent, if necessary
	- Follow-up
	  • Results of diagnostic tests received, if applicable
	  • Record is updated with results
	  • Provider reviews results
	  • Patient is contacted, if necessary

1.5 Use the help feature in PrimeSUITE. Pages 11–12	- Use of Help from menu bar - Other means of accessing help feature - User's Guide

chapter **review**

MATCHING QUESTIONS

Match the terms on the left with the definitions on the right.

_____ 1. **[LO 1.2]** interoperability

_____ 2. **[LO 1.3]** application

_____ 3. **[LO 1.3]** care provider

_____ 4. **[LO 1.1]** clearinghouse

_____ 5. **[LO 1.1]** electronic claims submission

_____ 6. **[LO 1.1]** encounter form

_____ 7. **[LO 1.3]** point of care

_____ 8. **[LO 1.1]** Practice Management software

_____ 9. **[LO 1.3]** speech recognition

_____ 10. **[LO 1.1]** demographics

a. a form generated at the completion of an office visit, a portion of which details the patient's diagnosis, procedures and services performed, and charge for each procedure/service

b. filing of a healthcare claim using a computer rather than paper

c. technology that digitally transcribes spoken words

d. specialized computer software that performs administrative and billing procedures in medical offices

e. documented patient information such as age, sex, and race

f. procedures that take place at the time of care, rather than at a remote location or at a point in time after care is complete

g. person, usually a physician, who performs healthcare services requiring specialized education and training

h. software with a unique purpose, such as word processing, or used for a specific industry

i. a single database to sync multiple unrelated functions or systems

j. service that assists in claims processing by standardizing billing and performing error checks

MULTIPLE-CHOICE QUESTIONS

Select the letter that best completes the statement or answers the question:

1. **[LO 1.1]** EHR/EMR software is more comprehensive than Practice Management software because it:
   a. is computerized.
   b. contains more menu options.
   c. includes clinical documentation.
   d. submits insurance claims.

 Enhance your learning by completing these exercises and more at http://connect.mcgraw-hill.com!

2. **[LO 1.3]** PrimeSUITE:
   a. allows for ePrescribing.
   b. has mobile applications.
   c. assists in information exchange.
   d. all of these

3. **[LO 1.1]** A patient is entered into the patient list:
   a. once.
   b. twice.
   c. after a procedure.
   d. each time he or she is seen.

4. **[LO 1.2]** In the long term, costs will _____ when transitioning to an electronic health record system.
   a. increase
   b. decrease
   c. stay the same
   d. disappear

5. **[LO 1.4]** The process of moving a patient from appointment making through check-out is called:
   a. patient cycle.
   b. patient process.
   c. patient flow.
   d. patient records.

6. **[LO 1.3]** Clinical documentation of a patient's visit is known as the:
   a. Superbill.
   b. progress note.
   c. medical claim.
   d. point of care.

7. **[LO 1.1]** An encounter form is also known as a/an:
   a. EHR.
   b. history.
   c. claim form.
   d. Superbill.

8. **[LO 1.1]** The _____ is a form used to bill patient claims in physician offices.
   a. CMS-1500
   b. ICD-10
   c. CPT
   d. UB-04

9. **[LO 1.2]** One factor that might contribute to slow acceptance of EHRs is:
   a. security fears.
   b. laziness.
   c. fear of change.
   d. space concerns.

10. **[LO 1.5]** PrimeSUITE's User Guide is accessed through the _____ feature.
    a. Help
    b. Information
    c. Lookup
    d. Query

11. **[LO 1.3]** Which of the following illustrates clinical information collected through an EHR?
    a. insurance policy
    b. plan of care
    c. research effects
    d. regulatory guidelines

12. **[LO 1.2]** _____ is not easily attained when using a manual record system.
    a. Communication
    b. Data capture
    c. Interoperability
    d. Maintenance

SHORT ANSWER QUESTIONS

1. **[LO 1.4]** List the steps included in patient flow of information.

2. **[LO 1.2]** Outline at least three advantages to electronic health records as discussed in the text.

3. **[LO 1.1]** What is Practice Management software?

4. **[LO 1.3]** What feature of PrimeSUITE allows practitioners to access clinical trials and other research?

5. **[LO 1.5]** If you needed to use PrimeSUITE's Help feature to look up how to register a patient, how would you do it?

6. **[LO 1.4]** What is the first step in the patient flow of information?

7. **[LO 1.1]** Why is a claim form completed for every patient visit?

8. **[LO 1.3]** Mobile EHR applications are currently available on what mobile devices?

9. **[LO 1.2]** Define interoperability and give an example of how it might be used in the healthcare field.

10. **[LO 1.2]** List three advantages of EMRs.

11. **[LO 1.1]** What is electronic claims submission? Why is this the preferred method of claims submission?

12. **[LO 1.1]** List at least three main applications found in a typical Practice Management program.

13. **[LO 1.4]** What is the final step in the Front Desk/Check-In process?

 Enhance your learning by completing these exercises and more at http://connect.mcgraw-hill.com!

APPLYING YOUR KNOWLEDGE

1. **[LO 1.2]** Your medical office is preparing to transition from a paper-based office to an electronic one; you are really excited about this change. One day you receive an email from one of your colleagues, Sari Murray, negatively discussing the change and wondering why things cannot stay how they are now. Your colleague is looking to you and asking your opinion on the upcoming transition. Write an email back to Sari discussing your thoughts on the change to electronic records.

2. **[LOs 1.1, 1.3, 1.5]** Which of PrimeSUITE's many EHR applications do you feel is the most beneficial or useful? Explain your answer.

3. **[LO 1.4]** Denisse Cruz arrives at your office for her annual check-up appointment with Dr. Smith. Discuss what will happen with Denisse as she moves through each step of patient flow.

4. **[LOs 1.2, 1.3]** A patient is admitted to the hospital with a constant, severe migraine headache. After numerous tests, no cause for the headache can be determined. Discuss how EHRs might help diagnose this patient.

5. **[LOs 1.1, 1.2, 1.3]** Contrast a typical day in a paper-based office with a day at an office that uses Practice Management software.

6. **[LOs 1.1, 1.2, 1.3, 1.4, 1.5]** The medical office you work in recently transitioned into an electronic office and is implementing Practice Management software. You are excited about this change and are learning all you can about the new technology. However, some of your coworkers are having trouble grasping the basics, and are now saying they don't want to use the software at all. What steps could you take to assist your struggling coworkers?

Health Data Structure, Collection, and Standards

Learning Outcomes

At the end of this chapter, the student should be able to:

2.1 Describe the role of six healthcare professionals who maintain or use practice management and electronic health record applications.

2.2 Explain the difference between data and information.

2.3 Identify computer-based health information media.

2.4 Relate how screen-based data collection tools are used in healthcare.

2.5 Demonstrate how individual data elements are collected.

2.6 Describe electronic health record applications.

2.7 Identify laws, regulations, and standards that govern electronic health information.

2.8 Distinguish between practice management software and hospital health information software.

Key Terms

American Recovery and Reinvestment Act of 2009 (ARRA)

Clinical decision support

Certification Commission for Health Information Technology (CCHIT)

Data

Healthcare administrator

Health information exchange (HIE)

Healthcare systems administrator

Health Insurance Portability and Accountability Act (HIPAA)

Health Information Technology for Economic and Clinical Health (HITECH) Act

Information

Institute of Medicine (IOM)

Meaningful use (MU)

National Health Information Network (NHIN)

National Provider Identifier (NPI)

Office of the National Coordinator for Health Information Technology (ONC)

Personal health record (PHR)

Picture Archiving and Communication Systems (PACS)

Protected health information (PHI)

Regional extension center (REC)

Regional Health Information Organization (RHIO)

Structured data

Unstructured data

The Big Picture

What You Need to Know and Why You Need to Know It

As a healthcare professional you will be one of many who will be selecting, maintaining, and using electronic health record and management software. Knowing who within the organization is using the software and how they are using it is important to selecting a system that meets the needs of the organization. The collection of data must be done efficiently while meeting the documentation requirements of licensing and accrediting agencies, as well as insurance carriers (including Medicare), and conforming to the legal definition of an electronic health record. We will begin this chapter by reviewing the professionals involved and the positions they may hold within the organization. Then, the concepts of data structure, collection, and standards will be introduced in preparation for a more detailed level of instruction found in the remaining chapters of the text. We will also cover how data is collected, the tools used to collect the data, how data is transformed into information, and the regulations and standards that dictate the collection, maintenance, use, and storage of health information in an electronic form.

Health Information Management spans a wide range of functions and processes within a healthcare organization. Just about every decision is based on statistics that are largely collected from the health records of a facility. The data that is captured will result in information that is used by care providers to make decisions regarding patient care and to justify reimbursement. In addition, various levels of administrators will use information in risk management activities, budgeting, strategic planning, quality assessment, and financial reporting. Report writing will be discussed in greater detail in the chapter covering decision and compliance support.

Table 2.1 depicts a few of the medical professions within healthcare, the education or certifications they may hold, and the responsibilities they may have as pertains to the collection and use of data. This is not an exhaustive list, as there are myriad other positions such as therapists, laboratory technicians, and radiology technicians, just to name a few. Those listed are the positions held by individuals who will most likely be involved in selecting, implementing, maintaining, and using the electronic systems in a healthcare facility.

During the selection process, it is imperative that people with knowledge of health information standards, structure, and content be involved. The health information professional fulfills this role, particularly in hospitals. In addition, administrative staff who are responsible for the effective operation of the entire organization, including facility- or enterprise-wide information systems, are key to the process as well. That is not to say that individual department managers (laboratory, nursing, radiology, etc.) do not have a say—but the administrator(s) responsible for those departments may be the key players in the early stages of system selection.

In large practices, there may be an office manager or other administrative staff member with a health information background or credentials who will oversee the process. In smaller offices, the services of a consultant may be used, or the EHR vendor may have the health information expertise to oversee the process.

TABLE 2.1	Medical Professions within Healthcare	
Profession	**Certifications**	**Description**
Health Information and Informatics	• Registered Health Information Administrator (RHIA) • Registered Health Information Technician (RHIT) • Certified Health Data Analyst (CHDA) • Certified in Healthcare Privacy and Security (CHPS) • Certified Professional in Health Information and Management Systems (CPHIMS)	• Work in any healthcare setting, but most often in acute care or specialty hospitals • Work in healthcare-related professions such as consultants, software trainers and installers, government agencies, insurance companies, and law offices • Associate's, bachelor's, and master's degrees available • Many healthcare facilities, particularly hospitals, require certification Positions held in the following areas: • Health Information Department managers • Information Technology and Systems • Project management • Software analyst • Implementation support • Information system design • EHR implementation and management • Data analyst • Documentation management • Privacy/security • Release of healthcare information • Risk management • Compliance • Utilization management • Quality Assessment/Assurance • Cancer Registrar • Medical staff coordinator
Health Information Specialty Areas (HITPro™)	Require completion of non-degree educational programs that prepare students to sit for competency exams in: • Clinician/Practitioner Consultant • Implementation Manager • Implementation Support Specialist • Practice Workflow & Information Management Redesign Specialist • Technical/Software Support Staff • Trainer	• The most recent health information/informatics roles • May work in any healthcare facility, inpatient or outpatient • Each competency exam is specific to a particular role that plays a part in meaningful use of the electronic health record (EHR)
Coding professionals	• Certified Coding Associate (CCA) • Certified Coding Specialist (CCS) • Certified Coding Specialist-Physician (CCS-P) • Certified Professional Coder (CPC) • Certified Professional Coder-Hospital (CPC-H) • Certified Interventional Radiology Cardiovascular Coder (CIRCC®)	• Work in all healthcare settings • Work in healthcare-related settings such as consulting firms, software vendors, insurance companies • Certificate or associate's degree Positions held in the following areas: • Medical Coder • Reimbursement specialist • Insurance biller • Chargemaster specialist • Insurance claims specialist

(continued)

Profession	Certifications	Description
Medical Assistants	• Certified Medical Assistant (CMA) • Registered Medical Assistant (RMA)	• Typically employed in physicians' office or other outpatient setting • Requires associate's degree or certificate • Perform clinical duties such as prepping patients, taking vital signs, taking medical histories, assisting physician during exams, explaining minor procedures and giving instructions based on physician's orders, and collecting specimens • Perform administrative duties such as answering phone, making appointments, registering patients, maintaining health records, handling correspondence, filing health insurance claims, scheduling outpatient services, arranging referrals, and managing the office in general • May hold positions as office managers or business managers within a medical practice
Healthcare Administrators	• Certified Health Care Facility Manager (CHFM) • Fellow of the American College of Healthcare Executives (FACHE) • American College of Medical Practice Executives (ACMPE) Certification • Certified Practice Manager (CPM) • Certified Medical Practice Compliance Specialist (CMPCS) • Certified Physician Practice Manager (CPPM®)	• Work in all healthcare organizations • Bachelor's or master's degree typically required • Plan, organize, coordinate, and direct facility or department operations Positions held with the following titles: • Hospital administrator • Chief Information Officer/Manager • Project manager • Department manager • Office manager • Office administrator • Compliance officer
Care Providers	• Physicians (Doctor of Medicine [MD]), Doctor of Osteopathy (DO) • Physicians' Assistants (PA, PA-C) • Certified Nurse Practitioners (CNP) • Certified Registered Nurse Midwives (CRNM)	• Work in any healthcare setting • Requires advanced education, licensure, and possibly certification • The only medical professionals who can diagnose a patient, order diagnostic testing and therapeutic (including medications) measures
Nursing	• Registered Nurse (RN) • Licensed Practical Nurse (LPN)	• Provide direct care to patients • May also hold non-direct care positions in Utilization Management, Risk Management, Quality Assessment, and general management positions within a healthcare facility • Nursing Informatics • Requires associate's or bachelor's degree at a minimum; management positions and informatics positions may require a master's degree

2.1 The Professionals Who Maintain and Use Health Information

In the inpatient setting, the **healthcare administrator** may be a chief executive officer (CEO), chief operating officer (COO), chief financial officer (CFO), or chief information officer (CIO). These individuals typically have a bachelor's or master's degree (preferred) in healthcare administration and are responsible for overseeing several departments (or the entire organization). Their degree is most likely in healthcare administration, healthcare management, or health systems administration. These individuals concentrate on the big picture—the operation of the organization as a whole. **Healthcare systems administrators** are concerned with how all automated systems, including the electronic health record, affect individual departments—for example: Will all the information needs of the board of directors and administration to supply adequate, easily obtainable decision support data be met? Will the clinicians have fast, easily accessible, accurate clinical information? Is the system secure and does it meet all standards and regulations? The healthcare systems administrator may be known as the chief information officer and will typically have a great deal of knowledge and experience related to the technical aspects of automated systems.

In a hospital setting, the Director of the Health Information Department and the Chief Information Officer work closely. Each plays a key role in the selection of the product. Health Information Professionals have basic clinical knowledge, technical knowledge of automated systems, and expertise in record-keeping practice, putting them in a position to lead automation of health information efforts. Depending on the level and content of his or her education, a health information management professional may hold the position of chief information officer. Traditionally, the data itself has been the health information manager's main concern, and the use of the actual technology has been the chief information officer's domain. The staff of the health information department will need to enter, maintain, and retrieve data from electronic health records and may be certified by the American Health Information Management Association (AHIMA). Various certifications are listed in Table 2.1, as well as other certifications for health information professionals. The most recent development in health information careers and competencies is the recognition of competency exams in specialty areas which are also explained in Table 2.1.

In a medical office or other outpatient setting, healthcare administrators may have the same titles as are used in the inpatient setting, or they may be called Office Manager, Office Administrator, Business Manager, and the like. These individuals are keenly aware that electronic systems can greatly enhance the efficiency of an office, or can just as easily be a negative force that causes inefficiencies; therefore, they are at the forefront of selecting and maintaining electronic systems that meet the needs of the practice and its practitioners. Certification of professionals in the outpatient setting is just as important as in the inpatient setting.

Healthcare professionals such as medical assistants, nurses, medical coders and billers, and other administrative professionals will be using the software in a medical practice and will want it to be "user friendly," since they will be required to enter and retrieve data quickly yet accurately. The office administrator (manager) will be gathering information from the practice management and EHR systems to ensure claims are filed and paid accurately and in a timely manner, to ensure requirements of managed care organizations are

Healthcare administrator A leadership position within a healthcare facility, including chief executive officer, chief operating officer, chief financial officer, chief information officer, or other higher level management positions. May also be referred to as healthcare manager or health systems manager.

Healthcare systems administrator A leadership position specifically responsible for the information technology (IT) functions within an organization or facility.

Meaningful Use Part of the requirements of the Health Information Technology for Economic and Clinical Health (HITECH) Act which is meant to increase the use of an electronic health record through monetary incentives provided the EHR is used in a meaningful way to improve patient care.

met, and to ensure compliance with **Meaningful Use (MU)** requirements. Meaningful Use will be discussed throughout this worktext.

The American Health Information Management Association (AHIMA), the American Association of Medical Assistants (AAMA), the American Medical Technologists (AMT), the Healthcare Information and Management and Systems Society (HIMSS), and the Physician Office Management Association of America (POMAA) are all professional associations offering certifying exams; providing members with up-to-date, relevant information about their respective fields; and offering continuing education opportunities, networking opportunities, publications, and career assistance. Each has an extensive website accessible by a search of the name.

Check Your Understanding

1. What roles might be held by a healthcare administrator?
2. What is the difference between a medical assistant and an office administrator?

2.2 Data versus Information

Data A single, raw fact such as a patient's name, height, or weight. Often used interchangeably with information, though they are not synonymous terms.

Information Raw facts that, when viewed as a whole, have meaning. Example: a report of all patients treated at Memorial Medical Center with a principal diagnosis of streptococcal pharyngitis (strep throat), sorted by patients' age.

Throughout this worktext you will see the terms **data** and **information**. They are often used interchangeably, but they are not entirely the same. Look up each term in a dictionary, and you will see within the definitions that the terms are almost interchangeable or synonymous. Think of it this way, though—data is a single fact, such as the patient is *60 years old*, or that the *patient is female*, or the *patient is African American*. Single facts come together to form information. For example, the fact that Elena Jones is allergic to penicillin is a piece of data. But, add to that piece of data the fact that she breaks out in hives, has difficulty breathing, and required an emergency room visit for her last allergic reaction and we have information about Elena and her allergy to penicillin. It is vitally important that each piece of data is accurate, valid, and timely to ensure that the information resulting from the data is also accurate, valid, timely, and in a usable format to ensure quality medical care.

Unstructured data Data in the form of words or audio files that cannot be tracked. Examples include emails, written narratives, and audio files from speech recognition technology.

Structured data Data that fits a particular model or format, which can be tracked and may be part of a database. Examples include ICD-10-CM/PCS codes, CPT codes, a patient's temperature, or a patient's age.

Data may be **unstructured** or **structured**. Examples of unstructured data are a dictated report, a written progress note, voice files, or scanned images of original documents. In this unstructured format, it is difficult, if not impossible, to track or trend statistics, or to share information with healthcare agencies, public health agencies, or insurance carriers. Structured data—such as standard templates that are used to collect the elements of the dictated report or progress note, bar codes to identify types of reports or individual files, or numeric codes that equate to a written diagnosis or procedure—allow computers to process the data into usable information.

Check Your Understanding

1. Define data.
2. Differentiate between structured and unstructured data.

Prior to there being an electronic health record system, clinicians relied on one medium to collect and access information about patients—paper. Many pieces of paper make up the health record, and records of patients are often several inches thick. Paper records are contained in a folder that is filed numerically by a medical record number or alphabetically by the patient's last name. It is not that paper is no longer in use, but electronic media is gaining acceptance in the healthcare community. And in the coming years, the electronic health record will be a requirement rather than a choice thanks to the **Health Information Technology for Economic and Clinical Health (HITECH) Act**, which will be addressed later in this chapter. Many health insurance plans are making electronic **personal health records (PHR)** available to their subscribers. A PHR contains a person's health history, immunization status, current and past medications, allergies, and instructions given by a care provider; it often includes patient education materials as well. Though insurance carriers may provide the means to keep a PHR online, this does not replace the legal health record kept by the patient's care provider.

Electronic health records provide physicians with **clinical decision support** software, which is used to access current information about a disease or condition. This technology alerts the care provider to possible medication interactions, gives treatment options based on results of clinical trials or research, and alerts the provider that a patient may have a particular diagnosis based on the data found in his or her electronic record. Not so long ago, physicians were opposed to this technology, thinking it was "cookbook medicine"; this is no longer the case, since great advances in the diagnosis and treatment of illnesses occur so quickly, making it very difficult or impossible to keep up with the most recent studies, findings, and recommended treatments. Thus, decision support applications within an EHR software package help to keep physicians up to date as well as improve the quality of care given to patients.

Physicians can use computerized models within the EHR to show where a patient's rash is located, for example, rather than a crudely drawn picture of a patient's back (Figures 2.1 and 2.2).

The use of videos or DVDs is not new technology, although they are now used more often to educate patients about the procedure they are about to undergo than are handouts or educational booklets. The care provider may choose to show patients a video while they are in the office, or provide a link to a video for patients to view from their home computer. Using this type of media ensures that the information used to educate patients is consistent.

Most EHRs now provide educational materials for patients, and the educational materials can be specific to a particular patient's conditions,

Health Information Technology for Economic and Clinical Health (HITECH) Act A portion of the American Recovery and Reinvestment Act (ARRA) that is meant to increase the use of an electronic health record by hospitals and physicians through a monetary incentive program.

Personal health record (PHR) A record, kept by the patient, that contains a person's health history, immunization status, current and past medications, allergies, and instructions given by a care provider; it often includes patient education materials as well.

Clinical decision support Allows access to current treatment options for a disease, through electronic or remote methods. Alerts the care provider to possible medication interactions, gives treatment options based on results of clinical trials or research, alerts provider that a patient may have a particular diagnosis based on the data found in the patient's electronic record.

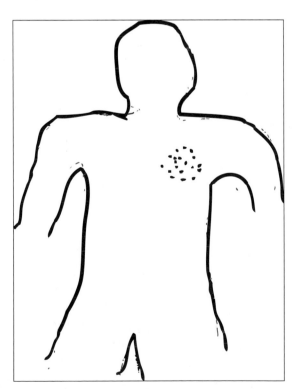

Figure 2.1 Drawing of placement of rash on patient's back as it would have appeared in a paper health record

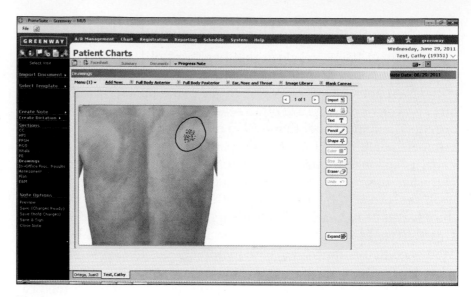

Figure 2.2 **Computer-generated drawing of placement of rash on patient's back**

including treatment options, medications, etc. The educational materials may be printed out for the patient, or they can be provided through a secure portal that the patient accesses from home.

Physicians and administrators may want to visually present findings of a study or to consult with another physician and show a patient's disease progression. This can be done through use of software that has been available for years—presentation software such as Microsoft Power-Point® or Open Office IMPRESS. Spreadsheets are often useful in making a point as well. EHR software provides the ability to visually chart changes in a patient's vital signs, for example, and show trends or statistical changes. Patient care and treatment is greatly enhanced with the ability to track vital signs over time, thus alerting the care provider to changes in a patient's condition.

Let us look at a particular scenario. Patti Wolfe has been seeing Dr. Raszkowski for the past five years. She has been faithful about having a yearly physical exam. For the past four years, her blood pressure has increased on each visit. In 2008, her blood pressure was 130/80; in 2009, it was 135/82; in 2010, it was 130/83; and in 2011, it was 140/88. Seeing this steady climb, Dr. Raszkowski explained the situation to Mrs. Wolfe, and started her on a treatment regimen. Without this quick visual of her blood pressures, the subtle changes may not have been picked up by the physician, and her high blood pressure could have gone untreated.

Speech (voice) recognition technology is a medium that has been available for many years and has steadily gained in popularity. This software translates what a provider is saying and types those words into text. Whereas physicians used to dictate into a microphone and a medical transcriptionist would type the words, using word processing software, with voice recognition software the physician still dictates, but the software captures his or her words, then converts speech into text. The software is not 100 percent accurate, however, and in the world of medicine, it needs to be. Thus, a human being must still review the final document for accuracy. With speech recognition, the medical transcriptionist's role has changed from transcriber to editor.

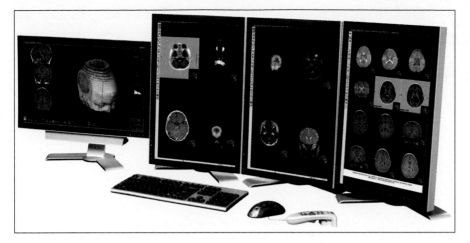

Figure 2.3 DS Systems, Inc. PACS

Picture Archiving and Communication Systems (PACS) allow providers to view images such as x-rays, scans, ultrasounds, and the like. Originally used as a means to store x-ray film, PACS make it possible for providers to remotely view x-ray film to aid in clinical decision support. The improved image quality using PACS as well as the ability to add alerts or reminders based on the findings noted in PACS greatly improve patient care. Figure 2.3 illustrates a typical PACS used to view radiologic images.

Picture Archiving and Communication Systems (PACS) Computerized system for enhanced viewing and sharing of images such as x-rays, scans, ultrasounds, and mammograms.

Check Your Understanding

1. In the past, physicians marked the location of a patient's pain by drawing on a picture of a body. With the advantage of EHRs, what are they now able to do?
2. What does PACS stand for?
3. What do PACS allow providers to do?

2.4 Screen-Based Data Collection Tools

Those who are entering (also known as capturing) data typically do so on a computer screen. It may be done on a desktop computer, a laptop, a notebook computer, or a personal digital assistant (PDA). Each of these pieces of hardware will be discussed in a later chapter but the commonality between them is that data can be entered and then retrieved by using a computer screen. Think of the screen as the replacement for paper. Advantages include the portability of the hand-held devices, the ability to have multiple monitors showing different images at the same time, and the ability to customize a screen based on user preference. With paper records, there is typically an order in which the individual papers are filed within the folder, but not all care providers prefer that same order. Take a look at the two screens showing a patient's history in Figures 2.4 and 2.5—you see that the same information is collected but that the information is in different places on the screen.

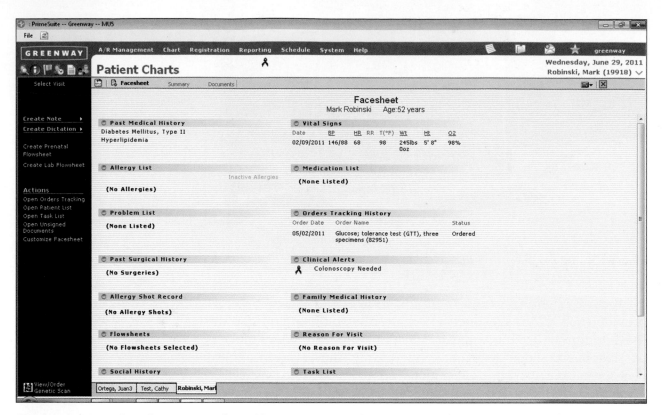

Figure 2.4   Facesheet format as preferred by one care provider

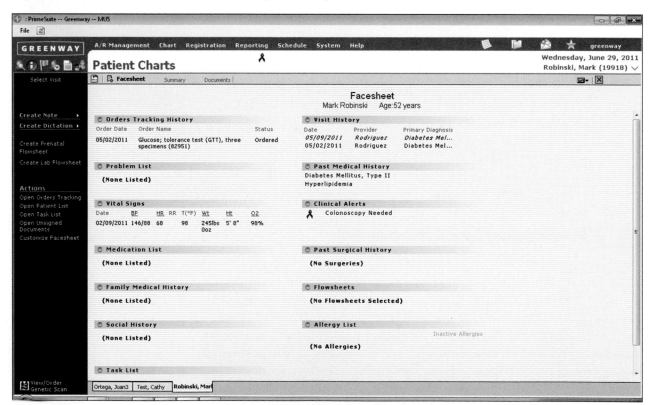

Figure 2.5   Facesheet format as preferred by a different care provider

Check Your Understanding

1.   What types of computers are used for data capture?
2.   What are some advantages of screen-based data collection tools?

So, we have this data, but how did we get it in the first place? It all starts when the patient makes an appointment with a physician's office or comes to the hospital for an emergency department visit, outpatient laboratory, outpatient surgery, or inpatient admission. We collect identifying information verbally from the patient (or representative), or we ask the patient to complete a form (or a combination of both). See Figure 2.6 for an example of a registration form.

Greensburg Medical Center
REGISTRATION FORM
(Please Print)

Today's date:	Care Provider:

PATIENT INFORMATION

Patient's last name:	First:	Middle:	❑ Mr. ❑ Mrs.	❑ Miss ❑ Ms.	Marital status (circle one) Single / Mar / Div / Sep / Wid

Is this your legal name? ❑ Yes ❑ No	If not, what is your legal name?	(Former name):	Birth date:	Age:	Sex: ❑ M ❑ F

Street address:	Social Security no.:	Home phone no.:

P. O. Box:	City:	State:	ZIP Code:

Occupation:	Employer:	Employer phone no.:

E-mail address :	Cell phone:

Race:	Ethnicity:	Primary language:	Religion:

Other family members seen here:

INSURANCE INFORMATION
(Presentation of Insurance Card is required at time of each visit)

Person responsible for bill:	Birth date: / /	Address (if different) :	Home phone no.: ( )

Is this person a patient here? ❑ Yes ❑ No

Occupation:	Employer:	Employer address:	Employer phone no.: ( )

Is this patient covered by insurance? ❑ Yes ❑ No

Please indicate primary insurance	❑ McGraw-Hill Healthmark Insurance	❑ BlueCross/Shield	❑ [Insurance]	❑ [Insurance]	❑ [Insurance]

❑ [Insurance]	❑ Workers' Compensation	❑ Medicare	❑ Medicaid *(Please provide card)*	❑ Other

Subscriber's name:	Subscriber's S.S.no.:	Birth date: / /	Group no.:	Policy no.:	Co-payment: $

Patient's relationship to subscriber:	❑ Self	❑ Spouse	❑ Child	❑ Other	Effective Date:

Name of secondary insurance (if applicable):	Subscriber's name:	Group no.:	Policy no.:

Patient's relationship to subscriber:	❑ Self	❑ Spouse	❑ Child	❑ Other

IN CASE OF EMERGENCY

Name of local friend or relative (not living at same address) :	Relationship to patient:	Home phone no.: ( )	Work phone no.: ( )

The above information is true to the best of my knowledge. I authorize my insurance benefits be paid directly to the physician. I understand that I am financially responsible for any balance. I also authorize [Name of Practice] or insurance company to release any information required to process my claims.

Patient/Guardian signature _____ *Date* _____

Figure 2.6 Patient registration form

The patient's past medical, surgical, social, and family histories are collected and entered into the EHR as well. Figure 2.7 illustrates documentation in PrimeSUITE; each of the areas, when clicked on, includes more detailed information about the patient. Medication allergies, current medications, and immunization history are typically captured as part of the past medical history. The history is taken from a history form and/or the patient is asked questions in order to capture those data elements in the EHR.

The care provider then documents the history of present illness (HPI) and performs and documents a physical exam. He or she views all of this information to make an assessment of the patient (make a diagnosis) and then determines a treatment plan (also called a plan of care).

In addition, the patient's previous health records are often used as a source of data. This information may be sent to the facility in a paper format, which is later scanned into the patient's health record, or the information can be retrieved electronically, eventually becoming part of the patient's record.

Check Your Understanding

1. Besides a patient's medical, social, surgical, and family histories, what other information is captured for entry into his or her EHR?

2. Can a patient's previous health records be used as a source of data? Explain your answer.

3. Name two ways that identifying information is collected from a patient.

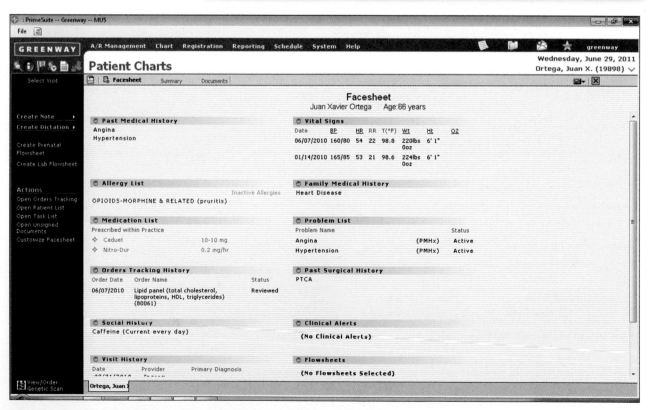

Figure 2.7 PrimeSUITE documentation of patient's past medical history

A health record that is in electronic form is referred to as an electronic health record (EHR) and sometimes an electronic medical record (EMR). The Office of the National Coordinator for Health Information Technology (ONC), however, differentiates between the two, based on a white paper by Garets and Davis. According to Garets and Davis, the EMR is the legal patient record that is created within any healthcare facility (hospital, nursing home, ambulatory surgery facility, physician's office, etc.). The information in that EMR relates solely to that episode of care, and the EMR is the data source for the EHR. The individual records feed into the EHR so that healthcare providers, patients, employers, and insurance carriers can access a patient's health records as appropriate and in accordance with **Health Insurance Portability and Accountability Act (HIPAA)** regulations. Only those who have a need to know should access the information found in a patient's record.

Let us look at an example. Alison Holt is seen in the emergency room of Memorial Hospital on July 15, 2009. An EMR is compiled for that visit. She also has an EMR for an inpatient stay in Memorial Hospital from October 5 to October 10, 2009. There are additional EMRs for Alison Holt that pertain to various physician office visits and outpatient diagnostic testing. Then, in April 2010, Ms. Holt sees a pulmonary specialist who needs to review her previous health records. Her providers and the hospitals she has been admitted to are able to share information through a **Regional Health Information Organization (RHIO)**, which includes healthcare organizations in her area that exchange patient information in order to improve care. This **health information exchange (HIE)** resulted in the quick and easy sharing of her medical history with the pulmonary specialist. Her individual records thus became part of an EHR. In effect, an EHR allows for the exchange of information among caregivers and others (insurance, employers, etc.) who have a need to know, but in a secure environment and according to certain standards.

In 2003, the **Institute of Medicine (IOM)** defined the functions of an EHR. The eight core functions are:

- health information and data
- result management
- order management
- decision support
- electronic communication and connectivity
- patient support
- administrative processes and reporting
- reporting and population health

We will no doubt continue to use the terms EMR and EHR interchangeably, but it is important to remember that in order for the benefits of the EMR to be realized, an EHR must exist. Without the EMR, the EHR, by definition, would not exist.

for your information **fyi**

The Garets and Davis paper can be found at http://www.providersedge.com/ehdocs/ehr_articles/Electronic_Patient_Records-EMRs_and_EHRs.pdf

Health Insurance Portability and Accountability Act (HIPAA) Passed in 1996, this act includes regulations that afford people who leave their employment the ability to keep their insurance or obtain new health insurance even if they have a pre-existing medical condition. Also sets standards for storing, maintaining, and sharing electronic health information while ensuring its privacy and security.

Regional Health Information Organization (RHIO) Healthcare organizations in a geographic area that exchange health information with the goal of improving patient care, reducing duplication, and reducing unnecessary costs.

Health information exchange (HIE) The movement or sharing of information between healthcare entities in a secure manner, and in keeping with nationally recognized standards.

Institute of Medicine (IOM) An independent, non-profit, nongovernmental organization that works to provide unbiased and authoritative advice to decision makers and the public.

Check Your Understanding

1. The legal patient record created for one episode of care is known as the _____.
2. Who is allowed to access the information contained in a patient's record?

Protected health information (PHI) Any piece of information that identifies a patient, including a patient's name, date of birth, address, email, telephone number, employer, relatives' names, social security number, medical record number, account numbers tied to the patient, fingerprints, photographs, and characteristics about the patient that would automatically disclose his or her identity. PHI also includes any clinical information about an identified patient.

2.7 Laws, Regulations, and Standards

Health Insurance Portability and Accountability Act (HIPAA)

As a healthcare professional, you will get used to the fact that there are many outside influences that affect how and why we do our jobs. We will start our journey through the agencies, regulations, and laws that govern the keeping and exchange of health information with HIPAA, although many laws and standards have come before it. HIPAA stands for Health Insurance Portability and Accountability Act. HIPAA was passed on August 21, 1996, with a multifaceted purpose. It included regulations that afforded people who left their employment the ability to keep their insurance or obtain new health insurance even if they had a pre-existing medical condition. It also set standards for several aspects of storing, maintaining, and sharing electronic health information while ensuring the privacy and security of health information.

There are several rules that are addressed in HIPAA. With an effective compliance date of April 14, 2003, is the Privacy Rule. Its intent was to ensure the privacy of health information, and the use of **protected health information (PHI)**, which is information that identifies the patient. It is the Office of Civil Rights that enforces compliance with the Privacy Rule. The specifics of the Privacy Rule will be covered in more detail in the Privacy, Security, Confidentiality, and Legal Issues chapter; however, it is important to know that electronic data collection, maintenance, use, and storage are all governed by standards, and many of these come from HIPAA. Health records are legal documents and must be compliant with state and federal regulations as well as standards set forth by accrediting agencies and insurance carriers.

In February 2003, the Security Rules were published. The deadline for facilities to implement the security rules was April 20, 2005. The security standards require healthcare organizations to include safeguards (administrative, physical, and technological) that ensure health information is protected, that it is kept private, and that it is retrievable in the event that the integrity of the electronic system is compromised.

The Electronic Healthcare Transactions, Code Sets, and National Identifiers Rules required that medical providers who submit claims electronically be compliant with regulations requiring standardization of electronic collection and exchange of health information.

Hospitals, physicians' offices, and clearinghouses (entities that process medical claims prior to payment) were required not only to submit claims (and diagnosis and procedure codes) electronically, but also to receive information, such as remittance advices, from insurance companies electronically. Compliance was required by October 23, 2003. Another change went into effect on January 1, 2012, version 5010 of the Code Set Rule, and is part of the electronic transaction standards of HIPAA. This is an upgrade to version 4010, which had been in use since 2000. Like any other software, it had become outdated and was in need of upgrading. The driving force behind the effective date, though, was the impending ICD-10-CM/PCS change. In order to accept and transmit codes that are alphanumeric and that vary in length, new software was necessary; 4010 could not accommodate the new coding structure. In addition, version 5010 included improved instructions for the use of the **National Provider Identifier (NPI)** number, which is a unique identifier that must be used on insurance claims to identify the care provider and/or group practice that rendered care to the patient. The NPI implementation was the last of the original HIPAA regulations to take effect.

National Provider Identifier (NPI) A unique identifier that must be used on insurance claims to identify the care provider and/or group practice that rendered care to the patient.

HITECH Act

The Health Information Technology for Economic and Clinical Health (HITECH) Act is part of the **American Recovery and Reinvestment Act of 2009 (ARRA)**, which was signed into law by President Obama on February 17, 2009. The HITECH portion of ARRA is meant to increase the use of an EHR by hospitals and physicians. The incentive program, made possible through HITECH, includes $18 billion in funding for this purpose. Physicians and hospitals that show meaningful use of the information collected through use of an EHR will benefit from HITECH. The incentives can be used for implementation of new EHR systems, or upgrades to those that are already in place. Later in this text, we will demonstrate the meaningful use of data. There are three stages of meaningful use; the first is the collection and use of data, the second is the secure exchange of information, and the third is use of patient data to improve patient outcomes. Figure 2.8 depicts the HITECH interim final rule from the Health and Human Services (HHS) website.

American Recovery and Reinvestment Act (ARRA) Signed into law by President Obama on February 17, 2009; this economic "stimulus plan" includes provisions for the Health Information Technology for Economic and Clinical Health (HITECH) Act.

Office of the National Coordinator (ONC)

From ARRA also came the **Office of the National Coordinator for Health Information Technology (ONC)**. The ONC was created in 2004 through a presidential order, but was later mandated by legislation (HITECH). According to the ONC website "ONC is the principal Federal entity charged with coordination of nationwide efforts to implement and use the most advanced health information technology and the electronic exchange of health information"; its mission includes:

Office of the National Coordinator for Health Information Technology (ONC) The principal federal entity charged with coordination, implementation, and use of health information technology and the electronic exchange of health information.

- promoting development of a nationwide Health IT infrastructure that allows for electronic use and exchange of information that:
  —ensures secure and protected patient health information
  —improves healthcare quality
  —reduces healthcare costs

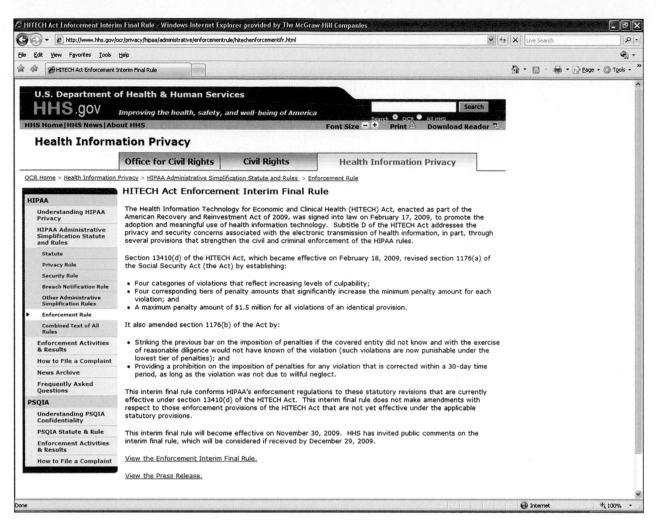

Figure 2.8   HITECH Act Enforcement Interim Final Rule

——informs medical decisions at the time/place of care

——includes meaningful public input in infrastructure development

——improves coordination of care and information among hospitals, labs, physicians, etc.

——improves public health activities and facilitates early identification/rapid response to public health emergencies

——facilitates health and clinical research

——promotes early detection, prevention, and management of chronic diseases

——promotes a more effective marketplace

——improves efforts to reduce health disparities

- providing leadership in the development, recognition, and implementation of standards and the certification of Health IT products
- coordinating Health IT policy
- strategic planning for Health IT adoption and health information exchange
- establishing governance for the Nationwide Health Information Network

National Health Information Network (NHIN)

The ultimate goal of using EHR technology is to improve patient care—sharing information to improve diagnosis, treatment, and prognosis—while doing so in an economically efficient manner. In order to share health information electronically, though, standards must be set, and policies must be adhered to. According to the ONC website, the **National Health Information Network (NHIN)** is "a set of standards, services, and policies that enable the secure exchange of health information over the Internet." (National Health Information Network: Overview)

Current activities of the NHIN include:

Nationwide Health Information Network (NwHIN)—"a set of standards, services, and policies that enable the secure exchange of health information over the Internet." (HealthIT.gov)

National eHealth Collaborative (NeHC)—created through a grant from the ONC, public-private partnership that enables secure and interoperable nationwide health information exchange to advance health and improve healthcare. "The broad mission of NeHC is threefold: consumer engagement in eHealth, health IT education, and HIE." (National eHealth Collaborative)

Direct Project—a project aimed at developing standards and services that will enable secure exchange of information on a local level among trusted providers to support stage 1 of the Meaningful Use incentives, which went into effect on January 1, 2011.

CONNECT—free, open source software that supports health information exchange.

Since the first edition of this text was written, there has been progress in healthcare reform in the United States. New reimbursement models are on the horizon, and with them comes more of an emphasis on competitiveness in providing healthcare, as well as more of a shared risk/shared reward system (Berry). Data is required in order to measure healthcare quality and the resulting quality measures are necessary to roll out these new models of reimbursement; therefore, the exchange of health information also becomes a necessity.

A downside to this, at least from the perspective of providers of healthcare, is a decrease in revenue from the standpoint that sharing health information will result in a reduction of duplicate testing and unnecessary tests or procedures.

Certification Commission for Health Information Technology (CCHIT) and Other Certifying Agencies

To ensure that health information is indeed shared securely, and that the shared information is being used for its intended purpose, the **Certification Commission for Health Information Technology (CCHIT)** was founded in 2004. Its purpose is to certify EHRs for functionality, interoperability, and security. A nongovernmental nonprofit organization, CCHIT began certifying EHR systems in 2004, and by 2009 over 200 systems had been certified. There is reference to the importance of

National Health Information Network (NHIN) A set of standards, services, and policies that enable the secure exchange of health information over the Internet.

Certification Commission for Health Information Technology (CCHIT) A nonprofit, nongovernmental agency whose purpose is to certify electronic health records for functionality, interoperability, and security.

certification within ARRA, specifically in the area of meaningful use of health information through the adoption of a certified EHR.

The Healthcare Information and Management Systems Society (HIMSS), a nonprofit organization that focuses on the use of information technology (IT) and management systems needed to improve heathcare, provides important information regarding the EHR on its website found at http://www.himss.org/ASP/topics_ehr.asp.

The Medicare and Medicaid EHR Incentive Programs require the use of certified EHR technology; a listing of certified EHR technologies can be found at http://onc-chpl.force.com/ehrcert. When you access this list, you will see that there are other EHR certifying agencies that will be discussed in a later chapter.

Regional Extension Centers

As part of HITECH, extension centers are funded by the federal government. The purpose of the extension centers is to lend technical assistance and guidance regarding best practices in the selection, implementation, and maintenance of an EHR that will satisfy the meaningful use requirements. Each **regional extension center**, or REC (pronounced R-E-C), is responsible for a geographic region within the United States and is a nonprofit entity. A map is available at http://www.hhs.gov/about/regionmap.html; click on your location to see what is happening in your area.

So you can see there are many outside entities to ensure that health information is shared so that safe, effective, quality medical care is provided, yet in a manner that allows for the security and privacy of that information exchange.

Regional extension center An organization that assists health-care providers with the selection and implementation of electronic health record systems.

Check Your Understanding

1. CCHIT is a _____ agency.
2. Name the four subcategories of HIPAA.
3. What does PHI stand for?
4. What office ensures compliance with the Privacy Rule?
5. Explain the necessity behind updating to HIPAA 5010.

2.8 Similarities and Differences between a Physician's Office and Hospital Information Systems

Regardless of the healthcare setting—inpatient or outpatient—every patient seen must have a health record that describes his or her history of present illness, past medical and surgical history, record of physical exam, record of treatment rendered, results of diagnostic tests, plan of care, and diagnoses. In a physician's office setting, the patient schedules an appointment, which is part of the registration process. In a hospital setting, a patient may arrive without an appointment for an emergency department visit, or to have outpatient lab work done, for example. In either case, appointments would typically be unnecessary or impossible. In other instances, such as for a CT scan, which requires a significant amount of time and specially trained staff, an appointment is necessary. And, in a hospital setting, a patient may be scheduled for an elective surgery such as cholecystectomy (removal of the gallbladder).

The steps taken to capture the fact that a patient was seen, no matter what the setting, are most easily (and accurately) done using computerization. In a physician's office, this is done using Practice Management (PM) software. In a hospital, this is called the Master Patient (person) Index (MPI) and it is part of the RADT (Registration, Admission, Discharge, Transfer) functions of the hospital's automated information system. Each patient is entered only once into the MPI, although there may be several visits (encounters) for each patient as a subset of the main entry. This allows the documentation of each individual visit to be filed in one place within the MPI.

Recent years have seen an increase in single hospitals and physician practices being purchased by large hospital systems. The single hospitals/offices then become part of an "enterprise." In some cases, the individual institutions or offices maintain their own records, and operate autonomously. In others, the MPI is shared (an enterprise-wide MPI), and more than likely will result in duplicate patients and an increase in incorrect data. Obviously, correct data in the MPI is always a priority, but when an enterprise-wide MPI is used, it becomes even more imperative to have staff that continually monitor for and clean up any inaccurate, duplicate, erroneous, or unreliable data. It also becomes more important for registration staff to do a thorough check of the MPI before adding a patient as new or before selecting an existing patient.

Practice Management software is used to handle the administrative functions in an office such as listing all patients who have been seen in that practice; capturing insurance and demographic information; entering charges and diagnosis and procedure codes; filing, maintenance, and follow-up of medical claims and collections (billing procedures); running statistical reports about the practice; and scheduling patients' appointments.

The capturing of the identifying information and the clinical documentation discussed earlier in this chapter becomes part of the electronic health record in both the hospital and physicians' offices.

The various functions performed are called by different names in different settings, but the goals are the same—registration of the patient and then compilation of a health record for every encounter the patient has in that facility or office.

Table 2.2 compares common jargon used in a hospital to that used in a physician's office.

The objective of an EHR is to capture timely, accurate, usable health information to ensure quality medical care; provide for coordination of care; support the medical necessity for diagnostic testing; protect the legal interests of the patient, provider, and hospital; collect data used in statistical reporting; and file insurance claims.

In order to select, implement, maintain, and use practice management software or the electronic health record, it is necessary to include professionals who understand not only how to use the software, but also what to look for when selecting software that will meet the stiff regulations that govern the keeping of health information. It is vitally important that this health information be maintained in a way that is

| TABLE 2.2 | Comparison of Outpatient to Inpatient Setting | |

Action	Physician's Office or Other Outpatient Setting	Hospital
Patient seeks care	Schedule patient or make an appointment	Register or admit a patient
Health record is compiled	End product is a SOAP note, progress note, or "chart"	End-product is a health (medical) record
Listing of all patients seen by the facility	Once the patient is registered one time, he/she appears in the Patient List	Once the patient is registered one time, he/she appears in the Master Patient (person) Index (MPI)
Patient has outpatient care	Each is called an encounter or visit	Each is called an encounter
Patient stays overnight	n/a	The patient is an admission or inpatient
Patient is finished with the encounter	Patient checks out	Patient is discharged

private, confidential, and secure, yet readily available when needed. In addition, the information needs to be accurate, reliable, and valid. Over the past several years, the federal government has affirmed that there is an urgent need for an electronic health record that will provide for more efficient, effective, and safe healthcare for Americans.

Check Your Understanding

1. SOAP notes are generally used in a/an _____ setting.
2. Could a patient ever have outpatient care in a hospital setting? If so, what is an episode of outpatient care called?
3. What term describes a hospital's historical list of patients?

APPLYING YOUR SKILLS

You have learned much about how healthcare is structured in the United States and the professionals who manage various aspects of healthcare, and have been introduced to the organizations that govern the electronic systems used in healthcare facilities. To tie all of this together, you will set out on a virtual scavenger hunt. Use the Internet to answer the following questions about your region of the country.

1. Find the website for a hospital near you. Who is the CEO?
2. By searching the Web or reading a newspaper or magazine article, find information related to healthcare, such as current cancer rate, death rate for a particular region, or proven treatment for a particular disease. What makes this information rather than data?
3. Using the Internet, find the regional extension center for your state.
4. Using the Internet, find the health information exchange for your state.
5. Find three hospitals or physician practices within a 100-mile radius of your home. For each, is the hospital or practice stand-alone or part of an enterprise system?

chapter 2 **summary**

LEARNING OUTCOME	CONCEPTS FOR REVIEW
2.1 Describe the role of six healthcare professionals who maintain or use practice management and electronic health record applications. Pages 22–24	- Healthcare professionals, their educational background, their certifications, and how they use health information: • Chief Information Officer • Health Information Professionals • Chief Financial Officer • Healthcare Administrators/Managers/Office Administrators • Care Providers • Nurses, Medical Assistants
2.2 Explain the difference between data and information. Page 24	- Often used interchangeably - Data is a single fact - Single facts come together to form information - Structured vs. unstructured data
2.3 Identify computer-based health information media. Pages 25–27	- Role of the Health Information Technology for Economic and Clinical Health (HITECH) Act in the adoption of an electronic health record - Define personal health record (PHR) - Electronic health record includes: • Decision support technology • Computerized models and images • Presentation aids • Voice recognition technology • Picture Archiving and Communication Systems (PACS)
2.4 Relate how screen-based data collection tools are used in healthcare. Pages 27–28	- Hardware used to collect health information includes: • Desktop computers • Laptop computers • Notebook computers • iPad • iPhone • Personal digital assistants (PDA) - Advantages include portability and customization
2.5 Demonstrate how individual data elements are collected. Page 29	- Data collected through use of forms or in person - Registration forms used as method of collecting patient identifying and demographic information - Patient history form used as method of collecting past medical, surgical, family, and social histories; allergies; medication history

(continued)

LEARNING OUTCOME	CONCEPTS FOR REVIEW
2.6 Describe electronic health record applications, Pages 29–32	- Differentiate between electronic medical record (EMR) and electronic health record (EHR) - Role of the Office of the National Coordinator for Health Information Technology (ONC) - Differentiate between Regional Health Information Organization (RHIO) and Health Information Exchange (HIE) - List the functions of the EHR as detailed by the Institute of Medicine (IOM)
2.7 Identify laws, regulations, and standards that govern electronic health information. Pages 32–36	- Identify the privacy, security, transactions, and code set rules of HIPAA - Define Protected Health Information (PHI) - Define National Provider Identifier (NPI) number - Describe the Health Information Technology for Economic and Clinical Health (HITECH) Act and its role in requiring electronic health records - Define meaningful use of data collected through use of an EHR - Describe the purpose of the Office of the National Coordinator for Health Information Technology (ONC) - Explain the National Health Information Network (NHIN) - Explain the Certification Commission for Health Information Technology (CCHIT) - Relate the purpose of regional extension centers (REC)
2.8 Distinguish between practice management software and hospital health information software. Pages 36–38	- Describe the functions of Practice Management software - Differentiate between RADT systems and EHR systems within a hospital setting - Discuss the use of a Master Patient (Person) Index and Patient List - Articulate the purpose of an EHR

chapter **review**

MATCHING QUESTIONS

Match the terms on the left with the definitions on the right.

_____ 1. **[LO 2.2]** data

_____ 2. **[LO 2.5]** health information exchange

_____ 3. **[LO 2.2]** unstructured data

_____ 4. **[LO 2.1]** healthcare systems administrator

_____ 5. **[LO 2.7]** meaningful use

_____ 6. **[LO 2.3]** clinical decision support

_____ 7. **[LO 2.8]** Master Patient Index

_____ 8. **[LO 2.7]** Protected Health Information

_____ 9. **[LO 2.7]** CCHIT

_____ 10. **[LO 2.6]** Institute of Medicine (IOM)

a. any piece of identifying or clinical information about a patient

b. an independent organization that is responsible for certifying electronic health records for viability

c. staff member whose responsibilities include management of a facility's IT functions

d. use of health information in an effective and efficient manner to improve patient care

e. a single fact often used interchangeably with information

f. an independent organization that works to provide advice and guidance to the public and healthcare decision makers

g. method of accessing current treatment options for a disease, through electronic or remote methods

h. the sharing of health information among various entities, using standardized and secure processes

i. record of the names of all patients seen in a hospital setting

j. details that cannot be tracked, such as emails and voice recognition technology audio files

MULTIPLE-CHOICE QUESTIONS

Select the letter that best completes the statement or answers the question:

1. **[LO 2.7]** The acronym HIE stands for:
   a. health information exchange.
   b. hospital information exchange.
   c. health information electronically.
   d. hospital institutional exchange.

 Enhance your learning by completing these exercises and more at http://connect.mcgraw-hill.com!

2. **[LO 2.4]** An advantage of using screen-based data collection tools is that the layout of the information can be:
   a. printed.
   b. deleted.
   c. shredded.
   d. customized.

3. **[LO 2.6]** The _____ defined the eight core functions of an EHR.
   a. National Institute of Health
   b. American Recovery and Reinvestment Act
   c. Institute of Medicine
   d. HITECH Act

4. **[LO 2.7]** Which of the following is a goal of HIPAA?
   a. establish standards for keeping of health information
   b. ensure patients receive timely treatment
   c. allow a person's insurance to transfer from one job to another
   d. guide how Picture Archiving and Communication Systems are used

5. **[LO 2.5, 2.8]** In a physician's office, patient data collection begins when:
   a. the patient exam begins.
   b. the patient calls to make an appointment.
   c. the medical assistant takes the patient's vital signs.
   d. the patient signs in at the front desk.

6. **[LO 2.3]** An advantage of EHRs is that patients are now able to _____ about procedures they are undergoing.
   a. hear lectures
   b. see diagrams
   c. ask questions
   d. view videos

7. **[LO 2.2]** Knowing that Jim Smith had a heart attack when he was 53 is an example of:
   a. data.
   b. information.
   c. support.
   d. technology.

8. **[LO 2.8]** When patients are finished with their encounter at a hospital, they:
   a. are admitted.
   b. check out.
   c. complete a SOAP note.
   d. are discharged.

9. **[LO 2.7]** If a hospital uses information gathered through their EHRs to justify the purchase of state-the-art equipment to improve patient care, they are:
   a. violating the Privacy Rule.
   b. engaging in meaningful use.
   c. abusing Protected Health Information.
   d. following CCHIT.

SHORT ANSWER QUESTIONS

1. **[LO 2.1]** Define the roles of the six healthcare professionals involved in EMR use.

2. **[LO 2.7]** What is the purpose of CCHIT?

3. **[LO 2.1]** Explain the differences among a healthcare administrator, healthcare manager, and health systems administrator.

4. **[LO 2.8]** List five objectives of an EHR.

5. **[LO 2.7]** HIPAA is an acronym for _____.

6. **[LO 2.6]** Contrast an EHR with an EMR.

7. **[LO 2.2]** Explain the difference between data and information, and give an example of each.

8. **[LO 2.3]** Why were so many physicians opposed to clinical decision support in the past?

9. **[LO 2.5]** List the four types of histories entered into a patient's electronic record.

10. **[LO 2.4]** Name two advantages of using screen-based data collection tools.

11. **[LO 2.1]** If someone has the letters "RHIA" after his or her name, what does that mean?

12. **[LO 2.8]** What does the RADT acronym mean in a hospital setting?

13. **[LO 2.7]** Explain the purpose of a regional extension center (REC).

14. **[LO 2.3]** Discuss at least one way that voice recognition technology can be used in a medical setting.

APPLYING YOUR KNOWLEDGE

1. **[LOs 2.3, 2.4, 2.6, 2.7]** Discuss any potential drawbacks to the full-scale use of EHRs, and explain what precautions or regulations have been put in place to deal with each drawback.

2. **[LO 2.7]** Incentives are a significant part of the HITECH Act. Discuss the advantages and potential disadvantages associated with using incentives as a tool for implementing EHRs.

3. **[LOs 2.2, 2.5]** In the following case study, determine what would be considered data and what would be considered information: New patient Alice Jones is a 32-year-old female who presents with chest pains. She tells you that, in the past, she has been diagnosed with rosacea and is allergic to latex. In addition, she has had surgery for a broken arm. She does not smoke; is a social drinker; and has no family history of heart problems.

4. **[LO 2.8]** A physician's office and a hospital employ different terminology and process flow when maintaining records and monitoring patient flow. Why is there no set protocol that is used by all healthcare settings?

 Enhance your learning by completing these exercises and more at http://connect.mcgraw-hill.com!

5. **[LO 2.4]** Describe a scenario where presentation software might be used in a physician's office practice.

6. **[LO 2.8]** Think about the five main objectives of an EHR. Which of the five do you feel would be most useful for care providers? For patients? For office managers? Explain your answers.

7. **[LO 2.7]** Visit one of the HIPAA Fast Facts websites located in the FYI box in Section 2.7. Summarize the information found on the website, and write a brief scenario that illustrates how the information could be put into practice at a physician's office or hospital.

8. **[LO 2.1]** Choose one of the professional associations listed in Section 2.1. Locate the association's website, and create an outline for a sample presentation you might give to your office staff that highlights the important aspects of that association's influence on health information management.

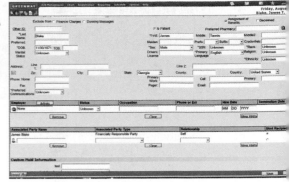

Content of the Health Record—Administrative Data

Learning Outcomes

At the end of this chapter, the student should be able to:

3.1 Identify administrative data elements.

3.2 Explain the administrative uses of data.

3.3 Explain the use of EHR data in an Accountable Care Organization (ACO).

3.4 Explain the use of the Master Patient (person) Index (MPI).

3.5 Apply procedures to register a new patient in PrimeSUITE.

3.6 Apply procedures to schedule a patient's appointment in PrimeSUITE.

3.7 Apply procedures to edit demographic information in PrimeSUITE.

3.8 Follow the steps performed upon patient check-in.

3.9 Apply procedures to capture insurance information in PrimeSUITE.

3.10 Locate the Help feature in PrimeSUITE.

Key Terms

Accountable Care Organization (ACO)
Administrative data
Chief complaint
Clinical Documentation Architecture (CDA)
CMS-1500
Continuity of Care Documents (CCD)
Data dictionary

Health Level Seven (HL7)
Library
Medical record number
Quality Reporting Document Architecture (QRDA)
Shortcut key
UB-04

The Big Picture

What You Need to Know and Why You Need to Know It

In previous chapters we talked about the importance of each patient having only one record in the EHR of that facility. Remember, though, that one record may have many individual encounters attached to it, one for each visit to the facility as a patient. In this chapter we will discuss the administrative data, including demographic (identifying) data that is collected about each patient, thus forming the master record or master patient index for each patient.

3.1 Administrative Data Elements

Administrative data Identifying information, insurance-related information, authorizations, and business correspondence found in a patient's health record.

CMS-1500 The form used by physicians' offices to submit insurance claims.

UB-04 The form used to submit insurance claims for hospital patients.

Administrative data is nonclinical data; it does not include data relative to the diagnosis, prognosis, treatment, or plan of care. Demographic data is a subset of administrative data and includes data collected to identify a particular patient. It includes the patient's full name, date of birth, gender, social security number, marital status, address, and phone number. Additional information that may be collected includes employer/student status, employer name and address, next of kin, race, ethnicity, and insurance policy name, policy number, and group number. In addition to identifying patients, many administrative data elements are required to complete insurance claim forms such as the **CMS-1500** and the **UB-04**, as required by HIPAA. The CMS-1500 form is used to bill outpatient encounters, and the UB-04 is used to bill hospital admissions/encounters. Both the CMS-1500 and the UB-04 are available on the Online Learning Center at http://www.mhhe.com/greenway2e.

Identifying information for inpatients and outpatients, as included in the core health data elements recommended by the National Center for Vital and Health Statistics in 1996, should include the data elements listed here:

- Full name
- Personal/unique identifier—this is also referred to as medical record number or chart number
- Account or billing number
- Date of birth
- Gender
- Race and ethnicity
- Residence (address)
- Marital status
- Current or most recent occupation (employer)
- Type of encounter (inpatient, emergency room visit, physician's office visit, etc.)
- Admission date (inpatient) or date of encounter (outpatient)
- Discharge date (inpatient)
- Facility identification (unique identifier of the medical office, hospital, outpatient surgery center, etc.)

- Type of facility/place of encounter (hospital, physician's office, surgi-center, etc.)
- Healthcare practitioner identification (outpatient)
- Provider location or address of encounter (outpatient)
- Attending physician identification (inpatient)
- Patient's expected sources of payment (Medicare, Medicaid, insurance, self-pay, etc.)
- Injury related to employment
- Total billed charges

These data elements are also included in the **Health Level Seven (HL7)** standards. HL7 allows different software packages to interface with one another, i.e., it allows them to share data. There are many different companies that develop healthcare applications and systems, and by writing the software according to HL7 standards, the applications "talk to each other"; otherwise the data would have to be entered separately for each. Hospitals or medical practices may have different vendors for different systems. For instance, there may be one service provider for the laboratory system, one for the pharmacy system, one for tracking incomplete records, etc. Through use of HL7 standards, if something is changed in one system, say the patient's telephone number, the change would be reflected in all three. This is a very important requirement, because without this standard language the interoperability (sharing data through a single database) would not be possible.

HL7 has been the most widely used and recognized standard in the healthcare industry. HL7 now recognizes new, more specific standards which include **Clinical Documentation Architecture (CDA)** and **Quality Reporting Document Architecture (QRDA)**. The CDA is used for an important piece of the Meaningful Use legislation in preparing **Continuity of Care Documents (CCD)** and the QRDA is important for quality reporting purposes as well as for sharing information between providers or facilities. The Continuity of Care Documents tie directly to one of the major goals of an electronic health record—that is, improving patient care and patient outcomes through information. The ability to electronically share important clinical data among caregivers, even those from different or even competitive healthcare facilities, is a step toward improving overall quality of care. Service providers (EHR and PM software vendors) are finding it more beneficial to work together to form new partnerships resulting in collaborative relationships rather than concentrating on selling their product(s) alone.

Commonwell Health Alliance is an example of how health information technology vendors are working together to collaborate with the ultimate goal of true interoperability of healthcare electronic systems. According to Commonwell's website, "The Alliance intends to be an independent, not-for-profit trade association that will support and promote the seamless interoperability of and access to patient data across the healthcare system."

Meaningful use will be covered in more detail in the chapter on Decision and Compliance Support in this worktext. Detailed explanation about the protocols themselves for HL7 is not necessary in this text, but will be covered in a more advanced information technology course.

Health Level Seven (HL7) A set of standards that makes sharing of data between or among healthcare entities possible.

Clinical Documentation Architecture (CDA) Developed by HL7, a document markup standard that specifies the structure and semantics of clinical documents such as discharge summary, operative report, etc. (Dolin).

Quality Reporting Document Architecture (QRDA) Based on HL7's approved Clinical Documentation Architecture (CDA), QRDA is a data standard used for reporting quality measure data and is EHR compatible across different health IT systems.

Continuity of Care Documents (CCD) A document exchange standard used to share patient summary information, such as in the case of a patient being referred from one healthcare provider to another.

One data element that is not included earlier but that should be collected is a patient's previous name, if applicable. This could be a maiden name or previous married name. Collecting this data element allows for cross-referencing of files. If a woman was previously seen at that facility under her maiden name, but is being seen for the first time using her married name, she should be listed only one time in the master list of patients.

In an outpatient setting, the data elements listed earlier are collected on a patient registration form, which is completed at the time care is established with that facility or office. The information should be verified with the patient each time he or she is seen to ensure that there has been no change in information, and that there have been no additions or deletions to the information. Examples would be change in address, telephone number, or marital status. In a hospital setting, the information may be required prior to a patient undergoing an elective admission, or would be collected face-to-face in the registration department when the patient presents for care.

Equally important when collecting sufficient identifying information is that each data element is consistently defined in the facility. Use of a **data dictionary** will ensure that each member of the registration staff has defined the data element correctly, and that only valid entries are made in a particular data element.

Let us look at a few examples. First, consider the possible data dictionary choices for marital status. The typical choices are single, married, separated, widowed, divorced, or unknown. If that is the definition of marital status in your facility, then those are the *only* choices available in the practice management system. Data dictionaries should be very specific. Each choice could be further defined. An example is the definition of "separated." Some facilities may consider a patient to be separated only if she presents a legal document stating such, and if she cannot do that, she is considered married for data collection purposes even though she considers herself to be separated in the legal sense. Another example is the patient's full name. In the facility's data dictionary the full name may be defined as the patient's last name, first name, middle name. Or, it may be defined as the last name, first name, middle initial. Thus, when a patient is registered, the name should be collected exactly as defined in that facility's data dictionary. Failure to follow the data dictionary definitions will result in unreliable data.

For consistency of wording and to save time, many fields in PrimeSUITE have a **library** of possibilities from which to choose. These are called drop-down menus. Examples of libraries would be: employers, common medications, religions, ethnicities, medical conditions, and elements of a physical exam. Clinical templates are also found in libraries (Figure 3.1).

3.2 Administrative Uses of Data

In addition to identifying a particular patient, administrative data is also used to satisfy HIPAA data requirements, which in turn are used to file electronic health claims for reimbursement. The CMS-1500 form is used to submit claims electronically for outpatient encounters, and the UB-04 is used to submit hospital claims. There

Data dictionary A document that specifies the format of each data field as well as a detailed explanation or definition for that field, which allows for consistency of data collection.

Library In computer software, a listing or choice of entities, for instance, employers, insurance plans, ICD-10-CM codes, or CPT codes.

are five major sections or levels on the claim form (refer to the CMS-1500 and UB-04 forms found at the Online Learning Center, http://www.mhhe.com/greenway2e):

1. Provider information
The name, address, national provider identifier (NPI) number, and telephone number of the provider.

2. Subscriber and patient information
This section includes information about the policyholder (subscriber) of the insurance and the patient identifying information.

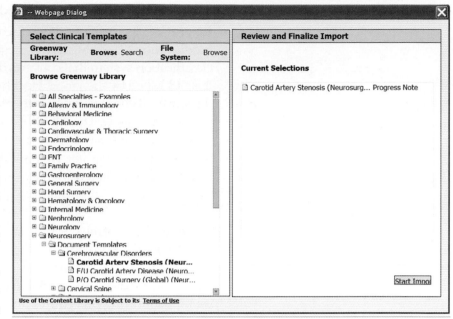

Figure 3.1 Library of clinical templates found in PrimeSUITE

These may be one and the same, if the patient is the policyholder (the primary insured). Below is a partial list of information collected but it is not limited to:

- Policyholder's (subscriber's) name
- Group or insurance plan name
- Identification (policy) number
- Patient's relationship to the policyholder

3. Payer information

- Group or insurance plan name
- Plan identification
- Address
- Assignment of benefits authorization (allows payment to be made directly to the provider)
- Release of information authorization (allows clinical information to be released to the insurance company)
- Referral number (if patient was referred by another provider)
- Prior authorization number (obtained when insurance plan requires procedures to be approved for payment in advance)

4. Claim details. A partial list of data includes:

- Individual account number or identification for that particular encounter
- Total charges submitted
- Place of service code
- Provider signature
- Details about the onset of the illness/accident
- Date(s) of service
- Amount collected from the patient

- Unique identifier (medical record number or chart number)
- International Classification of Diseases, 10th revision, Clinical Modification (ICD-10-CM) diagnosis codes. ICD-10-CM is a classification system that converts diagnoses into numeric form. It is published by the World Health Organization (WHO) and is the required code set for documenting diagnoses on all patients in any care setting. The ICD-10-CM code for a patient with type II diabetes mellitus with diabetic nephropathy is E11.21.
- Whether the encounter was due to an auto or other accident or was a work-related injury

5. Services

- Procedures performed as indicated by Current Procedural Terminology (CPT) codes. CPT codes convert written procedures and services into numeric form. It is published by the American Medical Association (AMA) and is the required code set for submitting procedures and services for outpatients. An example of a CPT code is 82247, which is the code for a total bilirubin test. For hospital inpatients, ICD-10-PCS codes are assigned to convert procedures into coded form. For example, the ICD-10-PCS code for a left heart catheterization is 4A023N7.
- Date(s) of service

Information collected in each of these major sections may overlap. For instance, the place of service code or dates of service code would be collected only once, but satisfies the claim details as well as the services section requirements.

Administrative data, as well as clinical data which describes the patient's diagnosis and procedures, may also be used to satisfy reporting requirements. Meaningful use of data was discussed in an earlier chapter reporting that the race and ethnicity of all patients is collected would be an example of the administrative use of data to satisfy meaningful use regulations. Other administrative data elements that are required to satisfy meaningful use are the patient's preferred language, gender, and date of birth. An example of a clinical data element that is collected from within the provider's documentation or in the health history would be the patient's smoking status (if the patient is 13 years of age or older). A report that includes the total number of patients living in a particular ZIP code with a diagnosis of COPD is an example of a report that uses both administrative and clinical data. Another would be the total number of patients between the ages of 13 and 50 years of age who are smokers and have a diagnosis of asthma. Either of these reports may be used by public health agencies or in educational materials used in a smoking cessation class.

3.3 Accountable Care

Accountable Care Organization (ACO) A healthcare model in which a group of healthcare providers and healthcare facilities form a partnership allowing them to provide high-quality, coordinated care to a patient population.

The Patient Protection and Affordable Care Act (ACA) is part of the healthcare reform legislation which was passed in 2010. Included in that piece of legislation is the formation of the **Accountable Care Organization (ACO)**. An accountable care organization is a healthcare model whereby a group of physicians, hospitals, and/or other healthcare providers (e.g., home health agencies) form a partnership that provides high-quality, coordinated care to a population of patients. The payment for the care is based on quality measures as opposed to the traditional fee for service model. Data is necessary to report the results of each quality measure (Washington).

ACO models include the Centers for Medicare and Medicaid Services (CMS) models and various commercial payer models.

The ACO models are reliant on the data gathered from individual providers' EHR systems. The exchange of health information that we discussed earlier is critical to the success of ACOs, since the point is coordination of care and the reduction of redundant or unnecessary treatments or diagnostics. Though this may result in a decrease in revenue for providers, it is essential if healthcare costs are to be contained. Health information professionals and practice managers play a major role in the ACO model, since quality data in the form of diagnosis and procedure codes, patient identification, etc., is essential in ensuring accurate quality measurement and data integrity.

3.4 The Master Patient (Person) Index (MPI)

The Master Patient (Person) Index, or MPI, contains the identifying or administrative data on each patient. The acronym MPI is used more in the hospital setting than in the outpatient setting, although the objective is the same: one file of all the patients seen in the facility, with each patient listed in the index only *once*. In a medical practice, this may be referred to as the Patient List or Master Patient List. Each patient then has a second level of information that reflects individual visits to the facility. For instance James Philips has been a patient at Memorial Hospital. He was admitted as an inpatient in January 2010 for appendicitis. He was then seen in the emergency department of the hospital in June 2010 for a fracture of his right radius. In September he underwent outpatient blood work ordered by his primary care physician. In this instance, James will have one entry in the MPI, but will have three individual encounters attached to his record (one inpatient, two outpatient encounters).

The MPI should be kept permanently, since it is the master list of all patients seen at a particular facility. In the hospital setting, records are filed by **medical record number**, which is a unique number assigned to each individual patient. Should the MPI be destroyed or unavailable for some reason, it would be difficult if not impossible to locate the patient's health record, if using paper records. Though physicians' offices typically file alphabetically by the patient's last name, best practice still dictates that a master index (list) of all patients be kept.

In some facilities or offices, the MPI is kept manually. With the move toward an electronic record, an electronic MPI is more the norm. Figure 3.2 is an example of a manual MPI card. Figure 3.3 is an example of the equivalent of an MPI entry in PrimeSUITE. Notice that in the electronic version, much more demographic information is collected and stored in this patient's master file than for the patient with the manual MPI card.

Medical record number A unique number assigned to each patient seen by a facility or office.

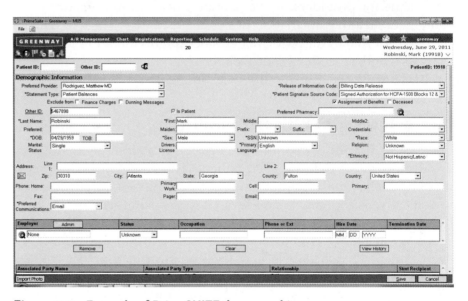

Figure 3.2   Master Patient Index (MPI) card

MEMORIAL HOSPITAL
7652 HORIZON WAY
ANYWHERE, TX 44555

Last Name, First Name, Middle Name		DOB	Gender Male
			Race Caucasian
			Medical Record Number
Philips, James Bernard		07/31/1990	07-45-85
Home Address			Telephone Number
1234 Oriole Way, Anywhere, TX 44555			555-555-3333
Previous Name			Social Security Number
n/a			123-45-6780

ADM/ENCOUNTER DATE	DISCHARGE DATE	TYPE OF SERVICE	PROVIDER
1/15/2010	1/28/2010	IP	Howard Hinkins, MD
6/22/2010	6/22/2010	ED	Sylvia Crowell, MD
9/30/2010	9/30/2010	OP	Lloyd Wright, Md

Figure 3.3   Example of PrimeSUITE demographic screen

Before any information, administrative or clinical, is entered for a patient, he or she must be registered in the practice management software, which, in turn, populates basic information in the EHR as well. This function is carried out in every healthcare setting. It is important to have pertinent information about the patient available to the office staff. In Exercise 3.1, perform the steps necessary to view this information on the desktop.

In a physician's office the registration process is completed by the reception staff. In the hospital setting this is part of the registration process. Some hospitals have a centralized registration department, meaning that regardless of the type of patient (inpatient or outpatient), all registration is done from a central location. Other hospitals have decentralized registration, meaning that there is an admissions department that registers inpatients, an emergency department registration area for emergency patients, a Radiology Department registration area for outpatient radiology patients, and so on. It is important for the office reception and scheduling staff to know what

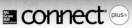  Go to http://connect.mcgraw-hill.com to complete this exercise.

PM EXERCISE **3.1**

The Patient Information Screen

Using a computer to store data about all patients allows us to retrieve that data more quickly and is more efficient than manual systems. There is certain data the healthcare professional needs to access often. In order to efficiently access this common information, the Desktop can be modified by changing the Patient Information Settings.

The Patient Information Settings screenshot shown in Figure 3.4 is the screen used to change the information settings.

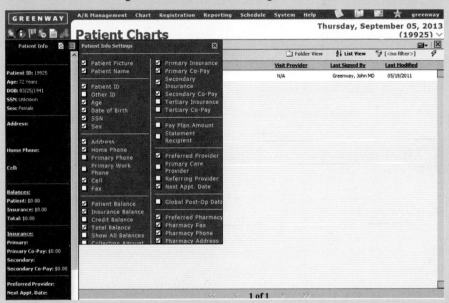

Figure 3.4 Patient Information Settings screenshot in PrimeSUITE

In this exercise, you will select common data elements to display on the Desktop screen.

Follow these steps to complete this exercise:

1. Click View Patient Info icon.
2. Click the Customize Patient Information icon.
3. Select Patient Picture.
4. Select Patient Name.
5. Select Patient ID.
6. Select Age.
7. Select Date of Birth.
8. Select SSN.
9. Select Sex.
10. Select Address.
11. Select Home Phone.
12. Select Cell.
13. Select Patient Balance.
14. Select Insurance Balance.
15. Select Total Balance.
16. Select Primary Insurance.
17. Select Primary Co-Pay.
18. Select Secondary Insurance.

(continued)

19. Select Secondary Co-Pay.
20. Select Preferred Provider.
21. Select Next Appt. Date.
22. Select Preferred Pharmacy.
23. Select Pharmacy Fax.
24. Select Pharmacy Phone.
25. Select Pharmacy Address.
26. Click View Patient Info icon again to close.

 You have completed Exercise 3.1

type of registration model is used by the local hospital(s) since communication with the registration staff is common. In Exercise 3.2 we will follow a patient through registration in a physician's office.

EXERCISE **3.2**   Go to http://connect.mcgraw-hill.com to complete this exercise.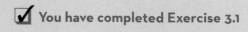

Register a New Patient

In this exercise, we will be registering a new patient, Alfredo J. Garza. He has called Greensburg Medical Center, asking if any of the providers were taking new patients. The healthcare professional tells him that Dr. Ingram, a Family Practice physician, is taking new patients and asks if he would like to establish care with Dr. Ingram. Since Mr. Garza does want to do so, the following steps are completed to register him in the Practice Management and EHR system of Greensburg Medical Center.

From the initial phone call, basic information such as full name, date of birth, address, and telephone number(s) is taken. He tells the healthcare professional that his name is Alfredo Jose Garza. He was born on 07/31/1945. His address is 117 Greenway Blvd, Carrollton, GA 30117, and his phone number is 770-555-5555.

The healthcare professional will mail Mr. Garza some paperwork to complete before he arrives for his appointment. Typically, the paperwork includes a form to collect administrative information, a past medical history form, and authorization forms. The administrative information includes information such as address, telephone number, next of kin, insurance information, ethnicity, race, etc. The insurance information is entered as soon as it is available so that verification of insurance can be done (more about insurance verification is in the Financial Management chapter).

For our purposes, we will assume that Mr. Garza completed the initial paperwork and brought it to the office before the day of his appointment with Dr. Ingram, as noted in Figure 3.5.

Follow these steps to complete the exercise on your own once you have watched the demonstration and tried the steps with helpful prompts. Use the registration form in Figure 3.5 to complete the following steps:

1. Click Search for Patient.
2. Type "Garza" in the *Last Name field.
3. Click the *First Name field.
4. Type "Alfredo" in the *First Name field.

PrimeSUITE Tip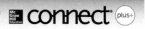

Information must be entered in test mode exactly as it appears in the source documentation. For instance, the telephone number must be entered as 770-555-5555.

Greensburg Medical Center
REGISTRATION FORM
(Please Print)

Today's date: August 18, 2013	Care Provider: Dr. Ingram

PATIENT INFORMATION

Patient's last name:	First:	Middle:	x Mr. ☐ Mrs.	☐ Miss ☐ Ms.	Marital status (circle one)
Garza	Alfredo	Jose			(Single) / Mar / Div / Sep / Wid

Is this your legal name?	If not, what is your legal name?	(Former name):	Birth date:	Age:	Sex:
☒ Yes ☐ No			07/31/1945	68	☒ M ☐ F

Street address:	Social Security no.:	Home phone no.:
117 Greenway Blvd.		770-555-5555

P. O. Box:	City:	State:	ZIP Code:
	Carrollton	GA	30117

Occupation:	Employer:	Employer phone no.:
Project Manager	Greenway	770-555-6666

E-mail address: ajgarza@greenwaymedical.com	Cell phone: 770-555-7777

Race: declined   Ethnicity: Hispanic   Primary language: Spanish   Religion: Catholic

Other family members seen here:

INSURANCE INFORMATION

(Presentation of Insurance Card is required at time of each visit)

Person responsible for bill:	Birth date:	Address (if different):	Home phone no.:
Alfredo Garza	07/31/1945		

Is this person a patient here?   ☒ Yes   ☐ No

Occupation:	Employer:	Employer address:	Employer phone no.:

Is this patient covered by insurance?   ☒ Yes   ☐ No

Please indicate primary insurance	☒ McGraw-Hill Healthmark Insurance	☐ BlueCross/Shield	☐ [Insurance]	☐ [Insurance]	☐ [Insurance]
☐ [Insurance]	☐ Workers' Compensation	☐ Medicare	☐ Medicaid (Please provide card)	☐ Other	

Subscriber's name:	Subscriber's S.S. no.:	Birth date:	Group no.:	Policy no.:	Co-payment:
Alfredo Jose Garza		07/31/1945	6500	GAR5679009	$ 20.00

Patient's relationship to subscriber:	☒ Self	☐ Spouse	☐ Child	☐ Other	Effective Date: 01/06/2013

Name of secondary insurance (if applicable):	Subscriber's name:	Group no.:	Policy no.:
None			

Patient's relationship to subscriber:	☐ Self	☐ Spouse	☐ Child	☐ Other

IN CASE OF EMERGENCY

Name of local friend or relative (not living at same address):	Relationship to patient:	Home phone no.:	Work phone no.:

The above information is true to the best of my knowledge. I authorize my insurance benefits be paid directly to the physician. I understand that I am financially responsible for any balance. I also authorize [Name of Practice] or insurance company to release any information required to process my claims.

Patient/Guardian signature	Date

Figure 3.5   Alfredo Garza registration form

(continued)

5. Click the Middle Name field.
6. Type "Jose" in the Middle Name field.
7. Click Search.
8. Click OK.
9. Click the Date Of Birth field.
10. Type "07/31/1945".
11. Click the Sex drop-down menu.
12. Click Male to select it.
13. Click the Home Phone field.
14. Type "770-555-5555".
15. Click the Work Phone field.
16. Type "770-555-6666".
17. Click Add New.
18. Click Yes.
19. Click Registration drop-down menu.
20. Click Information.
21. Click *Race: drop-down menu.
22. Click Declined to select it.
23. Click *Primary Language: drop-down menu.
24. Click Spanish to select it.
25. Click Religion: drop-down menu.
26. Click Catholic to select it.
27. Click *Ethnicity: drop-down menu.
28. Click Hispanic or Latino to select it.
29. Click Address Line 1 field.
30. Type "117 Greenway Blvd.".
31. Click Zip: field.
32. Type "30117".
33. Press "Tab".
34. Click Cell: field.
35. Type "770-555-7777".
36. Click Email: field.
37. Type "ajgarza@greenwaymedical.com".
38. Click *Preferred Communications: drop-down menu.
39. Click Email to select it.
40. Click the Search Employers icon.
41. Type "Greenway" in the Employer Name: field.
42. Click Search.
43. Click Select.
44. Click Status drop-down menu.
45. Click Full-time to select it.
46. Click the Occupation field.
47. Type "Project Manager".
48. Click Save.

 **You have completed Exercise 3.2**

In PrimeSUITE, the "Appointment Scheduling" function is used to make the appointment with the provider who has been assigned to that patient. In Alfredo Garza's example, he was a new patient, and was assigned to Dr. Ingram.

In an office setting, the healthcare professional will need to know the reason for the visit in order to allot enough time for the visit. For example, a follow-up visit for hypertension is going to take less time than a physical exam. The scheduler or healthcare professional will also ask for convenient days and times before beginning the search for the appointment. In a hospital setting, outpatient procedures such as CT scans or MRIs are scheduled in advance, and the process is similar.

Each care provider is set up in the PM system to show his or her typical schedule. For instance, Dr. Ingram may prefer to start the day at 9:00 a.m., break for lunch from noon to 1 p.m., and end his day at 5:30 p.m. Dr. Pueblas, on the other hand, may prefer to start seeing patients at 8 a.m., break from seeing patients between 11 and 11:30 a.m. to return phone calls and perform administrative tasks, see patients from 11:30 a.m. until 1:00 p.m., and then break for lunch from 1:00 p.m. until 2:00 p.m. Her last appointment of the day is scheduled for 4:30 p.m. In addition, some care providers prefer to do complete physical exams only in the morning. Many offices leave open appointment times for urgent visits. Patients who do not show up for an appointment, or who cancel at the last minute, can wreak havoc on a schedule!

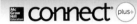 Go to http://connect.mcgraw-hill.com to complete this exercise. EXERCISE 3.3

Schedule an Appointment

Recall that we registered Mr. Garza in Exercise 3.2, so his name is located in PrimeSUITE's master patient list. The healthcare professional asked Mr. Garza which day(s) of the week work best for him. He does not have a preference of day, but he would like to be seen soon, so the healthcare professional starts the search beginning with September 2. Since Mr. Garza is establishing care with this office, the type of visit he will have is a Routine Office Visit (ROV). He will be having a complete exam. By selecting the correct type of visit, the amount of time allotted for that visit is automatically assigned by the system. In this case, it will be a 30-minute appointment. He then states that a morning visit on a Wednesday is best for him, so 9:30 on September 4th is selected by the healthcare professional. Mr. Garza also stated that he was having shortness of breath, so that will be entered as his **chief complaint**, which is the reason (in the patient's own words) that he has made the appointment.

Now we will perform the process of scheduling an appointment for Alfredo Garza.

Follow these steps to complete the exercise on your own once you have watched the demonstration and tried the steps with helpful prompts.

1. Click Search for Patient.
2. Type "Garza" in the *Last Name field.

 PrimeSUITE Tip

In PrimeSUITE, when the search function is used, the first patient who meets the criteria entered (in this case, the last name Garza) is highlighted. By clicking anywhere on the line of the patient you are actually looking for, then clicking Select, you will choose the correct person.

Chief complaint The reason for which a patient has made an appointment (usually in his/her own words, for instance, "I have a sore throat.").

(continued)

3. Click Search.
4. Click the line with the patient record for Alfredo Jose Garza.
5. Click Select.
6. Click Appointment Scheduling.
7. Click check box next to Dr. Ingram's name.
8. Click check box next to Greensburg Medical Center.
9. Click *From Date: field.
10. Type "09/02/2013" in the *From Date: field.
11. Click View Schedules.
12. Click the Next Day blue arrow.
13. Click the Next Day blue arrow again.
14. Click the plus sign next to Routine Office Visit to expand it.
15. Click the Scroll bar.
16. Drag the ROV - New Patient Complete Exam icon to the 09:30:00 AM time slot.
17. Click Chief Complaint: field.
18. Type "shortness of breath".
19. Click Save.

☑ **You have completed Exercise 3.3**

3.7 | **Editing Demographic Data**

People move, their last names change, their emergency contact information changes—just about anything except their first name and date of birth can change at one time or another. It is important that an office always have up-to-date information on a patient.

At the time of check-in, many offices will print out the identification page and have the patient review it either on a yearly basis or even every time a patient is seen. If changes need to be made, the patient communicates them to the office staff, and the information is edited appropriately. To save paper, some offices have a computer terminal where the patient can view the information on the screen, or the healthcare professional may just swivel her screen around for the patient to view and either verify that there are no changes necessary or tell her what information does need to be changed.

EXERCISE **3.4**   Go to http://connect.mcgraw-hill.com to complete this exercise.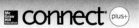

Edit Demographic Information

In this exercise, Mr. Garza realizes that he has moved since initially completing the registration paperwork; he calls in to the office to give his new address. He tells the healthcare professional that his address is now 2024 Peachtree Parkway, Carrollton, GA 30117.

Follow these steps to complete the exercise on your own once you've watched the demonstration and tried the steps with helpful prompts.

1. Click Search for Patient.
2. Type "Garza" in the *Last Name field.
3. Click Search.
4. Click Jose.
5. Click Select.
6. Click Information from the Registration drop-down menu.
7. Click the Address Line 1: field.
8. Double-click the current address listed in the field.
9. Type "2024 Peachtree Parkway".
10. Press "Tab".
11. Click Save.

☑ **You have completed Exercise 3.4**

3.8 Checking in a Patient

One of the advantages of using PM software is the ability to track a patient's flow through the office. The flow starts when the patient checks in. As a patient, you are aware of this part of the process—it is when you either sign your name on a log sheet or verbally inform the healthcare professional that you have arrived. This process is used in a physician's office setting, but would not necessarily have a use in the hospital environment other than in the outpatient registration area.

The typical flow is the following:

Patient checks in at front desk > patient is seen by clinical support team (MA or nurse) > patient is seen by the care provider (physician or physician's assistant or nurse practitioner) > patient stops at the cashier or check-out desk > billing processes begin.

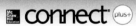

Go to http://connect.mcgraw-hill.com to complete this exercise.

PM | **EXERCISE** | **3.5**

Check in a Patient Who Has Arrived

In the following demonstration, Alfredo Garza has arrived and he has just signed the log, which alerts the healthcare professional to check him in for his appointment.

Follow these steps to complete the exercise on your own once you have watched the demonstration and tried the steps with helpful prompts.

1. Click Garza, Alfredo J.
2. Click Close.
3. Click *Visit Type drop-down menu.
4. Click Routine Office Visit.
5. Click *Service Location drop-down menu.
6. Click Greenway Clinic.
7. Click Check-In.

☑ **You have completed Exercise 3.5**

Although a medical practice or hospital is in business to care for patients, in the end, it is also just that—a business. In order to stay financially viable, there must be organized, effective policies and procedures in place to ensure cash flow and fiscal success.

You will learn about the intricacies of setting up fee schedules, billing insurance plans, and collection procedures in another course. In this exercise, though, you will learn about the information that must be collected for any patients who have a private or group insurance plan or who participate in a government health plan.

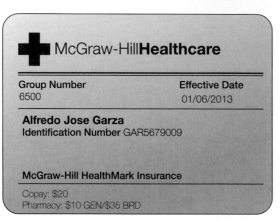

Figure 3.6   Sample insurance card

Figure 3.6 is a sample insurance card. This card should be presented each time a patient arrives for an encounter. An office may scan the front and back of the card as an image that will reside in PrimeSUITE, or they may photocopy the front and back of the card and keep it in the patient's chart.

The information must be entered in PrimeSUITE exactly as it appears on the insurance card. For instance, say Alfredo Jose Garza does not use his first name; instead he uses A. Jose Garza. But his insurance card reads Alfredo Jose Garza. In PrimeSUITE, or any other PM software, he should be entered as Alfredo Jose Garza.

Any typographical errors within PrimeSUITE will result in a delayed or denied claim. That will slow payment, which is not good business practice for the office!

EXERCISE   3.6   PM

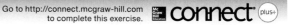

Go to http://connect.mcgraw-hill.com to complete this exercise.

Capture Insurance Information of a Patient

In the exercise that follows, Mr. Garza has presented his insurance card to the healthcare professional and he has completed the insurance information on his registration form (Figure 3.5). Mr. Garza only has coverage through one insurance company, so that is the **primary insurance** (the first insurance that is billed).

Follow these steps to complete the exercise on your own once you have watched the demonstration and tried the steps with helpful prompts.

1. Click Priority drop-down menu.
2. Click Primary to select.
3. Click "Click here to search for plan".
4. Click Insurance Co: drop-down menu.
5. Click the Insurance Co. drop-down menu to continue.
6. Click McGraw-Hill HealthMark Insurance.
7. Click Search.
8. Click Select.
9. Press "Tab".
10. Press "Tab".
11. Type "GAR5679009" in the Policy Number text box.

12. Press "Tab".
13. Type "6500" in the Group Number text box.
14. Press "Tab".
15. Type "01/06/2013" in the Effective Date text box.
16. Press "Tab".
17. Type "t" in the Expiration Date text box.
18. Click Save.
19. Click View/Edit Patient Flags icon.
20. Click Copay $20.
21. Click Save.

☑ **You have completed Exercise 3.6**

3.10 Utilize the Help Feature

The "HELP" feature is a staple of almost any computer software program. What is important is that you *use* the Help feature when you need to. For many of us, it is easier to ask someone how to perform a particular function than to search for the solution ourselves. The problem is—the person you are asking may give you the incorrect answer, or you may be in a position where you need an answer fast and there is no one around to ask. It shows initiative and will also help you to remember the steps more easily if you seek out the answer on your own. Consider this analogy—you remember how to get to a particular destination when you have driven there yourself rather than as a passenger, correct? The same applies here. You will remember and *understand* the process if you look up the steps on your own.

   **EXERCISE** 3.7

Go to http://connect.mcgraw-hill.com to complete this exercise.

Use the Help Feature

In this scenario you are fairly new to Greensburg Medical Center, but you have been there for several weeks and you are comfortable using Prime-SUITE. You would like to make the process easier, and one of your coworkers has told you about using **Shortcut keys** (keys that link directly to a function rather than choosing it from a menu). She has told you about some of the more common ones, but you would like to know more, so you go to PrimeSUITE Help for more guidance.

   Follow these steps to complete the exercise on your own once you have watched the demonstration and tried the steps with helpful prompts.

1. Click PrimeSuite Help.
2. Click Shortcut Keys.

Shortcut keys Keys that link directly to a function rather than choosing from a menu.

☑ **You have completed Exercise 3.7**

Selecting the Help feature will connect you to the PrimeSUITE User's Manual. Features you may typically use are:

- Getting Started and navigating PrimeSUITE Help
- PrimeSUITE Topics
- Frequently Asked Questions (FAQ)
- Work Flow Solutions

Also readily available in PrimeSUITE Help is material that speaks to the newest upgrades in functionality, and also a listing of what Greenway has determined to be the most frequently asked questions about topics (see Figure 3.7).

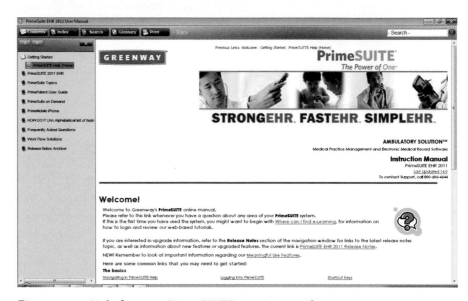

Figure 3.7   Help feature, PrimeSUITE user's manual

APPLYING YOUR SKILLS

In this chapter we discussed how important accurate data is. Let's take a look at a situation that is not all that uncommon.

Cindy, at Dr. Clark's office, is in the midst of checking in a patient, Diana G. Pike, while also listening to her supervisor, Emily, giving her instructions about something unrelated. Mrs. Pike filled out the new patient registration form and mentioned to Cindy that she is a new patient. Mrs. Pike has a seat, and Cindy is completing her registration. She types in the last name of Pike and sees that there is a Diana Pike in the system. Diana G. Pike has a date of birth of 9/18/1957 and lives at 367 Elmwood Drive, Carollton, GA. Diana Pike has a date of birth of 8/18/1957 and lives at 387 Elmhurst Drive, Carollton, GA. She assumes someone inaccurately entered Diana Pike into the system, and enters information about today's appointment under Diana Pike's record in the master patient index.

Is there a problem? If so, what is it? How could it have been avoided? What impact could this have on other steps of the process?

chapter 3 **summary**

LEARNING OUTCOME	CONCEPTS FOR REVIEW
3.1 Identify administrative data elements. Pages 46–48	– Demographic data is identifying data – Administrative data includes demographic data as well as additional nonclinical data – A data dictionary is necessary to ensure consistency and reliability of data – CMS-1500, UB-04, and HIPAA regulations dictate much of the administrative data captured

3.2 Explain the administrative uses of data. Pages 48–50	– Insurance purposes (file claims)
	– Satisfy regulatory requirements and meaningful use
	– Five sections of the claim form
	  • Provider
	  • Subscriber
	  • Payer
	  • Claim detail
	  • Services

3.3 Explain the use of EHR data in an Accountable Care Organization (ACO). Pages 50–51	– Patient Protection and Affordable Care Act (ACA)
	– Definition of an ACO
	  • A new healthcare reimbursement model
	  • Partnership between healthcare providers to provide high-quality, coordinated care
	– Reimbursement is based on quality measures, not fee for service
	– Need data from EHR to report results of each quality measure
	– ACO model is used by Medicare and some commercial insurance plans
	– Health information professionals as well as office administrators must ensure quality data collection and reporting

3.4 Explain the use of the Master Patient (person) Index (MPI). Pages 51–52	– A means of tracking that a patient was seen in a healthcare facility – Only one entry per patient • Each encounter has its own entry, filed under the patient's master entry – Medical record (chart) number is unique to each patient—links the patient to his/her health record – Can be manual or electronic – Is kept permanently

LEARNING OUTCOME	CONCEPTS FOR REVIEW
3.5 Apply procedures to register a new patient in PrimeSUITE. Pages 52–56	– Patient must have an entry in the Master Patient Index or patient list before any other functions can occur (scheduling, patient's chart, etc.) – Registration process occurs in every healthcare setting – Registration process ultimately results in the patient being a part of the MPI – In the physician office setting this is done by a healthcare professional – In hospital setting this is done by a registration department
3.6 Apply procedures to schedule a patient's appointment in PrimeSUITE. Pages 57–58	– Before scheduling an appointment, a provider has to be assigned, if a new patient, or select the patient's usual provider – Must know the reason for the visit in order to allot sufficient time for the visit – Select a date and time that works for the patient
3.7 Apply procedures to edit demographic information in PrimeSUITE. Pages 58–59	– All information about a patient must be current and correct – Verification of demographic and administrative information is done by administrative personnel at the time a patient checks in – Information is edited, added, or deleted as appropriate

3.8 Follow the steps performed upon patient check-in. Page 59	– Knowing where the patient is in the flow through the office is important to maintain efficiency
	– Typical flow:
	  • Patient checks in at reception desk
	  • Patient is called back to the exam room by the healthcare professional
	  • Patient is seen and examined by the provider
	  • Patient checks out
	  • Claim process begins

3.9 Apply procedures to capture insurance information in PrimeSUITE. Pages 60–61	– Capturing complete, correct insurance information is vital to cash flow and financial success – Require patients to present their insurance card on every visit – Information in the practice management system must match what is on the insurance card

3.10 Locate the Help feature in PrimeSUITE. Pages 61–62	– Help feature is available in any software
	– User's Manual includes:
	  • Getting Started and navigating PrimeSUITE Help
	  • PrimeSUITE Topics
	  • Frequently Asked Questions
	  • Work Flow Solutions

chapter review

MATCHING QUESTIONS

Match the terms on the left with the definitions on the right.

_____ 1. **[LO 3.3]** chief complaint

_____ 2. **[LO 3.2]** ICD-10-CM

_____ 3. **[LO 3.1]** CMS-1500

_____ 4. **[LO 3.1]** administrative data

_____ 5. **[LO 3.1]** Clinical Documentation Architecture

_____ 6. **[LO 3.4]** Master Patient Index

_____ 7. **[LO 3.1]** UB-04

_____ 8. **[LO 3.1]** Continuity of Care Documents

_____ 9. **[LO 3.1]** library

_____ 10. **[LO 3.1]** data dictionary

a. information, such as a patient's gender and date of birth, that is required to be collected under HIPAA

b. list of correct definitions for a facility's unique terms and jargon

c. form used to submit insurance claims in a healthcare office

d. in terms of computer software, a comprehensive listing of related entities to choose from, such as ICD-10 codes

e. form used to submit insurance claims in a hospital setting

f. permanent roster of all patients ever seen in a healthcare setting

g. reason for a patient's appointment; may determine the length of an exam visit

h. HL7 standard that outlines the format of clinical documentation, such as reports and discharge summaries

i. document exchange standard that guides how patient information is shared among providers and healthcare settings

j. comprehensive listing of national, numeric diagnosis codes

MULTIPLE-CHOICE QUESTIONS

Select the letter that best completes the statement or answers the question:

1. **[LO 3.1]** _____ data includes demographic data.
   a. Clinical
   b. HIPAA
   c. Administrative
   d. Financial

 Enhance your learning by completing these exercises and more at http://connect.mcgraw-hill.com!

2. **[LO 3.4]** Anna Jacobs presented to the ER of County Hospital three times in the past year. She will appear in County's MPI:
   a. once.
   b. twice.
   c. three times.
   d. four times.

3. **[LO 3.1]** Which of the following is NOT an example of demographic data?
   a. Full name
   b. Primary physician
   c. Social security number
   d. Date of birth

4. **[LO 3.2]** Administrative data is used to satisfy _____ requirements.
   a. CCHIP
   b. HITECH
   c. HIPAA
   d. ONC

5. **[LO 3.5]** Before a patient can be treated at a healthcare setting, she must be:
   a. prepped.
   b. registered.
   c. logged.
   d. admitted.

6. **[LO 3.4]** How long should a facility's Master Patient Index be kept?
   a. three years
   b. five years
   c. seven years
   d. permanently

7. **[LO 3.1]** Recording a patient's previous or married name might help with:
   a. cross-referencing data.
   b. compiling family history.
   c. legal proceedings.
   d. Privacy Rule compliance.

8. **[LO 3.10]** One of the common Help features is:
   a. Work Flow Help.
   b. Quick Start Guide.
   c. Frequently Asked Questions.
   d. Topical Outline.

http://connect.mcgraw-hill.com

9. **[LO 3.5]** _____ is part of a patient's administrative information found on a registration form.
   a. Occupation
   b. Chief complaint
   c. Provider number
   d. Co-pay amount

10. **[LO 3.1]** Patient demographic information should be verified:
    a. at initial visit.
    b. at each visit.
    c. once a year.
    d. when the patient initiates a change.

11. **[LO 3.9]** An insurance claim may be denied if the receptionist fails to:
    a. collect a patient's co-pay.
    b. make a copy of the patient's insurance card.
    c. enter all data correctly.
    d. have the patient sign the front-desk log.

12. **[LO 3.6]** _____ is part of the appointment scheduling feature of PrimeSUITE.
    a. Occupation
    b. Chief complaint
    c. Provider number
    d. Co-pay amount

13. **[LO 3.3]** Accountable Care Organizations rely on EHR:
    a. data.
    b. functionality.
    c. compliance.
    d. format.

14. **[LO 3.2]** A facility's collection of patient data might be used to satisfy _____ requirements.
    a. data dictionary
    b. meaningful use
    c. incentive
    d. interoperability

15. **[LO 3.7]** Editing a patient's mailing address is accomplished by using:
    a. drop-down menus.
    b. free-text fields.
    c. Help topics.
    d. patient flags.

 Enhance your learning by completing these exercises and more at http://connect.mcgraw-hill.com!

16. **[LO 3.4]** In a hospital's health information department, patient records are most often filed by:
    a. patient's last name.
    b. number of patient encounters.
    c. provider identification number.
    d. medical record number.

17. **[LO 3.8]** Patient check-in is:
    a. essential for claims processing.
    b. important for efficient patient tracking.
    c. done in the patient chart.
    d. an optional function in PrimeSUITE.

18. **[LO 3.2]** Information such as a policyholder name and insurance plan name appear in the _____ section of a claim form.
    a. payer
    b. provider
    c. services
    d. subscriber

SHORT ANSWER QUESTIONS

1. **[LO 3.3]** What is the role of an Accountable Care Organization?

2. **[LO 3.5]** What is the difference between centralized and decentralized registration centers in a hospital setting?

3. **[LO 3.9]** What is a co-pay?

4. **[LO 3.7]** List at least three ways that an office can obtain updated patient information.

5. **[LO 3.1]** Why is it important that every staff member in a facility uses terminology consistently?

6. **[LO 3.10]** List the four most commonly used features of PrimeSUITE's Help feature.

7. **[LO 3.6]** Explain why the receptionist needs to ask the reason for a patient visit when scheduling an appointment.

8. **[LO 3.2]** The CMS-1500 form is used to submit claims for _____ encounters while the UB-04 form is used to submit _____ claims.

9. **[LO 3.7]** Discuss the importance of reliable, up-to-date patient information.

10. **[LO 3.10]** Discuss why being able to use PrimeSUITE's Help feature is so important.

11. **[LO 3.1]** List at least five required pieces of demographic information collected for each patient.

12. **[LO 3.8]** Fields such as Visit Type, that contain a list of options to choose from, are known as what type of menus?

13. **[LO 3.4]** What is a medical record number?

14. **[LO 3.2]** List the five major sections on a standard claim form.

15. **[LO 3.5]** A patient may _____ to provide certain optional pieces of information if he or she feels uncomfortable.

16. **[LO 3.9]** List at least three things typically found on a patient's insurance card.

APPLYING YOUR KNOWLEDGE

1. **[LOs 3.5, 3.6, 3.7, 3.8, 3.9, 3.10]** Which of the PrimeSUITE exercises completed in this chapter do you think will be used most often in the office setting? Explain your answer.

2. **[LOs 3.1, 3.2, 3.7]** As the receptionist for Greenway Clinic, you recently mailed an informational letter to all patients listed in your MPI. One morning you come into work and see Alfredo Garza's letter marked "Return to Sender, Address Unknown" sitting on your desk. What do you do?

3. **[LOs 3.1, 3.2]** Discuss why administrative data such as race, ethnicity, and preferred language might need to be reported to satisfy meaningful use requirements.

4. **[LO 3.4]** The text mentions that if a MPI was inaccessible or unavailable for any reason, it would be nearly impossible to locate a patient's record. With the reality of computer system freezes and crashes, would this not be an argument against maintaining an electronic MPI? Explain your answer.

5. **[LOs 3.1, 3.2, 3.4]** One of your colleagues has been asked to update the office's data dictionary. She remarks that she does not see why having the data dictionary is so important, because most terms are easily understood by most people in the office. How would you explain to her, with examples, the importance of a solid data dictionary for your practice?

6. **[LOs 3.5, 3.6, 3.7, 3.8]** Discuss the advantages of using a practice management tool such as PrimeSUITE to complete tasks such as patient registration and appointment scheduling.

7. **[LOs 3.4, 3.5, 3.7]** Why is it important to search for a patient in the MPI before adding the person as a new patient? Explain the consequences of having a patient entered more than once.

8. **[LO 3.3]** Discuss the potential benefits and risks associated with the use of Accountable Care Organizations.

9. **[LO 3.1]** Visit the Commonwell Health Alliance website, at www.commonwellalliance .org. Discuss how they intend to increase the interoperability of EHR systems. Additionally, explain why interoperability is so important when using EHRs.

 Enhance your learning by completing these exercises and more at http://connect.mcgraw-hill.com!

4

Content of the Health Record—the Past Medical, Surgical, Family, and Social History

---

| Learning | Outcomes |

At the end of this chapter, the student should be able to:

4.1 Outline the use of forms as data collection tools.

4.2 Execute a step-by-step procedure to document past medical, surgical, family, and social histories in PrimeSUITE.

4.3 Examine the necessity of properly documenting and correcting inconsistent or unclear information.

4.4 Apply procedures to document vital signs in PrimeSUITE.

| Key | Terms |

Past family history
Past medical history
Past surgical history

Review of systems (ROS)
Social history
Vital signs

What You Need to Know and Why You Need to Know It

Before patients are seen by the care provider, they first meet with the healthcare professional to go over the reason for the visit and to capture historical information about their health status. In this chapter we will cover the types of history collected. We will also cover *why* knowing this information is so important in the care of the patient. As with all documentation in a health record, the history must be accurate because often the past history plays a part in the diagnosis and treatment of the current condition. The history generally begins with the chief complaint, which is documented in the patient's (or legal representative's) own words.

4.1 Forms as Data Collection Tools

Take a moment to think of forms that you have completed recently. Most likely they were on paper, and you can probably think immediately of one that was long, cumbersome, and took quite a bit of thought to complete. You can also think of one or two that were organized well, easy to complete, and seemed rather logical. The same goes for forms that are on screen rather than on paper. When we speak of paper forms, we refer to "boxes" that we are filling out. On screen, these boxes are called fields. In most healthcare settings, at this point in time, much of the information gathered from a patient will continue to be accomplished through use of a paper form, and then that information will be transferred to the patient's EHR. Thus, it is important that the design of the paper forms be logical to minimize the amount of time it takes to transfer the information and to minimize the likelihood of having missing or incorrect information end up in the EHR. As the transition to an electronic record progresses, patients will increasingly complete the forms electronically, though paper forms will not disappear completely since there will always be patients who do not want to complete the forms electronically due to lack of a computer, lack of computer literacy, or privacy concerns.

When designing a form, keep in mind the following:

- Name the form—give it a title that correlates to the information gathered on the form.
- Name of the office or facility.
- Each page of a multipage form should include the patient's name and the medical record number or chart number to guard against intermingling the records of patients with the same or similar names and to guard against documentation errors in general.
- The information collected should be relevant to the purpose of the form. Only information that is necessary should be collected—a medical history form in a dermatologist's office will probably not include the patient's menstrual history, for

example. If that information were needed for some reason, it could still be added elsewhere in the patient's record.

- Related information should be adjacent—for instance the street address, city, and ZIP code of a patient's address would be located adjacent to one another on the form.
- Clearly mark the field names (also called labels) by use of bolding, colored font, or italics.
- Separate the form into sections, if it is a lengthy form.
- Completion of the form should be easy for the person completing it; in other words it should be obvious whether the answer to each field should be written on the same line as the field heading or needs to go in the line below.
- Each piece of information should be requested only once on a given form.
- Provide sufficient space for the answer to each field.
- Typically, do not duplicate questions that are answered on other forms; an exception to this would be medication allergies— this question is often asked on more than one form due to the importance of the information. It may slip a patient's mind when completing a form at home but he or she will recall the allergy later in the interview process.

Following these guidelines will make it easy for the patient to complete the form. A thoroughly completed form will benefit the care provider as well. Care providers need complete, accurate information quickly, and so proper development of data collection tools— whether on paper or on screen—should be an important task in any healthcare setting.

The registration form used in the Administrative Data chapter is an example of a form that has individual fields in block format. The medical history form in Figure 4.1 is an example of one that has a more free-form format rather than individual fields.

As noted earlier, though forms do exist today, many "paperless" offices are requesting their patients to complete their history form online. Think of the last time you applied for a job or when you applied to the college you are attending. Most likely you did so online rather than with a paper application. The rules noted here about ease of completion apply to online forms as well as paper forms. You have no doubt experienced the frustration of completing a confusing, lengthy form online!

4.2 The Past Medical, Surgical, Family, and Social Histories

Past medical history Previous medical condition(s) for which the patient has been treated.

A patient's **past medical history** often contains information that is pertinent to his current health status. It is important that the care provider be aware of the patient's past medical history, which includes:

- Medical conditions (past and current) for which the patient has been treated or which he or she is experiencing

GREENSBURG MEDICAL CENTER — MEDICAL HISTORY FORM

PATIENT NAME	DOB	MEDICAL RECORD NUMBER

PLEASE ANSWER THE FOLLOWING QUESTIONS THOROUGHLY. IF A QUESTION DOESN'T APPLY, PLEASE ENTER N/A OR PLACE A LINE IN THAT AREA.

PRESENT MEDICAL CONDITION (why are you being seen today)

_____

_____

_____

ALLERGIES/REACTIONS TO MEDICINES/FOODS:

NAME OF MEDICATION/AGENT	TYPE OF REACTION

MEDICATIONS: Enter all prescription and non-prescription medicines, herbal remedies, vitamins, or birth control medications here:

MEDICATION	DOSE	HOW OFTEN?	TAKEN FOR?

PERSONAL MEDICAL HISTORY: Please check all conditions you have had (with approximate date or year)

Heart Disease ____ _____   Cancer ____ _____ Type _____

Heart attack ____ _____   Diabetes ____ _____ Type _____

Hypertension ____ _____   Thyroid ____ _____ Type _____

Stroke ____ _____   Bleeding Disorder ____ _____ Type _____

High cholesterol _____ _____   Other ___ _____

Depression/Suicide Attempt ___ _____   Other ___ _____

Alcoholism _____   Other ____ _____

1

Patient Name _____ DOB _____ Med. Record Number_____

SURGICAL HISTORY: Please indicate all procedures or surgeries you have had (with approximate date or year)

Type of surgery	Date (year)	Name of surgeon

FAMILY HISTORY: Please place a check under the family member who has had any of the conditions:

CONDITION	Mom	Dad	Sib.	Child	Other	CONDITION	Mom	Dad	Sibling	Child	Other
Alcoholism						Environmental allergies					
Anemia						Loss of hearing					
Anesthesia problem						Heart problems (heart attack, coronary artery disease, congestive heart failure)					
Arthritis						Hypertension					
Asthma						High cholesterol					
Bleeding problem						Mitral valve disorders					
Cancer, breast						Lupus					
Cancer, colon						HIV/AIDS					
Cancer, melanoma/basal cell						Kidney disease					
Cancer, ovarian						Mental health disorders					
Cancer, prostate						Migraine headaches					
Cancer, other						Osteoarthritis					
Depression						Rheumatoid arthritis					
Type I Diabetes						CVA (stroke)					
Type II Diabetes						Cerebral hemorrhage					
Eczema						Thyroid disorder					
Seizure disorder or epilepsy						Other					
Glaucoma						Other					

IMMUNIZATION HISTORY: Please indicate date (or best guess) of last immunization for:

Hepatitis A ____ Hepatitis B ____ Measles ___ Mumps ___ Rubella ___ Pneumovax (pneumonia) ___

Tetanus (Td) ____ MMR _____ Chicken pox _____ Flu ____Other _____

SOCIAL HISTORY

Tobacco Use

Cigarettes (current use) ☐ yes ☐ no If yes, packs per day _____ for _____ years

Cigarettes (past use) ☐ yes ☐ no   If yes, no. of years _____; quit when? _____

2

Other current tobacco use: ☐ snuff/chew ☐ pipe ☐ cigar

Other past tobacco use: ☐ snuff/chew ☐ pipe ☐ cigar

Alcohol Use

Do you drink alcohol? ☐ yes ☐ no If yes, no. of drinks per week _____

Recreational Drug Use

Do you use any recreational drugs? ☐ yes ☐ no If yes, what and how often? _____

_____

Physical Activity

How often do you exercise? _____ times/week

Are you relatively active (engage in recreational sports, take stairs daily, job involves standing, walking often, etc). ☐ yes ☐ no

SOCIOECONOMIC HISTORY

Occupation _____ Student status ☐ Full time ☐ Part time

Education Completed : ☐ High School graduate ☐ College graduate ☐ Graduate School

Marital Status ☐ Single ☐ Married ☐ Separated ☐ Divorced ☐ Widowed

REVIEW OF SYSTEMS   Answer the following questions for any current problems you are experiencing:

Constitutional: Are you experiencing?

____ Fever/chills/nigh-sweats   ____ Tiredness/weakness

____ Unexpected weight gain/loss   ____ Excessive thirst or urination

____ Tiredness/weakness   ____ Difficulty falling or staying asleep

Eyes, Ears, Nose, Throat and Mouth   *Skin*

____ Change in vision   ____ Rash

____ Difficulty hearing/ringing in ears   ____ Change in moles

____ Teeth/gum problems

____ Hay fever or allergies

Cardiovascular   *Respiratory*

____ Chest pain or discomfort   ____ Cough/wheeze

3

____ Leg pain during exercise   ____ Difficulty breathing/shortness of breath

____ Palpitations (racing heart)

Gastrointestinal   *Genitourinary*

____ Abdominal pain   ____ Frequent urination during night

____ Blood in stool   ____ Leaking urine

____ Nausea/vomiting/diarrhea   ____ Vaginal bleeding (not related to period)

Musculoskeletal   ____ Discharge from penis

____ Muscle/joint pain   *Breasts*

Neurological   ____ Lump or discharge

____ Headaches   *Psychiatric*

____ Dizziness/light-headed   ____ Anxiety/stress

____ Numbness   ____ Depression

____ Memory Loss   *Blood/Lymphatic*

                   ____ Lumps

                   ____ Easily bruises/bleeding

Is there anything you want the doctor to address with you today? _____

_____

WOMEN'S HEALTH HISTORY

No. pregnancies _____ No. deliveries _____ No. abortions ___ No. miscarriages _____

Date of last menstrual period _____ Frequency of periods _____ Length _____

_____   _____
Patient's Signature   Date

FOR INTERNAL USE ONLY (ENTER DATE REVIEWED AND INITIALS) ANY CHANGES, ADDITIONS, DELETIONS SHOULD BE DOCUMENTED ABOVE, DATED AND INITIALED.

4

Figure 4.1   Medical history form

- Date of onset and date resolved for each
- Known allergies (particularly to medications) as well as the actual reaction
- Immunization status, particularly in children
- Current list of medications, including name, dosage, frequency, and reason it is being taken
- A **review of systems (ROS)**, that is, a body system inventory of symptoms he or she may be having

Many offices include the patient's current condition on the history form, or the particulars of the current condition may be documented in the progress note for the visit. The information about the current condition includes:

- Chief complaint (the reason the patient is being seen that day; generally speaking, the reason for the appointment)
- History of present illness: location of the condition (for example, pain in the right shoulder); type of pain (ache, sharp pain, etc.); severity (mild, severe); duration (how long the complaint has been present); and any associated signs and symptoms (for example, difficult to raise arm above head when pain is present)

The **past surgical history** includes information about procedures the patient has undergone. If a patient, Carolyn Wright, is experiencing right lower quadrant pain, yet her history shows she had an appendectomy 14 years ago, the care provider will concentrate diagnostic testing for other possibilities. Past surgical history includes:

- Name of operation or procedure
- Reason for procedure
- Date that the procedure was performed (may be approximate)
- Name of surgeon who performed the procedure
- Anesthesia reactions or complications, if any

The **past family history** includes information that will alert the care provider to any conditions that may affect the patient's overall health now or in the future. For example, Neil Alexander is a 45-year-old patient who has been experiencing chest pains and shortness of breath. He notes that his father and paternal grandfather both had a myocardial infarction (heart attack) before the age of 50. In this case, that information is important to the care provider in order to make diagnostic and treatment decisions for the patient. Past family history includes:

- Name of condition(s)
- Family member(s) who had the condition(s)
- Sometimes, whether immediate family members (parent, sibling) are still alive and, if not, the date/cause of death

The **social history** is important because the care provider needs to know the patient's habits in order to assess possible causes of

Review of systems (ROS) A body system–by–body system inventory of any symptoms the patient is having or has had based on a series of questions asked by the care provider.

Past surgical history Previous surgical procedure(s) the patient has undergone, the approximate date(s), name of surgeon, reason for procedure(s), and complications, if any.

Past family history Documentation of conditions and diseases found in immediate family members (e.g., diabetes mellitus, cancer, or heart disease).

Social history Lifestyle or social habits of the patient.

conditions or potential health concerns that could arise as a result of the habits or the lifestyle of a patient. An example would be a patient who is overweight, works in a sedentary job, and has noted that she does not exercise or participate in any other strenuous activity. That patient would be at risk for heart disease, stroke, and other serious medical conditions. Elements of a social history include:

- Smoking history—past or current use
- Other tobacco use (snuff, pipe, cigar, for example)
- Alcohol use—current or past
- Recreational drug use
- Socioeconomic data—occupation, education, marital status
- Sexual activity and use of protection
- Exercise and physical activity

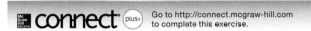

Go to http://connect.mcgraw-hill.com to complete this exercise.

EXERCISE 4.1

Enter a Patient's Past Medical History

In this exercise, we will be following the past medical history of a patient, Amy Peterson. She has arrived and checked in for her appointment with Dr. Rodriguez at Greensburg Medical Center. The healthcare professional has called Mrs. Peterson back to the exam room for the initial portion of the visit. Mr. Peterson has accompanied the patient to the appointment, and is in the exam room as well. The healthcare professional begins by accessing Amy Peterson's Facesheet screen in PrimeSUITE as noted in Figure 4.2.

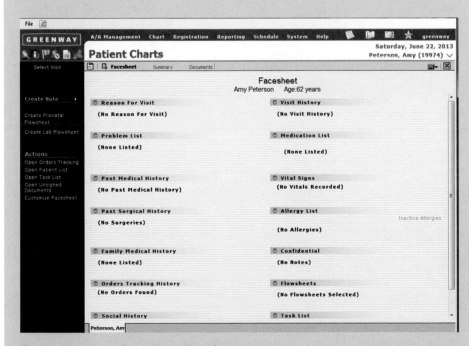

Figure 4.2   Amy Peterson's Facesheet

(continued)

The reason for the visit, confusion, already appears on the screen because that information was collected at the time the appointment was made. The healthcare professional will verify that information, and change it if necessary before going on to the Past Medical History. In our scenario, that information is correct. The reason for the visit is also known as the chief complaint and it is the reason, as noted by the patient, that an appointment was made with the care provider.

The healthcare professional clicks on the Past Medical History screen from the Facesheet.

Though a medical history form had been completed last year, the healthcare professional asks Mrs. Peterson about any other conditions she has. Mrs. Peterson and her husband confirm that she has osteoporosis and osteoarthritis, but no other medical conditions. The healthcare professional asks about any previous surgeries. Mr. Peterson responds that she had an appendectomy back in 1971 and she had a cataract removed from her right eye in 2007. They are the only surgical procedures Mrs. Peterson has had, but she does have one child, so the healthcare professional asks Mrs. Peterson about her reproductive history. Mrs. Peterson says that she was pregnant once and has one child. The pregnancy was a full-term pregnancy.

Follow these steps to complete the exercise on your own once you have watched the demonstration and tried the steps with helpful prompts. Use the information provided in the scenario to complete the information.

1. Click the Past Medical History radio button.
2. Check Osteoarthritis.
3. Check Osteoporosis.
4. Click PSHx.
5. Check Appendectomy.
6. Click details.
7. Type "1971".
8. Click OK.
9. Check Cataract removal.
10. Click details.
11. Type "2007".
12. Click Notes: field.
13. Type "right eye".
14. Click OK.
15. Click RHx.
16. Click the Total Preg field.
17. Type "1".
18. Double-click the Full Term field.
19. Type "1".
20. Click Close.

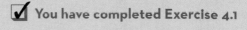 **You have completed Exercise 4.1**

Enter a Patient's List of Current Medications

In this exercise the patient's current medications are entered. Part of the functionality of PrimeSUITE is the differentiation between those medications prescribed by Greensburg Medical Center and those prescribed by another provider or bought over the counter.

This process begins by accessing Mrs. Peterson's Facesheet in PrimeSUITE and then selecting Medication List (see Figure 4.2). Mrs. Peterson shares with the healthcare professional that she takes ibuprofen for her osteoarthritis. She takes 800 mg tablets, 3 times a day. She also takes glucosamine chondroitin every day. These are tablets as well, and she takes the 750–600 mg tablets. She is also taking alendronate, which is a drug for post-menopausal osteoporosis prevention. These are taken in tablet form as well, 35 mg one time a week.

Follow these steps to complete the exercise on your own once you have watched the demonstration and tried the steps with helpful prompts. Use the information provided in the scenario to complete the information.

1. Click the Medication List radio button.
2. Click Record Medication.
3. Type "ibuprofen" in the Medication Name: field.
4. Click ibuprofen.
5. Click Osteoarthritis.
6. Click Oral.
7. Click 800 mg Oral Tablet.
8. Click OK.
9. Click Sig field.
10. Click take 1 tablet (800 mg) by oral route 3 times per day with food label.
11. Click OK.
12. Click Record Medication.
13. Type "glucosamine chondroitin" in the Medication Name: field.
14. Click glucosamine-chondroitin.
15. Click 750-600 mg Oral Tablet.
16. Type "2" in the take field.
17. Click by oral route field.
18. Click QD.
19. Click Done.
20. Click Add Another.
21. Type "alendronate" in the Medication Name: field.
22. Click alendronate.
23. Click Post-Menopausal Osteoporosis Prevention.
24. Click 35 mg Oral Tablet.
25. Click OK.
26. Click Save.

 You have completed Exercise 4.2

Go to http://connect.mcgraw-hill.com to complete this exercise. connect plus+

Enter a Patient's Known Drug Allergies

Mrs. Peterson has an allergy to amoxicillin. Knowing the patient's medication allergies is a very important piece of information. Not knowing her allergies, and prescribing a drug that she is allergic to, could cause a very serious reaction. Her allergy to amoxicillin will be documented in the Allergies List section of the Facesheet (see Figure 4.2).

Follow these steps to complete the exercise on your own once you have watched the demonstration and tried the steps with helpful prompts. Use the information provided in the scenario to complete the information.

1. Click Allergy List radio button.
2. Click Add.
3. Type "amox" in the Allergen: field.
4. Click amoxicillin.
5. Click OK.
6. Click the check box next to **amoxicillin** to select it.
7. Click Close.

☑ **You have completed Exercise 4.3**

4.3   Handling Inconsistent or Unclear Information

As we discussed earlier, a patient's history is gathered by use of a form as well as through an interview with the patient. Sometimes, what a patient has documented on the history form is contradictory to what comes out during the interview. When entering any information about a patient, for instance if you are reviewing a past medical history with the patient, and you see on the past medical history form that the patient had an appendectomy in 1997 yet she tells you verbally that she has never had any surgeries, you need to question the patient to determine the correct answer. Though the patient completed the form, she could have checked the wrong box on the form, or she may have forgotten that she had the surgery. Sometimes, patients choose not to tell the healthcare professional or care provider all of the facts. Often, the healthcare professional senses the fact that the patient is being evasive or is only partly answering questions. It is part of the healthcare professional's role to act in such a way that instills trust; communicating *why* these questions are being asked is often all that is needed for a patient to become more comfortable. The fact that there is a discrepancy (or that there is information missing) should never be ignored, and should be documented. The medical practice or hospital must have written policies on how to handle such situations.

An example of a policy statement regarding inconsistent information is: *In the event that an error or inconsistency is found in a health record or in the information given verbally by a patient/legal representative, an attempt should be made to verify the information and document same. The circumstances surrounding the discrepancy should be documented sufficiently in the health record to explain the situation thoroughly.*

PrimeSUITE, as in other EHR software, has built-in mechanisms to amend, delete, or add documentation. Though a change to documentation may occur, the original version of the documentation is always retrievable. In the previous example regarding the discrepancy about the patient's surgery, the explanation of the discrepancy can be documented in a details box that is found in the past surgical history section of the record. Later in this worktext, we will further examine correcting and amending entries and will test your knowledge through PrimeSUITE exercises.

4.4   Documenting Vital Signs

The patient's **vital signs** are taken by the healthcare professional—some offices take them before completing the history and others take them after. PrimeSUITE software includes a very helpful feature—the ability to see a patient's vital signs over time The tracking of the vital signs can be seen in graph form or chronologically. This will help the provider assess such conditions as hypertension or significant weight gain (or loss).

Like the history documentation, entering the vital signs is done from the vital signs section of the Facesheet.

The vital signs include the patient's blood pressure, heart rate, respiratory rate, temperature, height, weight, body mass index (BMI), and oxygen saturation. Technically, height and weight are not vital signs, but both are taken around the same time as the vital signs and are therefore included in that section of the record.

Vital signs Measurements taken (temperature, heart rate, respiratory rate, blood pressure, height and weight, and sometimes body mass index) to determine the status of basic body system functions.

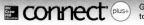 **EHR**   **EXERCISE**   **4.4**

Go to http://connect.mcgraw-hill.com to complete this exercise.

Enter a Patient's Vital Signs

PrimeSUITE allows documentation of the position the patient is in when the blood pressure is taken. The positions include sitting, standing, or lying down.

In our example, the healthcare professional is in the process of taking Amy Peterson's vital signs. She asks Amy to sit on the exam table and takes her blood pressure. The reading is 110/65. Her heart rate is 68 beats per minute (bpm) and regular, with a respiratory rate of 22. Mrs. Peterson's temperature is 97.6 F. Her weight was taken before coming into the exam room, and she weighed 135 pounds. She is 5 feet 2 inches (62 inches) tall. Her oxygen saturation today is 99%.

Follow these steps to complete the exercise on your own once you have watched the demonstration and tried the steps with helpful prompts. Use the information provided in the scenario to complete the information.

1. Click the Vital Signs radio button.
2. Click Add New Vitals.

(continued)

for your information **fyi**

The body mass index (BMI) is now a standard entry in most health records. BMI is a formula showing body weight adjusted for a patient's height. A healthy BMI is between 18.5 and 24.9. EHR software will automatically compute the BMI once the patient's height and weight are entered in the vital signs.

3. Click the Systolic field.

4. Type "110".

5. Click the Diastolic field.

6. Type "65".

7. Click the Heart Rate field.

8. Type "68".

9. Click the Respiratory Rate field.

10. Type "22".

11. Click the Temperature field.

12. Type "97.6".

13. Click the Weight field.

14. Type "135".

15. Click the Height in inches field.

16. Type "62".

17. Click the Oxygen Saturation field.

18. Type "99".

19. Click Add Vitals.

20. Click Close.

21. Click the Facesheet tab to confirm that you have viewed the screen.

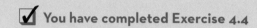 **You have completed Exercise 4.4**

At this point in the process, the patient has been taken to the exam room, vital signs have been taken, and she is ready to be seen by the care provider.

APPLYING YOUR SKILLS

In this chapter's Applying Your Skills, you will work through three different exercises without exact step-by-step instructions. Feel free to use similar exercises as noted in the scenario to complete the steps. Go to http://connect.mcgraw-hill.com to complete the exercises. The source document for these exercises is available in the Appendix for this book.

AYS Exercise 4.1: Schedule an Appointment in PrimeSUITE

You receive a phone call from Jeannie E. Lawrence asking for an appointment with Dr. Rodriguez. She is new to the area and asks if Dr. Rodriguez is taking new patients, since he was suggested by a friend of hers. She wants to be seen because she has been having increasing joint pain, especially in her knees. Dr. Rodriguez is accepting new patients, so you set up an appointment for her at 10:00 a.m. on September 4, 2013. (Hint: Use the steps found in Exercise 3.3 as a guide.)

AYS Exercise 4.2: Enter Data to Register Patient

Jeannie E. Lawrence arrives for her appointment, and completes her registration form. Enter the demographic information found on Mrs. Lawrence's form in PrimeSUITE using Connect Plus. (Hint: Use the steps found in Exercise 3.2 as a guide.)

AYS Exercise 4.3: Enter a Patient's Social History Data

You are in the exam room with Mrs. Lawrence, taking her social history. The conversation with Mrs. Lawrence goes as follows:

Healthcare professional: "Mrs. Lawrence, do you drink alcoholic beverages?"

Mrs. Lawrence: "Yes, occasionally I have a beer."

Healthcare professional: "How often do you drink beer and how many?"

Mrs. Lawrence: "I usually have two beers just on weekends."

Healthcare professional: "Do you now or have you ever smoked cigarettes?"

Mrs. Lawrence: "I smoked a pack a day until 2005, now I have one about once a month."

Healthcare professional: "Do you now or have you ever used recreational drugs?"

Mrs. Lawrence: "No, I've never done that."

Complete Mrs. Lawrence's social history in PrimeSUITE using Connect Plus. (Hint: Use the steps found in Exercise 4.1, but remember, this time you are entering her social history!)

chapter 4 **summary**

LEARNING OUTCOME	CONCEPTS FOR REVIEW

4.1 Outline the use of forms as data collection tools. Pages 71–72	– Paper form versus computer screen
	– When designing a form, keep the following in mind:
	  • name the form
	  • name of the office or facility
	  • patient's name on every page
	  • purpose of the form
	– Keep related information close together on the form
	– Clearly mark field headings
	– Lengthy forms should be separated into sections
	– Ease of completion and of reading
	– Don't duplicate information on the form
	– Sufficient space for answers on paper forms

4.2 Execute a step-by-step procedure to document past medical, surgical, family, and social histories in PrimeSUITE. Pages 72–78	– All histories are important in the assessment of patients – Past medical history includes: current and past medical conditions; allergies; medications; immunization status; chief complaint; history of present illness; review of systems – Surgical history includes all surgeries or procedures the patient has had and the dates (approximate) – Past family history is collected to assess whether the patient is predisposed to certain conditions – Social history is collected to determine if patient may be at a greater risk for certain conditions
4.3 Examine the necessity of properly documenting and correcting inconsistent or unclear information. Pages 78–79	– Office or facility must have clear policies to deal with inconsistent information – When a discrepancy is found and the patient is present, ask which is correct; amend the record according to policy – If the correct information is not certain, document that as well

4.4 Apply procedures to document vital signs in PrimeSUITE. Pages 79–80	– Vital signs include:
	  • blood pressure
	  • temperature
	  • heart rate
	  • respiratory rate
	  • height
	  • weight
	  • body mass index
	  • blood oxygen
	– PrimeSUITE will show vital signs over time, which may alert the provider to certain risk factors such as high blood pressure or significant weight loss or gain

chapter **review**

MATCHING QUESTIONS

Match the terms on the left with the definitions on the right.

_____ 1. **[LO 4.2]** review of systems

_____ 2. **[LO 4.2]** past surgical history

_____ 3. **[LO 4.2]** past medical history

_____ 4. **[LO 4.2]** social history

_____ 5. **[LO 4.2]** past family history

_____ 6. **[LO 4.4]** vital signs

a. patient information such as blood pressure and respiratory rate

b. patient information that includes immunizations and allergies

c. patient information that includes information such as frequency of drinking and smoking

d. comprehensive inventory of patient symptoms such as headaches, vision, heart palpitations, swelling of joints, etc.

e. patient information that includes past procedures and who performed the procedures

f. patient information that includes possibly inherited conditions

MULTIPLE-CHOICE QUESTIONS

Select the letter that best completes the statement or answers the question:

1. **[LO 4.1]** An on-screen item of data is known as a:
   a. box.
   b. crate.
   c. carton.
   d. field.

2. **[LO 4.3]** PrimeSUITE allows you to note discrepancies in the _____ box.
   a. details
   b. discrepancies
   c. information
   d. registration

3. **[LO 4.1]** It is important to keep the design of paper forms:
   a. cumbersome.
   b. detailed.
   c. logical.
   d. short.

4. **[LO 4.2]** Which of the following is NOT a required patient history?
   a. Family
   b. Birth
   c. Social
   d. Surgical

 Enhance your learning by completing these exercises and more at http://connect.mcgraw-hill.com!

5. **[LO 4.1]** Of the following, who will benefit from thoroughly completed paper forms?
   a. Care providers
   b. Patients
   c. Receptionists
   d. All of these

6. **[LO 4.2]** The patient's _____ history could possibly help predict a future health condition.
   a. family
   b. medical
   c. social
   d. surgical

7. **[LO 4.4]** A patient's vital signs are entered via PrimeSUITE's _____ screen.
   a. Facesheet
   b. History
   c. Patient
   d. Registration

8. **[LO 4.3]** Which of the following is an acceptable way of gathering a patient's history?
   a. Assessment
   b. Critique
   c. Discussion
   d. Interview

9. **[LO 4.1]** Which piece of information might be included multiple times on a form?
   a. Address
   b. Allergies
   c. Marital status
   d. Patient history

10. **[LO 4.1]** What information should you see on all forms in a patient chart?
    a. Name
    b. DOB
    c. Medical record number
    d. All of these

11. **[LO 4.2]** A patient's past surgical history includes the:
    a. approximate date of the procedure.
    b. name of the attending physician.
    c. patient's recovery time.
    d. type of sutures used.

12. **[LO 4.1]** For ease of completion, related information should be _____ on a form.
    a. adjacent
    b. duplicated
    c. labeled
    d. separate

13. **[LO 4.4]** What does BMI stand for?
    a. basic medical information
    b. body mass index
    c. body matter indicator
    d. base measurement index

14. **[LO 4.2]** Which of the following would include a patient's exercise regimen?
    a. Family history
    b. Medical history
    c. Social history
    d. Surgical history

15. **[LO 4.3]** Any discrepancies in patient information need to be:
    a. detailed.
    b. documented.
    c. filed.
    d. transcribed.

SHORT ANSWER QUESTIONS

1. **[LO 4.1]** Explain why it is important to keep the design of paper forms logical and orderly.

2. **[LO 4.2]** Explain why a patient's social history is important.

3. **[LO 4.1]** Why is it recommended that a patient's name and chart number/medical record number appear on each page of a multipage form?

4. **[LO 4.4]** List the vital signs that are typically taken at each patient visit.

5. **[LO 4.1]** Why, in the age of EHRs, is patient information still gathered mainly through the use of paper forms?

6. **[LO 4.2]** Differentiate between the social and family histories.

7. **[LO 4.3]** Why does a medical office need to have clear policies in place for dealing with discrepancies in patient information?

8. **[LO 4.4]** PrimeSUITE asks you to record what position—sitting, standing, or lying down— a patient was in when his or her blood pressure was taken. Why does this matter?

9. **[LO 4.2]** Why might so many patient histories need to be taken?

APPLYING YOUR KNOWLEDGE

1. **[LO 4.2]** Stephanie Lewis comes to your office for her annual wellness checkup. As the healthcare professional who will be doing her initial interview, create a list of questions you might ask Stephanie to obtain her social history.

2. **[LO 4.4]** How can the PrimeSUITE tracking feature assist you in analyzing a patient's vital signs over time? Give a specific example.

3. **[LO 4.1]** As an office manager for a large healthcare practice, you have been asked to design a new patient intake form. Sketch out your form's layout, keeping in mind the best practices discussed in the chapter.

4. **[LO 4.3]** Bob Larks is a new patient in your practice, and he brought his informational form with him on his first visit. During the patient history portion of his exam, he says that he does not drink, but while entering that information in Bob's chart you notice that his initial history stated that he was a "social drinker." What should you do?

5. **[LOs 4.2, 4.3]** As a healthcare professional, you are attempting to obtain the medical histories of your patient, Lisa Sanchez. However, you are having difficulty because Lisa is evading your questions and is refusing to respond. What could you do?

 Enhance your learning by completing these exercises and more at http://connect.mcgraw-hill.com!

Chapter **five**

5

Content of the Health Record—the Care Provider's Responsibility

---

Learning Outcomes

At the end of this chapter, the student should be able to:

5.1 Explain each element of a SOAP note.

5.2 Identify elements of the history of present illness (HPI).

5.3 Identify elements of the review of systems (ROS).

5.4 Identify elements of the physical exam (PE).

5.5 Describe the process of traditional dictation and transcription.

5.6 Illustrate the advantages of speech recognition technology.

5.7 Outline the benefits of ePrescribing.

5.8 Evaluate the benefits of computerized physician order entry (CPOE).

5.9 Support the necessity to track physicians' orders.

5.10 Examine the benefits of a problem list.

Key Terms

Computerized physician order entry (CPOE)
Discharge summary
ePrescribing
History of present illness (HPI)
History & Physical (H&P)
Interface
Physical exam (PE)

Point of care (POC)
Problem list
Scribe
SOAP note
Speech recognition technology
Voice recognition technology

What You Need to Know and Why You Need to Know It

In this chapter, the EHR is assessed from the care provider's perspective. In the PrimeSUITE demonstrations we will illustrate how a care provider captures clinical information.

Knowing where in the record certain information resides is important because it is often necessary for the medical assistant, biller, or other healthcare professional to access a care provider's documentation to answer a question for another care provider or for an insurance company, or to complete forms.

5.1 The SOAP Note

SOAP stands for **S**ubjective, **O**bjective, **A**ssessment, and **P**lan. It is a format for documentation that reflects a patient's visit (typically an office visit) in an orderly fashion—from the time the visit begins to the time it ends. The four areas are:

SOAP note An acronym for the documentation used in a care provider's office to record the patient's symptoms, signs, assessment (diagnosis), and plan of care.

Subjective (S): This is the information the care provider learns from the patient. The subjective findings are the patient's description of his or her symptoms. For instance, Philip James is seen in Dr. Connors' office today; he tells the doctor that he has had a cold and terrible headache for three days.

Objective (O): Objective findings include information the care provider gathers from performing a physical exam. For example, upon conducting a physical exam on Philip James, he notes the patient has tenderness above the eyebrows and just beneath the cheek bones when touched and a green nasal discharge. Objective findings also include measurable test results such as an x-ray finding or lab result.

Assessment (A): At this assessment stage, the care provider *assesses* the patient's signs and symptoms and results of his physical exam in order to make a diagnosis or diagnoses. The documented diagnosis for Philip James is acute sinusitis.

Plan (P): The plan is also known as the plan of care. The care provider will order any tests he feels are medically necessary, prescribe medications or recommend over-the-counter medications, order consultations with other care providers if necessary, educate the patient about his condition, and advise the patient of follow-up instructions. So, in Mr. James's case, Dr. Connors wrote an order for a CT scan of the sinuses. His instructions to Mr. James included drinking plenty of fluids and taking the next two days off from work. A prescription for a Z-Pak was ordered and he was given printed educational material about sinusitis (from the EHR software). He was told to schedule a follow-up appointment for 10 days from now.

An example of an instruction screen for a patient is found in Figure 5.1. In a paper record, the physician would handwrite the patient's record as seen in Figure 5.2.

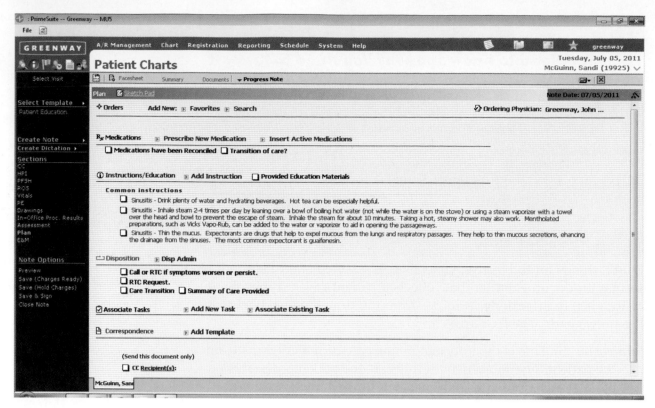

Figure 5.1   Example of patient instructions from PrimeSUITE

Look up the Patient's Plan of Care

In this exercise, it is necessary to access the plan of care Dr. Ingram ordered for Alfredo Garza. Dr. Ingram is on the phone and has asked you to look up the treatment plan for Alfredo Garza, since he has to return a call to Mr. Garza quickly and is not at a computer. Once the information is accessed, then you would read the documentation to Dr. Ingram.

Follow these steps to complete the exercise on your own once you have watched the demonstration and tried the steps with helpful prompts.

From the PrimeSUITE desktop, the patient's Facesheet is accessed and then the steps below are followed.

1. Click the Documents tab.
2. Click 09/04/2013. (Note the information in the Plan section.)

✓ **You have completed Exercise 5.1**

PrimeSUITE Tip PS

Unstructured data is not taken into consideration when PrimeSUITE calculates the charges for an office visit; structured data is included in the calculation of charges for the office visit.

In an electronic health record, these elements are documented, but rather than being handwritten, a combination of free-text writing and use of drop-down menus and standard text make documentation more thorough, consistent, easily retrievable, and legible. As you complete the exercises later in this chapter you will see that the SOAP elements just described are present in the EHR.

When a patient is admitted to a hospital, the care provider documents the subjective and objective findings, along with the results of a physical exam, in the **History & Physical** report, otherwise known as an **H&P.** The assessment and plan, as well as a recap of the patient's course in the hospital, would be documented in a **discharge summary** (or note). Throughout the stay, nurses document in the nursing notes section of the record and care providers document in the physicians' progress notes. When handwritten or typed, this is *unstructured data;* when an electronic health record is used and the responses are chosen from a pre-formatted field, such as from a drop-down menu, the data is *structured.*

History & Physical (H&P)
A report completed by a care provider which includes the reason(s) the patient is being seen or admitted; the history of present illness; the pertinent past medical, surgical, social, and family histories; other current conditions/diseases the patient is being treated for; the report of a physical examination; working diagnoses; and plan of care.

Discharge summary A report completed by a care provider which summarizes a patient's stay in the hospital. It generally includes the final diagnoses, a summary of the patient's course in the hospital, any procedures performed, recap of diagnostic results, and discharge instructions.

History of present illness (HPI) The patient's description of current complaints such as when the symptoms started, the location of the condition, quality of the symptoms, severity of the symptoms, anything that makes the symptoms better or worse, and additional symptoms the patient is experiencing.

5.2 The History of Present Illness (HPI)

The **history of present illness**, or **HPI**, is the patient's depiction of his or her current illness as told to the healthcare professional or care provider. The typical elements of an HPI are:

- Location of the condition (abdomen, arm, leg, head, etc.).
- Quality: pain is sharp, dull, or an ache, for example.
- Severity: rating of pain/itch/cough/nausea, etc. Often, patients are asked to rate their symptoms on a scale of 1 to 10 with 1 being barely noticeable and 10 being intolerable. This may also mean the severity in terms of bleeding, vomiting, or diarrhea—for instance, profuse bleeding from a laceration versus a small amount of bleeding.
- Timing/duration: how long the condition has been present—hours, days, weeks, months, for example.
- Modifying factors: alternating ice and heat on a painful area; effect of pain medication, etc.
- Associated signs and symptoms: for instance, the cold symptoms described by Philip James in Figure 5.2.

Read Philip James's SOAP note in Figure 5.2 again. Match the information listed in the subjective portion of the note to the typical elements of an HPI. Not all elements are collected on all visits—only those that are necessary based on the patient's chief complaint would be documented.

5.3 The Review of Systems (ROS)

The review of systems (ROS) is a body system–by–body system assessment of any signs or symptoms the patient is experiencing that may or may not be related to the reason for his visit. The ROS is not the same as a physical exam, because the ROS refers to the patient's own responses, not an objective assessment by the care provider. Often, the ROS is accomplished by the patient completing the medical history form that we discussed earlier. Or, the care provider may use that as a starting point and ask questions based on the patient's responses given on the form. The completion (or review) of the ROS

for your information **fyi**

Some typical questions asked during a ROS are:
Have you been having any unusual headaches?
Have you been having any blurry or double vision?
Have you had any change in bowel habits?
Have you had any swelling of your joints?

Patient: Philip James	DOB: July 31, 1991 Date of Service: 09/08/2013
S	Mr. James presented today because he has had a headache for the past three days. He has not received any relief from OTC decongestants or antihistamines. He describes the pain as more of an ache, though when he pushes on his forehead, it is painful. He has had cold symptoms for about a week, but his symptoms are getting worse, and on a scale of 1 to 10, he says that his pain is an 8. He has also noted that he has had two minor nose bleeds in the past two days.
O	Vital signs noted in his chart. All within normal limits. Head and face: physical exam of nasal passages reveals a moderate amount of green discharge from both nares. The patient is tender to the touch above each eyebrow and cheek bone. Chest is clear to percussion and auscultation. Heart: Regular rate and rhythm. Abdomen: Non-tender. This is the third time Mr. James has been diagnosed with a sinus infection in the past 18 months.
A	Acute sinusitis.
P	CT scan of sinuses to be done today or tomorrow at Memorial Hospital (order given to patient). Instructed to drink plenty of fluids and bedrest for two days. To return to office in 10 days for follow-up. Z-Pak single-dose pack was sent to The Corner Pharmacy via ePrescribe. Patient was given sinusitis literature.
	Jared Connors, MD 09/08/2013

Figure 5.2   Handwritten SOAP note

EXERCISE   5.2   EHR

Go to http://connect.mcgraw-hill.com to complete this exercise. connect plus+

Locate Alfredo Garza's Blood Pressure

In this exercise, Alfredo J. Garza stopped by the office and wants to know what his blood pressure was on his last visit. To look this up, you will access Alfredo Garza's chart.

You will start by going to Alfredo J. Garza's Facesheet. The Vital Signs are found there, and you do not need to leave the Facesheet to find his blood pressure readings.

Follow these steps to complete the exercise on your own once you have watched the demonstration and tried the steps with helpful prompts.

From the PrimeSUITE desktop, the patient's Facesheet is accessed and then the steps below are followed.

1. Click the Vital Signs radio button.
2. Click the blood pressure reading to highlight it.

Once you locate the vital signs, you will tell Mr. Garza that on his visit of September 4, 2013, his blood pressure reading was 160/80.

 You have completed Exercise 5.2

PrimeSUITE Tip PS

Click on the radio button next to the words Vital Signs, *not* on the words themselves.

is an integral component in assessing the patient's overall health as well as gaining a better picture of any additional signs or symptoms that may be related to the patient's chief complaint. In addition, the ROS plays a role in how much the patient will be charged for the visit, since it takes into account the care provider's time and medical expertise during an office visit. Regardless of whether the history form is already completed and the care provider reviews it or whether the care provider completes the form herself during an office visit, there must be some form of documentation to show that the ROS was done or reviewed in order to receive reimbursement for it. The particulars of procedure coding, charging, and reimbursement will be covered briefly in a future chapter of this worktext and in another course.

Usually, a care provider will start at the head and work down through the body to the lower extremities. Following are the typical organs and/or body systems that may be reviewed as well as examples of questions that may be asked for each:

- General, also referred to as Constitutional (how the patient is feeling in general, any complaints or concerns, and a recap of vital signs)
- Skin (any rashes or wounds that will not heal, any unusual moles or markings that have appeared, etc.)
- Head, Eyes, Ears, Nose, and Mouth (headaches, double vision, blurring of vision, ringing of ears, earache, nosebleeds, dry mouth, dental issues)
- Throat (persistent sore throat, difficulty swallowing)
- Breasts (whether monthly self-exams are done, any changes, lumps, nipple discharge)
- Respiratory (difficulty breathing, shortness of breath)
- Cardiovascular (any chest pain, palpitations, or fluttering)
- Gastrointestinal (any problems with stomach pain, constipation, diarrhea; any changes in stool, signs of blood in stool)
- Genitourinary (any problems voiding, cloudiness of urine, changes in color or odor of urine, difficulty starting to urinate, nighttime urination, signs of blood in urine)
- Musculoskeletal (any pain in joints or extremities, difficulty walking)
- Neurologic (any dizziness, lightheadedness, difficulty with memory, cognition, coordination, or severe headaches)
- Endocrine (if female, any problems with menses, any swelling of the thyroid)
- Psychological (depression, changes in mood)
- Hematologic/Lymphatic (any unexplained or profuse bleeding, any swelling of lymph glands)
- Allergies (problems with environmental allergies; any known allergies or reactions to medications)

In PrimeSUITE and most EHR software, the ROS choices are determined by the patient's chief complaint or the corresponding body system. Not every ailment requires a thorough ROS. For instance, for a patient being seen with cold symptoms, the care provider may just review the head, eyes, ears, nose and throat (HEENT), and chest (which essentially makes up the respiratory system) and would typically have no need to review the breasts, neurological, psychological, or reproductive systems.

Figure 5.3 shows the master ROS file in PrimeSUITE and Figure 5.4 shows the full ROS.

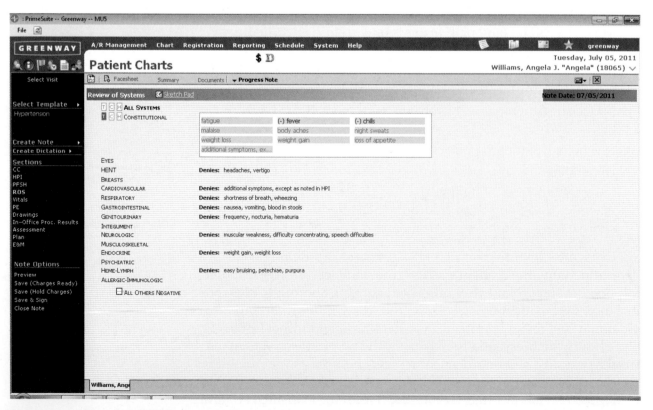

File ☑

GREENWAY A/R Management Chart Registration Reporting Schedule System Help 📄 📖 🖼 ★ greenway

Review of Systems Admin

Thursday, September 05, 2013
McGuinn. Sandi (19925) ⌄

Current Selection: **Cardiovascular**

Edit
Options 💾

☐ Constitutional
☐ Eyes
☐ HENT
☐ Breasts
☐ Cardiovascular
☐ Respiratory
☐ Gastrointestinal
☐ Genitourinary
☐ Integument
☐ Neurologic
☐ Musculoskeletal
☐ Endocrine
☐ Psychiatric
☐ Heme-Lymph
☐ Allergic-
   Immunologic

Comprehensive Review

☑ (-) chest pain	☑ irregular heart beats	☑ rapid heart rate
☑ (-) syncope	☑ dyspnea on exertion	☑ orthopnea
☑ paroxysmal nocturnal ...	☑ lower extremity edema	☑ cyanosis
☑ varicosities	☑ venous cords	☑ claudication
☑ lightheadedness	☑ orthostatic symptoms	☑ additional symptoms ...

Import | Export | Replace with Greenway
Default

Figure 5.3   PrimeSUITE Review of Systems Administration screen—Constitutional Section

Figure 5.4   Completed ROS

Each office must construct a master ROS file; but each care provider chooses the content of each ROS screen and how it displays. Thus, in PrimeSUITE, the ROS screens are user-based and can be customized to each user's needs or preferences. (Figure 5.4 shows a completed ROS in narrative form.)

EXERCISE 5.3

Add New Options to the ROS

Even though the PrimeSUITE ROS Admin function is very comprehensive, there may be times when your practice will want to customize specific sections by adding new choices or adjusting existing ones. This is done through the ROS Admin screen.

1. Click the Chart drop-down menu.
2. Click Review of Systems Admin.
3. Click the Constitutional box.
4. Click Edit Options.
5. Type "stomach cramps" in the Add New Options field.
6. Click the plus sign.
7. Click the Scroll bar.
8. Double-click malaise.
9. Type "tiredness".
10. Click OK.
11. Click Save.

You have now customized your ROS Admin screen. If you are the office manager in charge of customizing the practice's screens, you could click Export at the bottom of the screen to share it with other users; those users can then import the changes into their profiles.

 You have completed Exercise 5.3

5.4 The Physical Exam

The **physical exam (PE)** is performed by the care provider. As we discussed earlier, in a physician's office that would be the physician, physician's assistant, nurse practitioner, or nurse midwife. The extent of the physical exam is typically driven by the patient's chief complaint, or the reason the patient is being seen today. If a patient is being seen for an annual physical exam, then it will be more extensive than the PE performed for a patient who is being seen with a chief complaint of a splinter in the right ring finger.

The care provider will also determine the extent of the PE based on the patient's responses to the ROS questions. If the patient with the splinter in the right ring finger has also been falling more than usual, then the PE will be more extensive and may also include the musculoskeletal and neurologic systems.

Figure 5.5 depicts a written physical exam that would be similar to one found in a paper health record. Figure 5.6 shows a physical exam as documented using PrimeSUITE.

Physical exam (PE) An examination of the patient's body for signs of disease.

PHYSICAL EXAM

Alexis Shaw is a 25-year-old African American female being seen today for her annual physical. Her ROS has been reviewed; and is unremarkable.
HEENT: Scalp clear; eyes and ears within normal limits; Nose: Some congestion noted; throat: post-nasal drip noted.
Chest: Lungs clear to auscultation, no wheezes or rales.
Cardio: Heart rate and rhythm normal; no murmurs.
Abdomen: Soft, non-tender, no guarding or rebound noted.
Skin: No rashes, broken skin, or open wounds. Nails: bites her nails, but otherwise unremarkable.
Breasts & Genitalia: Deferred – she has an appointment with her GYN in two months. Her LMP was April 15 of this year. Periods are normal.
Extremities: Range of motion intact; no swelling.
Neuro: Within normal limits.

Figure 5.5   Written PE

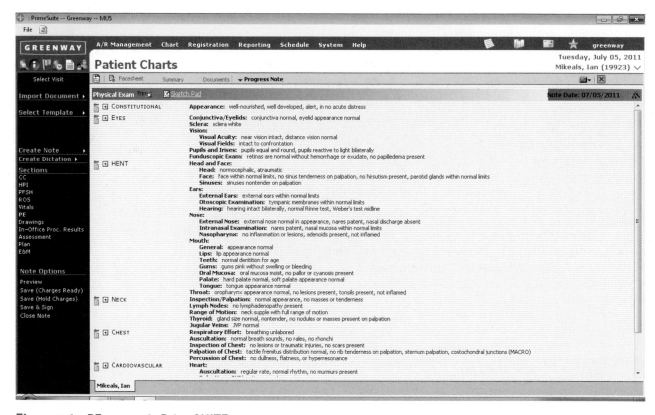

Figure 5.6   PE as seen in PrimeSUITE

The healthcare professional who needs to know the results of a patient's physical exam to answer questions, complete forms, or handle insurance issues will need to access the patient's physical exam.

Though an EHR results in more detailed, timely documentation, it is still labor intensive for the care provider and it is possible that patients could leave with the perception that the physician was more interested in the computer than in them. To counter this, many physicians, hospitals, emergency departments, and clinics are utilizing **scribes** to enter data into the EHR. The scribe works only under the supervision of the care provider and must have knowledge of medical terminology, human disease, and pharmacology. Excellent keyboarding skills including speed and most importantly accuracy are a must. The care provider is ultimately responsible for the information

Scribe An assistant who enters data either in writing or electronically into the health record as the care provider verbally dictates recent findings.

entered into the EHR. The entries made by the scribe are electronically signed or attributed to the scribe, but the care provider must countersign the documentation. Best practices dictate that the care provider not countersign any notes until after reading and verifying their accuracy.

The use of scribes is not a new practice. Many care providers have long used scribes to document in their paper or electronic records. Dermatologists, for example, are not only examining skin with their eyes, but also have to hold measuring tools and a magnifier, and therefore cannot stop to document each lesion. A scribe is needed to document as the dermatologist verbally describes each lesion. The same applies to an ophthalmologist, who uses instruments to examine a patient's eyes and therefore cannot stop to write or type in findings.

5.5 Medical Dictation and Transcription

With a manual record system, most care providers choose to handwrite their charts. That has often been problematic since handwriting is often illegible. A chart that is not legible could cause safety concerns and negative patient outcomes, and wastes time for the healthcare professional who cannot read the writing and has to track down the care provider for clarification. You have no doubt read or heard horror stories of wrong medications or wrong dosages being given to patients because of illegible handwriting. Health insurance companies may also deny payment based on illegible handwriting.

One solution many physicians used in the past was to dictate their notes into a recorder (hand-held or into a larger system via telephone), and a transcriptionist would then transcribe the physician's words into a typed document. Dictation used as a business tool dates back to the early 20th century, when Thomas Edison, Inc. and Columbia Graphaphone Company distributed their first versions of voice recorders known as the Ediphone and Dictaphone, respectively. Dictation has evolved considerably—from hand-held machines to less cumbersome systems that only require the use of a telephone.

The use of dictation and transcription software resulted in greater accuracy (because of better recording quality), faster turnaround time than the original dictation systems, and more advanced reporting capabilities, which allowed physicians' offices and hospitals to analyze the cost of dictation and transcription as a means of documentation.

The cost of dictation, and the required transcriptionists who translate the spoken word into the written word, are not inexpensive. As the technology progressed, so did the price of dictation systems. As the requirements of government agencies and insurance companies rose, as well as escalating malpractice and negligence cases, the need for better, faster documentation grew. But recording a physician's words on paper also needed to be done in a timely manner. The need for qualified transcriptionists grew, but were often in short supply.

5.6 Voice (Speech) Recognition Technology

Over the past 15 years or so, voice (speech) recognition technology has replaced traditional dictation to a great degree. **Voice recognition technology** is software that "learns" as it is used. In other words, it learns the voice and tone inflections of the dictator, and accuracy improves with time. **Speech recognition technology**, on the other hand, does not recognize individual voices. Many of you may already be using speech recognition technology and do not even realize it. For instance, your cell phone has a feature that allows you to voice dial; or you call your local cable company and have to go through a series of questions that you can respond to by "saying or pushing 3." Both are forms of voice recognition. In these two examples, a command is carried out based on your speech response. With voice recognition used in the medical environment, as the care provider dictates, the words appear on the computer screen. In true voice recognition systems, the software "learns" the dictator's voice. The words that end up on screen are not perfect; for instance, "there" may be typed rather than "their" or Xanax may be heard as Zantac. But, since medicine requires accurate information, the transcriptionist's role has become more of editor than transcriber. The transcriptionist may listen to the entire piece of dictation and compare it against what appears on the screen, or, once the system learns that physician's voice and becomes more accurate, the transcriptionist may only read what is on the screen to look for obvious errors.

The quality of transcription is higher with voice recognition (if the software recognizes the words correctly). Once physicians are comfortable with the use of voice recognition software, it may be less time consuming than dictation, and long-term costs are lower since in most instances the transcription costs are lower (especially if a transcription service has been utilized in the past). The greatest advantage, though, is speed of documentation. With traditional transcription, days could pass between the time a chart note was dictated and transcribed (known as turn-around time). With voice recognition, the documentation is instant—as the words are spoken, they are documented in the chart simultaneously. Of course, the chart should be reviewed and edited before the care provider authenticates (signs) the note, but the fact that there is a draft copy in the record so quickly is a strong benefit.

Most EMR/EHR software solutions have a voice recognition component.

for your information fyi

Nuance is a popular service provider of speech recognition technology. This YouTube video gives you a physician's perspective shows the dictation process using speech recognition. http://www.youtube.com/watch?v=5FOVFVh_Nuw&list=TLw0-tV2ksT5O

5.7 Electronic Prescribing (ePrescribing)

ePrescribing software is another component of the meaningful use requirements of HITECH. With ePrescribing, the care provider sends prescriptions to the patient's pharmacy electronically, at the **point of care** (occurring at the time the patient is being seen). Electronically sending prescriptions speeds up the process for the patient as opposed to the traditional method where the care provider hands the patient a written prescription, the patient takes it to the pharmacy, and then waits for it to be filled (or returns at a later time). Even if the prescription is called in by the office, the process takes longer than using ePrescribing.

Most importantly, quality of care is greatly improved with electronic prescribing; not only does the prescription itself go directly to the pharmacy, but also the patient demographics, insurance information, allergies, and medication history are sent as well. Care providers and pharmacists are alerted to possible food and drug interactions between medications that are currently prescribed or that the patient is already taking, and drug allergies and sensitivities are flagged. Also, medication dosing errors are avoided—for instance, if the care provider orders 250 mg of a particular drug for a 15-year-old patient, but the recommended dosage for that drug is 25 mg for a 15-year-old, an alert message would automatically appear, so that the care provider can make the correction before the prescription is sent through to the pharmacy. Prescription renewal requests are handled more efficiently too, since they are received electronically and there is no need to manually update the patient's chart. And of course, there are no more legibility issues—pharmacists do not have to make phone calls back to the office to ask what was written by the care provider; and the office staff does not have to take the time to track down the care provider or chart.

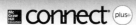 Go to http://connect.mcgraw-hill.com to complete this exercise. EXERCISE 5.4

Using ePrescribe

Before we look at the steps involved in using ePrescribe, we will cover the parts of a prescription. They are:

Drug name: The name of the drug in brand or generic form. For instance, HydroDIURIL is the brand name for hydrochlorothiazide (the generic name).

Dosage: The measurement of the amount of drug that is being administered. HydroDIURIL is prescribed in 25 or 50 mg doses to treat adult hypertension.

Sig: The "label" or instructions that the pharmacist needs to list on the prescription label. A common Sig for HydroDIURIL would be "Take one tablet by mouth, once daily."

In our scenario for ePrescribe, Alfredo J. Garza has called in for a refill of his prescription for Caduet (a medication for high blood pressure and angina).

Since this information would be found in the clinical part of the chart, Alfredo J. Garza's Facesheet is first accessed and then the Medication List. The care provider would typically carry out these steps unless he or she has given the healthcare professional a verbal order to do so.

Follow these steps to complete the exercise on your own once you have watched the demonstration and tried the steps with helpful prompts. Use the information provided in the scenario to complete the information.

1. Click the Medication List radio button.
2. Click View Medication History.
3. Click Caduet Oral Tablet 10-10 mg.
4. (Note the refill sent via ePrescribe.) Click Close.

Once we completed these steps, we found that Dr. Ingram ePrescribed a refill for Alfredo J. Garza.

 You have completed Exercise 5.4

5.8 Computerized Physician Order Entry (CPOE)

No treatment, diagnostic test, or medication administration is performed on any patient without a care provider's order. Using paper records, orders were traditionally either written by the care provider or given verbally and written in the patient's record by a nurse. Orders may be in written form or may be electronically submitted via **computerized physician order entry (CPOE)**. PrimeSUITE's functionality is called *Orders Requisition*. Through this function, orders can be printed or electronically submitted to an outside laboratory, medical equipment company, or hospital with **interface** capabilities with PrimeSUITE. The interface capability means that one computer system (or component) can accept and receive data from another system. The interface could refer to systems at different locations or within the same facility. Your office may have PrimeSUITE software for PM and EHR, but your laboratory system may be manufactured by a different vendor. If the computer programs for each are configured to exchange data without having to re-enter the data, then orders can flow directly to the laboratory system and the results can flow directly back to the EHR in PrimeSUITE.

A major advantage of CPOE functionality is built-in clinical decision support. Alerts appear when orders are entered for medications or treatment that may cause an adverse reaction to a drug or drugs that had previously been ordered for that patient. The same applies to dosing errors—if a care provider ordered 250 mg of a drug for a 10-year-old patient, but maximum dosage is 100 mg for that age group, then an alert would appear, and a potentially serious situation could be averted since the alert occurs prior to administration of the drug. Through use of CPOE, as long as the facility's data dictionary includes a comprehensive listing of medications and abbreviations used, the probability of medication errors is greatly reduced.

Regarding orders for diagnostic tests, once the order is carried out, for instance a Complete Blood Count (CBC), the results will be electronically sent to the care provider who ordered the lab test. Using CPOE is safer as well because there is no questionable handwriting or errors in transcribing the verbal orders of physicians to contend with—again, improving overall patient care.

5.9 Tracking Physicians' Orders

If a test is important enough to order, then learning the results of that test is equally important. Tests that are not carried out and reported in a timely manner can delay necessary care and also cause inefficiency in the business processes of an office. Having this functionality in an EHR system prevents communication breakdowns and unnecessary rework.

When an order has been completed and the results are ready for the care provider's review, she will receive notification on her Desktop. In Figure 5.7, note on the left side of the screen that the Lab Flowsheet tab shows one resulted order and has a red star next to it, meaning it is high priority. The care provider would click on the Orders tab to review the returned results.

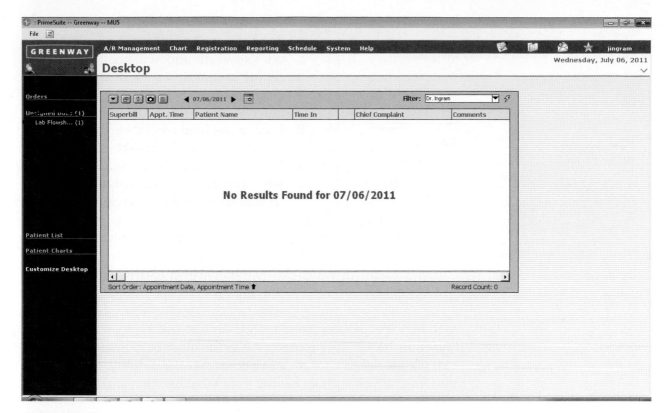

Figure 5.7   Results ready for review

Once the care provider clicks the Orders tab, all resulted orders will appear on the screen. In Figure 5.8 you can see that there is one order that has been resulted, and it is for a metabolic panel on Dr. Ingram's patient, Tom Gunn.

Figure 5.8   Resulted order

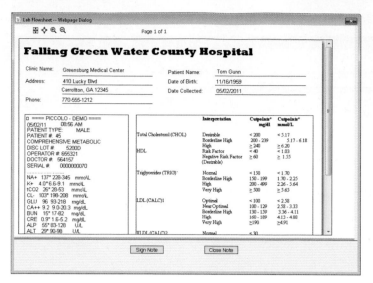

Figure 5.9   Detailed report and option to sign note

Dr. Ingram will want to see the detailed results, and to do so he clicks on View/Edit and will see the complete report; at that time he will also click Sign Note on the report to document that he has reviewed the results. Figure 5.9 illustrates a detailed report.

If, based on the results of the lab test, Dr. Ingram wants to order additional tests, prescribe a particular medication, or follow up with the patient soon, he will give additional orders to the healthcare professional to handle the situation accordingly.

Figure 5.10 represents the final screen the care provider sees. From it he can note whether the results were normal, abnormal, or a specific assessment, and can also send a follow-up task to one of the healthcare professionals in the office or to another care provider in the practice for review. These tasks can be done directly from the Order screen without having to exit that function and find another.

EXERCISE   5.5   EHR

Go to http://connect.mcgraw-hill.com to complete this exercise.   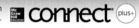 plus+

Locate the Status of an Order

In this exercise, Dr. Ingram is asking you about the results of Alfredo Garza's lab and radiology work. You will again go to the Facesheet of Alfredo J. Garza, but find the section titled Order Tracking History, since our goal is to find out whether or not Alfredo had the tests done, and if the results are in his chart.

Once the Facesheet is accessed, follow these steps to complete the exercise on your own once you have watched the demonstration and tried the steps with helpful prompts.

1. Click the Orders Tracking History radio button.
2. Click the View Lab Orders tab.
3. Click the View Imaging Orders tab.
4. Click View/Edit.
5. Click Imported - Document - Radiologic examination, chest; single X Ray.
6. Click Scroll down button.
7. Click Close Note.
8. Click Save & Close.

✔ You have completed Exercise 5.5

5.10   The Problem List

Problem list   A listing kept in the patient's health record of all current (active) and resolved medical conditions.

Another requirement of meaningful use is an up-to-date **problem list** of current and active diagnoses. Providing quality care means that current diagnoses or conditions should be followed on an ongoing basis until the problem is resolved, or at least until it is stable. Of course, there are some medical conditions, such as asthma or coronary artery disease, that may never resolve completely, but the care provider must ensure that the patient is stable and that his or her condition is not worsening. With the use of a problem list, as long as it is kept current, necessary testing or assessment of the condition does not "fall through the cracks." For instance, a patient may be seen today because of an upper respiratory infection, but has also been treated by the care provider for hypertension, and on today's visit the care provider notes that the patient's blood pressure is elevated. By clicking on Hypertension in the list of diagnoses included in the problem list, the care provider is able to quickly see the treatment history and prior blood pressure readings on that patient and then proceed accordingly. (See Figure 5.11 for an example of a problem list.)

Sometimes, the information included in the problem list is helpful to the patient as well as the care provider. The patient may have told the care provider something about his treatment or hospitalizations, and later forgets the details. By having this complete history, the medical office has the information readily available when needed.

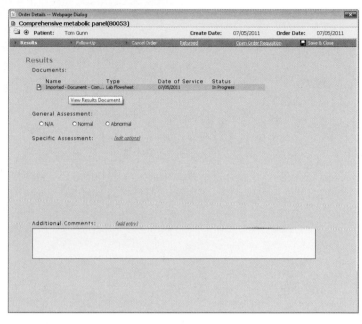

Figure 5.10 Order details screen

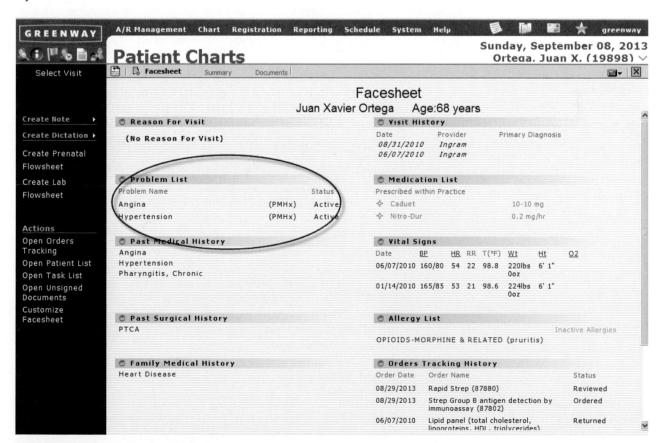

Figure 5.11 Example of problem list

Utilizing the Problem List

In the scenario we are about to view, Alfredo J. Garza has been treated for angina over the past few years. He was first diagnosed in 2005 and has been hospitalized at Memorial Hospital twice for it—once on August 31, 2010, and once on June 17, 2009. Mr. Garza has asked the office staff to complete a form that he needs for his employer. His employer needs to know if he has ever been hospitalized for angina and when. He does not recall the dates but does remember giving that information to Dr. Ingram on his last visit, so he hopes the information can be found in his record.

From the Facesheet of Alfredo J. Garza, the healthcare professional will click on angina from the Problem List area in order to get Mr. Garza the information he needs.

Once the Facesheet of the patient's chart is accessed, follow these steps to complete the exercise on your own once you've watched the demonstration and tried the steps with helpful prompts.

1. Under Problem List, click Angina.
2. Click OK. (Note the hospitalization dates.)

 You have completed Exercise 5.6

APPLYING YOUR SKILLS

In this chapter, we covered the usual contents of a SOAP note. Following are random sentences likely to be found in a provider's office note. After each sentence, note whether the sentence should be in the **S**ubjective, **O**bjective, **A**ssessment, or **P**lan portion of the office note. Again, these are random sentences, and will not come together to form a note for one particular patient.

1. A chest x-ray performed in the office showed an infiltrate in the right lower lobe of the lung.
2. Grace has been complaining of a pain in her right side, which is stabbing in nature.
3. The patient was given an order for an ultrasound of the kidneys and bladder, which she should have done in the next week or so.
4. Nephrolithiasis
5. The patient's blood pressure is 145/95.
6. "I am here because I've had a headache for three days that just won't go away."
7. The patient should continue physical therapy for two more weeks.
8. Right lower lobe pneumonia
9. Both pupils are equal and reactive.
10. The patient states she has tried Aleve, but her right knee pain has not improved.

chapter 5 **summary**

LEARNING OUTCOME	CONCEPTS FOR REVIEW
5.1 Explain each element of a SOAP note. Pages 87–89	– Subjective—the patient's description of the problem – Objective—the care provider's results of physical examination – Assessment—the diagnosis or diagnoses – Plan—the diagnostic tests or treatment plan for the patient
5.2 Identify elements of the history of present illness (HPI). Page 89	– Location of the condition (abdomen, arm, leg, head, etc.) – Quality of the symptoms – Severity of the symptoms – Duration/timing of the symptoms – Context under which symptoms occur – Modifying factors – Associated signs and symptoms
5.3 Identify elements of the review of systems (ROS). Pages 89–93	– Body system–by–body system assessment of any signs or symptoms the patient is experiencing that may or may not be related to the reason for his or her visit – Not the same as the physical exam
5.4 Identify elements of the physical exam (PE). Pages 93–95	– The extent of the exam is dependent on the patient's presenting symptoms (the chief complaint) – The physical exam relates to the findings of the care provider, not the patient, as in the ROS; for example, the patient complains of pain in the right lower abdomen, yet when the care provider presses on the right lower abdomen, the patient does not express feelings of pain
5.5 Describe the process of traditional dictation and transcription. Page 95	– Physician dictates medical notes into a recording device – Transcriptionist types the words using word processing software – Often takes days for the transcribed report to be filed in the patient's record
5.6 Illustrate the advantages of speech recognition technology. Page 96	– The provider's documentation immediately appears in the patient's record; no lag time between dictation and transcription – In the long term, may be less expensive than traditional dictation and transcription – Quality is higher than with traditional transcription (in most cases)
5.7 Outline the benefits of ePrescribing. Pages 96–97	– Less chance for medication errors – Potential food/drug interactions are identified – Fewer man-hours to complete the process – More convenient and less wait time for patients – Overall, better-quality care

LEARNING OUTCOME	CONCEPTS FOR REVIEW
5.8 Evaluate the benefits of computerized physician order entry (CPOE). Page 98	– Fewer errors in carrying out orders because they are no longer handwritten – Orders can be sent directly from the office to the laboratory or hospital – Safer for the patient—the order is sent by the care provider rather than verbally given to another healthcare professional to send on to the laboratory or hospital – If an interface exists, the results automatically come back to the ordering physician.
5.9 Support the necessity to track physicians' orders. Pages 98–100	– Patient care—knowing the results of the test in a timely manner, proper treatment can be started quickly
5.10 Examine the benefits of a problem list. Pages 100–102	– Timely follow-up of conditions – Serves as a reminder to the care provider to address problems on the patient's problem list – Information about each problem is located in one place

chapter **review**

MATCHING QUESTIONS

Match the terms on the left with the definitions on the right.

_____ 1. **[LO 5.1]** SOAP note

_____ 2. **[LO 5.8]** interface

_____ 3. **[LO 5.4]** scribe

_____ 4. **[LO 5.6]** voice recognition technology

_____ 5. **[LO 5.8]** computerized physician order entry

_____ 6. **[LO 5.2]** history of present illness

_____ 7. **[LO 5.7]** point of care

_____ 8. **[LO 5.10]** problem list

_____ 9. **[LO 5.7]** ePrescribing

_____ 10. **[LO 5.6]** speech recognition technology

a. Patient's description of current symptoms

b. EMR feature that is part of HITECH's meaningful use requirements

c. Software that recognizes spoken words and converts them into text

d. Immediate, real-time documentation of patient procedures

e. Comprehensive record of a patient's complaints and conditions

f. Documentation format that allows health-care professionals to capture all aspects of a patient encounter

g. The ability to access another provider's practice management software for patient care purposes

h. Assistant who enters the dictation of a care provider into a patient record

i. Software that automatically turns spoken words into text and learns voice inflections the more it is used

j. Electronic entry of care provider orders for direct transmission to appropriate departments

MULTIPLE-CHOICE QUESTIONS

Select the letter that best completes the statement or answers the question:

1. **[LO 5.2]** Which of the following is an element of the history of present illness?
   a. Duration
   b. Prevention
   c. Medication
   d. Treatment

 Enhance your learning by completing these exercises and more at http://**connect.mcgraw-hill.com**!

2. **[LO 5.3]** Which of the following would most likely require a complete review of systems?
   a. Annual exam
   b. Headache
   c. Mole on back
   d. Sore throat

3. **[LO 5.1]** Notes about a prescription ordered for a patient would appear in the _____ section of a SOAP note.
   a. subjective
   b. objective
   c. assessment
   d. plan

4. **[LO 5.3]** An ROS covers information likely documented in the:
   a. history of present illness.
   b. medical history form.
   c. physical exam.
   d. SOAP note.

5. **[LO 5.9]** PrimeSUITE has the capability to _____ the status of an order.
   a. assign
   b. generate
   c. query
   d. track

6. **[LO 5.6]** The biggest advantage of voice recognition software over manual transcription is:
   a. clarity.
   b. cost.
   c. ease.
   d. speed of turn-around time.

7. **[LO 5.1]** Information gathered during a provider's physical exam would appear in the _____ section of a SOAP note.
   a. subjective
   b. objective
   c. assessment
   d. plan

8. **[LO 5.6]** The more voice recognition software is used, the:
   a. faster it corrects mistakes.
   b. quicker it gets.
   c. more it learns voice inflections.
   d. slower it gets.

http://connect.mcgraw-hill.com

9. **[LO 5.8]** There must be a _____ to perform any tests or treatments.
   a. diagnosis
   b. referral
   c. care provider request
   d. SOAP note

10. **[LO 5.5]** A person hired to manually record a physician's spoken words is known as a:
    a. dictator.
    b. recorder.
    c. stenographer.
    d. transcriptionist.

11. **[LO 5.2]** Which of the following elements of an HPI are collected at a visit?
    a. All of them
    b. Duration, quality, and severity
    c. Location and severity
    d. Only those that apply to the patient's chief complaint

12. **[LO 5.4]** The extent of a physical exam largely depends upon which of the following?
    a. Age of patient
    b. Amount of time available
    c. Patient's chief complaint
    d. Patient's medical history

13. **[LO 5.10]** Meaningful use regulations require the keeping of an up-to-date:
    a. exam registry.
    b. order queue.
    c. problem list.
    d. provider note.

14. **[LO 5.7]** The use of ePrescribing is part of the requirements for:
    a. HIPAA.
    b. HITECH.
    c. HIM.
    d. HPI.

SHORT ANSWER QUESTIONS

1. **[LO 5.2]** List the typical elements of a history of present illness.

2. **[LO 5.5]** List at least three drawbacks of handwritten patient charts.

3. **[LO 5.3]** In order for a practice to receive reimbursement for an ROS, what must happen?

4. **[LO 5.4]** Explain the factors that might influence the extent of a physical exam.

 Enhance your learning by completing these exercises and more at http://**connect.mcgraw-hill.com**!

5. **[LO 5.1]** List the four sections of a SOAP note and give an example of each.

6. **[LOs 5.5, 5.6]** Why is there still a need for medical transcriptionists in an age of voice recognition software?

7. **[LO 5.3]** List the typical organs and body systems that would be covered in a complete review of systems.

8. **[LO 5.10]** List one reason a provider might use a patient's problem list.

9. **[LOs 5.3, 5.4]** Contrast an ROS with a PE.

10. **[LO 5.4]** List four types of medical providers who might perform a physical exam.

11. **[LO 5.8]** Explain what it means to have interface capabilities with PrimeSUITE. What benefits does interfacing have?

12. **[LO 5.9]** List three benefits of PrimeSUITE's order tracking capabilities.

13. **[LO 5.4]** Based on Alexis Shaw's physical exam as documented in the text, what is her chief complaint?

14. **[LO 5.6]** Contrast voice recognition with speech recognition.

APPLYING YOUR KNOWLEDGE

1. **[LOs 5.1, 5.2, 5.3, 5.4]** Patient James Frank presents for his appointment. He is complaining of fatigue and headaches. When Dr. Ingram examines him, he finds that James has an enlarged lymph node on the right side of his throat; his lungs are clear; his blood pressure is a little low at 100/68. Dr. Ingram suspects anemia or an underactive thyroid as the causes of James's fatigue, so he orders a comprehensive blood panel be done. Create a SOAP note that properly documents each piece of James Frank's visit with Dr. Ingram.

2. **[LO 5.6]** Your office is preparing to implement new voice recognition technology, and you have been tasked with creating some talking points and benefits to share with your peers. How could you go about explaining the benefits of voice recognition software?

3. **[LOs 5.7, 5.10]** Why would ePrescribing and an up-to-date problem list be addressed under meaningful use requirements?

4. **[LOs 5.7, 5.8, 5.9, 5.10]** Of the following PrimeSUITE capabilities—ePrescribing, CPOE, order tracking, and the problem list—which do you think is the most beneficial? Explain your answer.

5. **[LO 5.7]** Create two flowcharts: one that shows the progression of a manually written prescription, and one that shows the progression of a prescription entered using ePrescribing.

chapter **six**

Financial Management: Insurance and Billing Functions

Learning Outcomes

At the end of this chapter, the student should be able to:

6.1 Illustrate the need for a claims management process.

6.2 List the information contained in an encounter form (Superbill).

6.3 Apply procedures to update a patient's account in PrimeSUITE.

6.4 Demonstrate coding using ICD-10-CM/PCS and CPT codes in PrimeSUITE.

6.5 Examine the correlation between documentation and code assignment.

6.6 Describe Accountable Care Organizations.

6.7 Describe the information contained in a remittance advice or explanation of benefits.

6.8 Apply procedures to manage accounts receivable in PrimeSUITE.

6.9 Demonstrate the need for a compliance plan.

Key Terms

Abuse
Accountable Care Organization (ACO)
Accounts payable
Accounts receivable
Affordable Care Act (ACA)
Co-payment (co-pay)
Compliance plan
Deductible
Evaluation and Management (E&M)
Explanation of benefits (EOB)
Fee schedule

Fraud
Healthcare Common Procedure Coding System (HCPCS)
Insurance plan
Insurance verification
Managed care plan
Medical necessity
Remittance advice (RA)
Subscriber
Transactions

What You Need to Know and Why You Need to Know It

Physicians, hospitals, and any other healthcare facility are in business to take care of patients, first and foremost. However, they are also businesses. They have bills to pay just like any other business—payroll, rent or mortgage, utilities, supplies, insurance, and, yes, the providers themselves also need to be paid. The efficiency we have discussed in terms of providing patient care also applies to collecting monies owed to the office. The billing and collections process will be discussed in this chapter. Remember, though, that this is not a course on billing procedures. From this chapter you will gain an awareness of how billing and EHR applications are intermeshed using PrimeSUITE. The specifics of *how* to complete and file insurance claims, manage accounts, collect unpaid bills, and handle financial management in general will be covered in another course. The coding of diagnoses and procedures will also be covered in other classes, but when you finish this chapter you will understand how documentation, coding, and reimbursement are related.

Fee schedule The amount charged for services rendered in a physician's office by Current Procedural Terminology (CPT) code.

6.1 Claims Management—Why and How

Every patient seen in a healthcare facility is charged for the care he or she receives. Yes, some accounts are "written off"; in other words, the patient does not pay, but there still needs to be an accounting of the visit and the charges that were incurred for the visit. If this is not done, the business profile of the office would show an inaccurate picture of the number of patients seen, the procedures carried out, the charges incurred, and the amount of money collected. In other words, the statistics collected for that medical practice would not be valid because not all of the patients were included in the practice's database.

The financial well-being of a medical office is of great importance if the practice is to stay in business. Therefore, a process, or to be specific, a written claims management process, is necessary. Each step of the process must be carried out efficiently and effectively. This process includes written policies—how much is charged per service (**fee schedule**), the timing of filing claims, follow-up on unpaid claims, and collections procedures when claims are not paid must all be in writing. The importance of written policies will be addressed in the compliance section of this chapter.

The use of practice management (PM) software greatly improves the efficiency of a claims process because it allows for more accurate capturing of charges, submits automatic reminders, offers a variety of reporting options, and provides automatic follow-up of each account. There is far less chance of missed charges, missed payments, and payments being posted to the wrong account with a computerized system than a manual one. Just the ability to run reports on daily charges, daily payments, and accounts in collections increases the efficiency of the business processes.

Remember that each patient is entered only once in the practice's database of patients, but each patient may have more than one encounter (visit) attached to that master entry (see Figure 6.1). Each

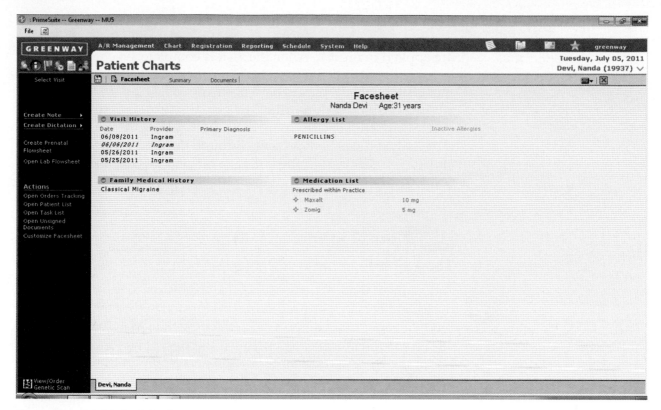

Figure 6.1   Multiple visits for one patient

visit has an account attached to it, and therefore, the claims process must be fulfilled for each of those accounts. Without PM software, just tracking insurance payments on one patient who is seen a couple of times a month would be a daunting task!

The patient's account for each visit begins when the patient makes the appointment. The healthcare professional asks for the expected source of payment at that time. If the patient is going to be paying out of pocket (no insurance), the payment policies of the office are discussed with the patient. Many patients have some type of insurance coverage, whether it be Medicare, Medicaid, TRICARE, private insurance, or group insurance, including managed care plans. **Managed care plans** promote quality, cost-effective healthcare through monitoring of patients, preventive care, and performance measures of providers. Physicians contract with managed care plans to provide care at a predetermined rate. If the patient is covered by insurance, **insurance verification** is completed by the office staff, usually before the patient arrives for his appointment, so that the office is reasonably sure that the patient is covered and that payment will come from some source. Verifying insurance is the process of contacting the insurance carrier and receiving validation of coverage for that patient, whether he owes a co-pay amount (due from the patient at the time of the visit), whether the visit and services ordered are covered by the insurance, and whether he has met his **deductible.**

Once the patient arrives for his appointment he checks in at the front desk. The patient is seen by a healthcare professional who takes the patient's vital signs and begins the documentation for the visit,

Managed care plan Insurance plan that promotes quality, cost-effective healthcare through monitoring of patients, preventive care, and performance.

Insurance verification The process of contacting the insurance carrier and receiving validation of coverage for that patient, deductible status, and co-pay amount.

Deductible The out-of-pocket payment amount that a policyholder must meet before insurance covers the service(s).

including chief complaint, history of present illness, and perhaps a history. The patient is then seen by the care provider and charges are applied to his bill. When the visit is complete, he checks out (in a hospital this is called *discharge*). The patient now has an account for that visit to which charges have been applied.

In a hospital setting, all of the above tasks are performed; however, there are specific rules that apply to insurance verification, especially if the patient presents through the emergency department and/or is in labor. Hospital billing is beyond the scope of this worktext, but a claim is filed with insurance.

6.2   Use of an Encounter Form

The Paper Encounter Form (Superbill)

A document that is often used in medical offices to capture the diagnoses and services or procedures performed, either as a hard copy piece of paper or is computer generated by the PM system, is known as an encounter form or a Superbill (this concept was introduced earlier in the worktext). The information on the Superbill will be transferred to a form known as the CMS-1500 claim form and used to bill an outpatient encounter.

Typically, a hard-copy Superbill (Figure 6.2) includes the following information, though it may contain more elements than those listed below:

- Name and address of the medical practice
- National Provider Identification number (NPI) number
- Patient's name
- Patient's chart number
- Date and time of visit
- CPT codes for common procedures performed in that office
- Diagnosis narrative (as written by the care provider)
- ICD-10-CM codes corresponding to each written diagnosis (not on all Superbills)

On this form, the provider documents the services that were rendered during the encounter. Even if a PM system is computerized, the paper form may still be printed. The patient's identifying information is already completed for the provider, and he or she checks off the CPT codes for the procedures that were performed and writes in the diagnosis or diagnoses the patient was treated for during that particular visit.

The Electronic Encounter Form

Figure 6.3 shows a Superbill Summary in PrimeSUITE for a patient, Tom E. Gunn, who is being seen for cholelithiasis (gallstones).

Notice that the charges are listed just under the visit information. There are five (5) CPT codes listed; these were introduced earlier and will be discussed in more detail later in this chapter. Each CPT code must "map" to a diagnosis code because the diagnosis

ENCOUNTER FORM

11/11/2016	11:15 am
DATE	TIME
Edwin Hsu	**HSUEDWI0**
PATIENT NAME	CHART #

OFFICE VISITS - SYMPTOMATIC

NEW

99201	OF--New Patient Minimal	
99202	OF--New Patient Low	
99203	OF--New Patient Detailed	
99204	OF--New Patient Moderate	
99205	OF--New Patient High	

ESTABLISHED

99211	OF--Established Patient Minimal	
99212	OF--Established Patient Low	X
99213	OF--Established Patient Detailed	
99214	OF--Established Patient Moderate	
99215	OF--Established Patient High	

PREVENTIVE VISITS

NEW

99381	Under 1 Year	
99382	1 - 4 Years	
99383	5 - 11 Years	
99384	12 - 17 Years	
99385	18 - 39 Years	
99386	40 - 64 Years	
99387	65 Years & Up	

ESTABLISHED

99391	Under 1 Year	
99392	1 - 4 Years	
99393	5 - 11 Years	
99394	12 - 17 Years	
99395	18 - 39 Years	
99396	40 - 64 Years	
99397	65 Years & Up	

PROCEDURES

12011	Simple suture--face--local anes.	
29125	App. of short arm splint; static	
29540	Strapping, ankle	
50390	Aspiration of renal cyst by needle	
71010	Chest x-ray, single view, frontal	

PROCEDURES

71020	Chest x-ray, two views, frontal & lateral	
71030	Chest x-ray, complete, four views	
73070	Elbow x-ray, AP & lateral views	
73090	Forearm x-ray, AP & lateral views	
73100	Wrist x-ray, AP & lateral views	
73510	Hip x-ray, complete, two views	
73600	Ankle x-ray, AP & lateral views	

LABORATORY

80048	Basic metabolic panel	
80050	General health panel	
80061	Lipid panel	
82270	Blood screening, occult; feces	
82947	Glucose screening--quantitative	
82951	Glucose tolerance test, three specimens	
83718	HDL cholesterol	
84478	Triglycerides test	
85007	Manual differential WBC	
85018	Hemoglobin	
85651	Erythrocyte sedimentation rate--non-auto	
86580	TB Mantoux test	
87040	Culture, bacterial; blood	
87076	Culture, anerobic isolate	
87077	Bacterial culture, aerobic isolate	
87086	Urine culture and colony count	
87430	Strep test	
87880	Direct streptococcus screen	

INJECTIONS

90471	Immunization administration	
90703	Tetanus injection	
96372	Injection	
92516	Facial nerve function studies	
93000	Electrocardiogram--ECG with interpretation	
93015	Treadmill stress test, with physician...	
96900	Ultraviolet light treatment	
99070	Supplies and materials provided	

FAMILY CARE CENTER
285 Stephenson Blvd.
Stephenson, OH 60089
614-555-0000

☐ DANA BANU, M.D.
☐ ROBERT BEACH, M.D.
☒ PATRICIA MCGRATH, M.D.

☐ JESSICA RUDNER, M.D.
☐ JOHN RUDNER, M.D.
☐ KATHERINE YAN, M.D.

NOTES

REFERRING PHYSICIAN	NPI	AUTHORIZATION #

DIAGNOSIS
J06.9, Acute URI

PAYMENT AMOUNT
$20 copay, check #1066

Figure 6.2   Paper encounter form (Superbill)

code shows **medical necessity** (the fact that there is a medical reason to perform that procedure). To the left of the CPT code column (highlighted in Figure 6.3), notice that there are symbols. There are many coding rules set down by Medicare and Medicaid, and most insurance companies have additional rules as well. The symbols you see are an advantage of using PM software; cash flow is not adversely

Medical necessity The fact that there is a medical reason to perform a procedure or service. Documentation exists in the patient's record to show there are sufficient signs, symptoms, or history to warrant the services provided.

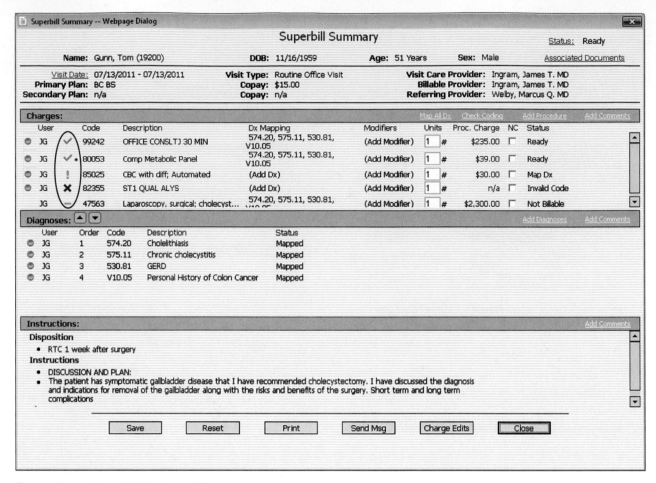

Figure 6.3 PrimeSUITE Superbill

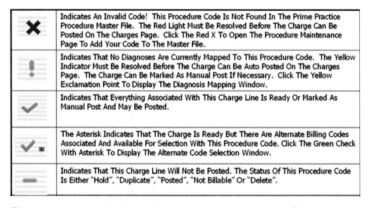

Figure 6.4 Symbols used on PrimeSUITE Superbill summary

affected when potential coding problems leading to denied claims are taken care of before the claim is filed. In Figure 6.4 you will find the legend for these symbols. For instance, a green checkmark denotes that there are no problems with that code and charges can be posted. A yellow exclamation point, on the other hand, means that no diagnosis code is mapped to that procedure code that would justify payment of the claim; until that is resolved, cash flow would be affected because the claim would be denied or returned for more information by the insurance company. A red "X" indicates that an invalid code appears on the Superbill and that payment would be denied or returned for more information.

6.3 The Claims Process Using PrimeSUITE

As noted, the process begins when the patient makes an appointment. But the charges do not start accruing until the patient presents for the appointment and services are rendered.

The first step, if the patient has insurance, is to collect the **co-payment**, otherwise known as the **co-pay**. In managed care plans particularly, this is the portion of the bill that is the responsibility of the patient. It is due at the time of the office visit. Many offices collect the co-pay at the time of arrival; others collect it when the patient checks out at the conclusion of the visit. For inpatient hospital visits, co-pays do not exist.

You will recall that one of the benefits of using PM software is the alerts that are generated. An alert is a reminder to do something. These alerts are generated based on the patient's **insurance plan**. For instance, a patient who has Medicare Part B would not pay a co-pay, so no alert would appear, but a patient with a managed care plan would, so the reminder would appear. Many offices refuse to see patients who do not pay their co-pay at the time of the visit. Look at Figure 6.5 to see an example of the co-pay reminder in PrimeSUITE.

Co-payment (co-pay) The amount due from the patient at the time of the office visit; typically a requirement of managed care plans.

Insurance plan The medical insurance contract under which a patient is covered; the extent to which services are covered. Also referred to as "the plan."

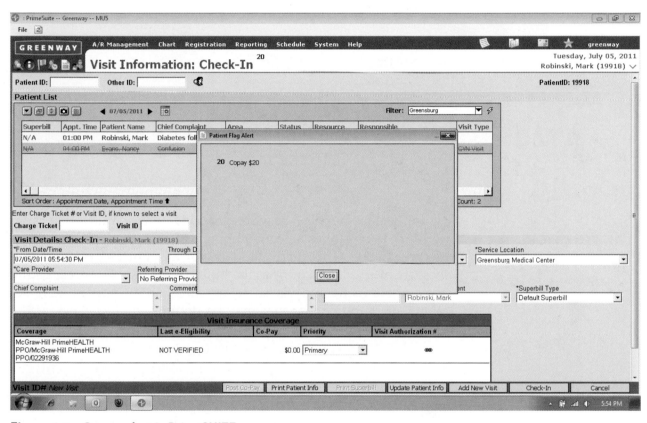

Figure 6.5 Co-pay alert in PrimeSUITE

Go to http://connect.mcgraw-hill.com to complete this exercise.

EXERCISE 6.1

Post a Co-payment to an Account

In this scenario, a patient, Mark Robinski, has just come in for his 1:00 p.m. appointment and has checked in at the front desk. The healthcare professional noted his arrival in PrimeSUITE by using the Visit Information Check-in screen. Mr. Robinski has a $20 co-pay, which he is paying for with his VISA® credit card, account number 7708363100. The credit payment itself is run through a different system; only the fact that it was paid with a credit card is noted in PrimeSUITE.

(continued)

Follow these steps to complete the exercise on your own once you have watched the demonstration and tried the steps with helpful prompts in practice mode. Use the information provided in the scenario to complete the information.

1. Click Visit Information: Check-In.
2. Click Close.
3. Click Post Co-Pay.
4. Click the Method drop-down.
5. Click Credit Card.
6. Click the Supplier drop-down.
7. Click Visa.
8. Click the Additional Info field.
9. Type "7708363100".
10. Click the Amount field.
11. Type "$20.00".
12. Click Save.
13. Click Yes.
14. Click OK.
15. Click Save.

☑ **You have completed Exercise 6.1**

In the next exercise, we will be checking on the status of a claim for Mark Robinski for an earlier appointment he had at Greensburg Medical Center. This might be done for any number of reasons—the patient may be inquiring, the billing staff may be investigating because his name and visit date appeared on an unpaid accounts report, or an office manager may be doing a quality check of the work performed by a member of the staff.

 EXERCISE 6.2 PM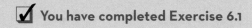

 Go to http://connect.mcgraw-hill.com to complete this exercise.

Given a Scenario, Look Up the Status of an Insurance Claim

The scenario is that Mark Robinski, while being seen on October 3, 2013, asks if the claim from his September 13 visit has been paid.

The healthcare professional will investigate by accessing the Accounts Receivable (A/R) Management menu, and then the claims management function. Accounts receivable includes money that is received by the medical practice including insurance payments or payments made by the patient. The patient's identification number (chart number) is needed for this step, and it is found in the upper right corner of every screen. Mr. Robinski's chart (ID) number is 19918.

Follow these steps to complete the exercise on your own once you have watched the demonstration and tried the steps with helpful prompts. Use the information provided in the scenario to complete the information.

1. Click Search for Patient.
2. Type "Robinski" in the *Last Name field.
3. Click Search.
4. Click Select.
5. Click Claims Maintenance.
6. Click Patient ID field.
7. Type "19918".
8. Click Search.
9. Click Scroll.
10. Click E - Paid In Full to note the claim status.

In this exercise, we have seen how to perform the co-pay posting function as well as how to find the status of a patient's claim using PrimeSUITE.

✓ **You have completed Exercise 6.2**

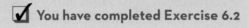

6.4 **Diagnosis and Procedure Coding Using PrimeSUITE**

In the medical field, care providers diagnose patients using medical terms, for instance, a myocardial infarction (heart attack), an upper respiratory infection (a common cold), or cholelithiasis (gallstones). They also perform tests to make a diagnosis, such as an EKG, a strep screen (for strep throat), or a lower GI series (x-rays to detect abdominal conditions). Therapeutic procedures (those that are done to alleviate symptoms or correct a condition) are done as well, for example, suturing a laceration, packing the nose to stop a severe nosebleed, or removing a cyst. Supplies are necessary to complete procedures or for treatment purposes. For instance, a suture kit is used to suture a laceration, serum is used to administer an injection, and a sling may be ordered for a patient with a sprain.

Though the care provider documents the diagnoses, procedures, or services in words, those words have to be converted to a numeric form in order to file claims to insurance companies and to keep statistics of the conditions treated and procedures performed at the office or facility.

We will discuss three types of codes that are used, and one new one that will be used beginning in October 2014.

First, let's look at diagnosis coding. Since 1979, the coding system used to translate diagnoses and procedures into numeric form has been the *International Classification of Diseases, 9th revision, Clinical Modification*, better known as ICD-9-CM. This coding system is 35 years old. Though it is updated yearly to reflect new diagnoses, remove obsolete ones, and capture the advances in technology, it is far overdue for a complete revision because it is simply not up to date with current medical diagnoses or available treatment options. The World Health Organization, in 1990, endorsed the newest version, ICD-10, and since 1994 it has been used in the majority of industrialized nations, with the United States being one of the exceptions.

The International Classification of Diseases (ICD) is used to classify diseases and conditions diagnosed in any healthcare setting. It is also used to record cause of death on death certificates. The United States will begin using ICD-10-CM and ICD-10-PCS, *International Classification of Diseases, 10th revision, Clinical Modification* and *International Classification of Diseases, 10th revision, Procedure Coding System* on October 1, 2014. Only hospitals are required to use ICD-10-PCS, but the two are often referred to as ICD-10-CM/PCS.

The United States has lagged behind in the adoption of ICD-10 in healthcare settings, due in large part to the high cost of converting current computer systems to accept ICD-10 rather than ICD-9 codes, time and cost involved in training staff in the use of ICD-10, and general questions of whether or not ICD-10 will meet the needs of the U.S. healthcare system. In the United States, coding enables the storage and retrieval of diagnostic information for clinical, epidemiological, and quality purposes as well as the compilation of morbidity and mortality statistics. This is its use in other nations as well, but in this country ICD-9 is also used for reimbursement purposes. The amount a hospital is reimbursed per patient stay is tied in part to each patient's diagnosis codes, or combination thereof. In hospital and outpatient settings, the ICD code correlates to the medical necessity of the procedures and services being done to or for patients. ICD-9 does not address the severity of a patient's condition, whereas ICD-10, though not perfect, does a better job of capturing a truer picture of the resources needed to care for a patient during a particular stay or encounter.

Another glitch that has held up implementation in this country is the coding of procedures in hospital settings, which is done now using ICD-9-CM. The CM means "clinical modification" and includes procedure codes. In other countries, the CM portion is not used. With ICD-10-PCS, the PCS stands for "Procedure Coding System," and contains the procedure codes that will be used by hospitals. Outpatient facilities, including physicians' offices, will continue to code procedures with Current Procedural Terminology (CPT).

The following table shows a comparison of how common diagnoses were coded in ICD-9-CM and how they will be coded in ICD-10-CM.

Narrative Diagnosis	ICD-9-CM Code	ICD-10-CM Code
Epistaxis (nosebleed)	784.7	R04.0
Urticaria (hives)	708.0	L50.0
Chest pain	786.50	R07.9
Diabetes mellitus	250.00	E11.9
Routine general medical exam	V70.0	Z00.00
Streptococcal sore throat	034.0	J02.0
Subarachnoid hemorrhage (stroke)	430	I60.9
Acute anterior wall myocardial infarction (heart attack)	410.11	I21.09
Cholelithiasis (gallstones)	574.20	K80.20

In PrimeSUITE, on the Assessment screen, both the ICD-9 and ICD-10 diagnosis codes will be displayed, as noted in Figure 6.6. Remember that ICD-10-CM codes can capture specificity that ICD-9-CM cannot. In the figures that follow, pay attention to the Barton's Fracture codes in ICD-9-CM as well as ICD-10-CM.

The care provider then selects a more specific code by checking appropriate diagnostic descriptors or modifiers, as seen in Figure 6.7.

Figure 6.8 shows the codes after all diagnostic modifiers (initial fracture, open, type 1, and right-side fracture location) were documented by the care provider. Notice that the Barton's Fracture code has stayed the same in ICD-9-CM, but is now S52.561B in ICD-10-CM.

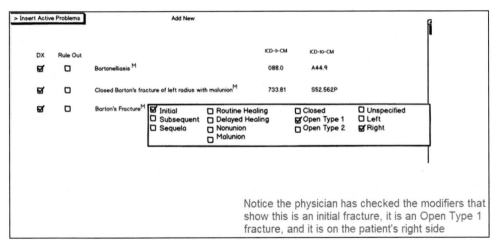

Figure 6.6   ICD-9 and ICD-10 diagnosis codes displayed for a patient's active problems

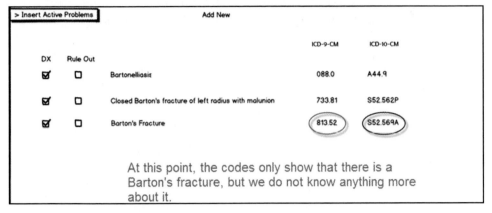

Figure 6.7   Increasing the specificity of the diagnosis of Barton's Fracture

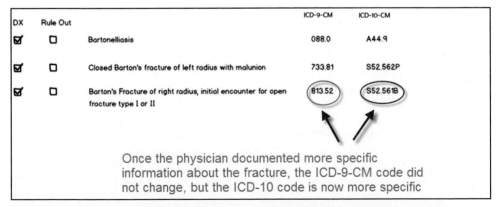

Figure 6.8   The final ICD-9-CM and ICD-10-CM codes for Barton's Fracture

Patients may have one diagnosis code or many for each encounter. Any conditions that were diagnosed, were treated, or required more nursing or care provider attention should be coded. The first listed diagnosis is most closely related to the reason the patient was seen for that encounter (the chief complaint).

The second code set we will discuss is Current Procedural Terminology, or CPT. It is Level 1 of the **Healthcare Common Procedure Coding System,** known as **HCPCS.**

In the physician's office setting, CPT codes are used to code procedures or services given to a patient. In a hospital setting, they are used for outpatient coding (emergency room, outpatient diagnostic testing, or ambulatory surgery, for example).

Examples of CPT codes in a physician's office include:

Code	Description
87430	Strep test
90703	Tetanus injection
71010	Chest x-ray
11100	Skin biopsy
99213	Detailed office visit of an established patient
99202	Low complexity office visit of a new patient

For procedure coding using ICD-10-PCS, these are only used in the hospital setting. Below are comparisons of ICD-10-PCS procedure codes to ICD-9-CM procedure codes. As you can see, ICD-10-PCS procedure codes are much different in ICD-10 than they were in ICD-9. Much more specificity can be coded in ICD-10 than we were able to capture in ICD-9 procedure codes. Again, in an outpatient setting, such as a physician's office, CPT is used to code procedures.

Narrative Procedure	ICD-9-CM Code	ICD-10-PCS Code
Splenectomy (removal of spleen)	41.5	07TP4ZZ
Salpingectomy (removal of fallopian tubes), bilateral	66.51	0UT74ZZ
Cholecystectomy (removal of gallbladder)	51.22	0FT40ZZ

HCPCS Level 2 codes are codes used to show tangible items provided such as suture kits, ambulance services, and orthotic devices (cane, splint, etc.). They are used in any healthcare setting.

Examples of HCPCS level 2 codes include:

Code	Description
A0998	Ambulance response and treatment without transport
E0105	Cane, triple or quad
A6453	Self-adherent elastic bandage

Healthcare Common Procedure Coding System (HCPCS) Coding system required by Medicare and Medicaid to document services and procedures (Level 1, Current Procedural Terminology, CPT) and equipment, supplies, and transport (HCPCS Level 2).

6.5 The Relationship between Documentation and Coding

Services rendered to a patient—whether they involve the face-to-face time with the physician, treatment, or diagnostic tests and procedures—cannot be billed to insurance unless they are medically necessary. That is to say, there need to be sufficient signs, symptoms, or history to warrant the services given. Therefore, the documentation in the record must support the need for any and all services and procedures. The EHR has been instrumental in making it possible for care providers to spend beneficial face-to-face time with their patients rather than spend time completing their records. Of course, documenting the patient's record while the patient is in the room also takes some finesse. The provider does not want to appear to be paying more attention to the computer screen than to the patient, but the longer the provider uses the computer to document, the more easily she is able to document, listen attentively, and converse with her patients all at the same time.

Performing services that are not necessary or coding services that were not actually performed both constitute insurance (including Medicare and Medicaid) **fraud.** Fraud is intentional deception, which in healthcare takes advantage of a patient, an insurance company, or Medicare or Medicaid.

Whether you are studying to become a health information professional, a medical assistant, or a medical coder and biller, you will take courses that are specific to coding, and you will spend a significant amount of time discussing accurate, appropriate coding as well as the guidelines that apply to the coding and billing functions.

In the next exercise, you will see how ICD-10 and CPT coding are assigned using the PrimeSUITE software.

Fraud Intentional deception, which in healthcare takes advantage of a patient, an insurance company, Medicare, or Medicaid.

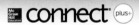 (plus+) Go to http://connect.mcgraw-hill.com to complete this exercise.   **EXERCISE 6.3**

Enter Diagnoses and Procedures to Locate ICD-10 and CPT Codes

Once a patient has been seen and examined by the care provider, a diagnosis is made. The written diagnosis is then transformed into a numeric code. In our example, it is done using a function of PrimeSUITE, but it can also be done manually, using code books. As we mentioned earlier, the diagnosis coding is done using ICD-10-CM and the procedures or services are coded using CPT and/or HCPCS Level 2.

In the example that follows, Dr. Ingram has just seen a patient, Mark Robinski. Remember, only the care provider can make a diagnosis. So, from the Patient Notes Progress Note screen, Dr. Ingram will be using the Assessments tab (found on the left side of the screen) to add a diagnosis for Mark Robinski.

Mark Robinski's diagnosis is diabetes mellitus, type 2, and Dr. Ingram ordered a fasting blood sugar. A diagnosis code (ICD-10-CM) and a

(continued)

procedure code (CPT) will be assigned in the following exercise. The software will automatically assign the codes, but it is important to read the description of the codes and compare it to the narrative diagnosis the care provider has made. You should never code more than what the care provider has documented.

Follow these steps to complete the exercise on your own once you have watched the demonstration and tried the steps with helpful prompts in practice mode. Use the information provided in the scenario to complete the information.

1. Click Assessment.
2. Click Add Diagnosis.
3. Click Search.
4. Click the Diagnosis Search field.
5. Type "diabetes".
6. Click Search.
7. Click Type Two Diabetes Mellitus Without Mention Of Complication.
8. Click OK.
9. Click Plan.
10. Click Search.
11. Click Search for Code.
12. Click the Procedure Code Search field.
13. Type "fasting blood".
14. Click Search.
15. Click Fasting Blood Sugar.
16. Click the Category drop-down.
17. Click Labs.
18. Click OK.

☑ **You have completed Exercise 6.3**

6.6 | Accountable Care Organizations

Affordable Care Act (ACA) Signed into law in 2010, the ACA that resulted in improved access to affordable healthcare coverage and protection from abusive practices by healthcare insurance companies. Gives consumers more control over their healthcare coverage and ties reimbursement to quality, patient satisfaction, and coordination of care.

Accountable Care Organization A reimbursement model where hospitals, physicians, other healthcare providers form partnerships whereby all are accountable for the quality of care, efficiency of medical services (to contain costs), and patient satisfaction. A pay for performance model of healthcare reimbursement.

The model of healthcare reimbursement for Medicare patients has been fee-for-service for years. In other words, services are rendered and hospitals and physicians are paid as long as the services were considered medically necessary. In the latest healthcare reform legislation, through a portion of the **Affordable Care Act (ACA)**, however, providers and hospitals are required to show that they are providing high-quality, coordinated care and are seeking patient input regarding their experience. In addition, positive patient outcomes and less redundancy of services are expected. In other words, reimbursement is tied to quality and efficient use of healthcare services as well as overall patient satisfaction.

When hospitals, doctors, and other healthcare providers formally work together to provide this high-quality care, the result is an **Accountable Care Organization (ACO).**

Accountable Care Organizations are groups of doctors, hospitals, and other healthcare providers (home health agencies or durable medical equipment companies, for example), who form a voluntary partnership that results in coordinated, high-quality care to their Medicare patients.

As of this writing, there are two ACO models from Medicare. The first is the Medicare Shared Savings program which transitions current Medicare fee-for-service providers to the ACO model; the second, Advance Payment ACO Model, is a supplementary incentive model that is only open to providers in the Shared Savings program.

Participation is voluntary and Medicare patients will not see any changes to their coverage because of a physician's or hospital's choice to become part of an ACO.

In order for care to be "coordinated," the hospital(s), provider(s), and ancillary service providers within the ACO must be able to share patient information. The EHR and interoperable systems make the sharing of this data possible. Approximately 30 quality measures will be monitored and are related to the patient's experience, care coordination, and patient safety. The higher the quality of care delivered, the higher the shared savings earned by the ACO.

Structured data (through ICD-10, CPT, and HCPCS codes) is necessary to measure quality, and the exchange of health information between and among members of the ACO is necessary to achieve coordination of care. Both are made possible through the electronic health record.

6.7 Accounts Receivable—Getting Paid

You may have heard the terms **accounts payable** and **accounts receivable** at some point in time. Accounts payable is money going out—paying the bills. Accounts receivable, on the other hand, is money coming in—in this context, it is the insurance companies' payment of claims that have been filed by Greensburg Medical Center. Of course, it is imperative that what is billed is paid, and that there is an accurate accounting of all **transactions**. Transactions are the posting of charges and the payment of claims.

Insurance companies submit payments to care providers and hospitals electronically (electronic claims transactions or submissions), by check, or by automatic deposit into the bank account of the office. But the amount of the payment may be for more than one patient's care. The insurance company submits the payment with a detailed accounting of the claims for which payment is being made. The document that accompanies the payment is called a **remittance advice (RA)** (see Figure 6.9). It may also be called an **explanation of benefits (EOB)**. Many insurance companies use the term remittance advice to describe the document that accompanies payment to the provider, and the explanation of benefits is generally the form the **subscriber** (the primary person covered by the insurance) receives to notify him of what was billed, what was paid, and what is owed by him.

Regardless of what it is called, the information typically included on an RA or EOB is listed on the following pages. Again, this is not a

Accounts payable Monies being paid from the medical practice, for instance to pay for supplies, rent, utilities, payroll, etc.

Accounts receivable Monies coming into a medical practice, for instance insurance payments or payments made by patients.

Transaction Posting of charges and the payment of claims in the Practice Management system to update patients' accounts.

Remittance advice (RA) A detailed accounting of the claims for which payment is being made by an insurance company. The remittance advice accompanies the payment from the insurance company.

Explanation of benefits (EOB) An explanation of the charges for services, the amount paid by the insurance company, and the amount due by the subscriber, which is sent to the subscriber (and also to the provider, in some instances).

Subscriber The primary person covered by an insurance plan.

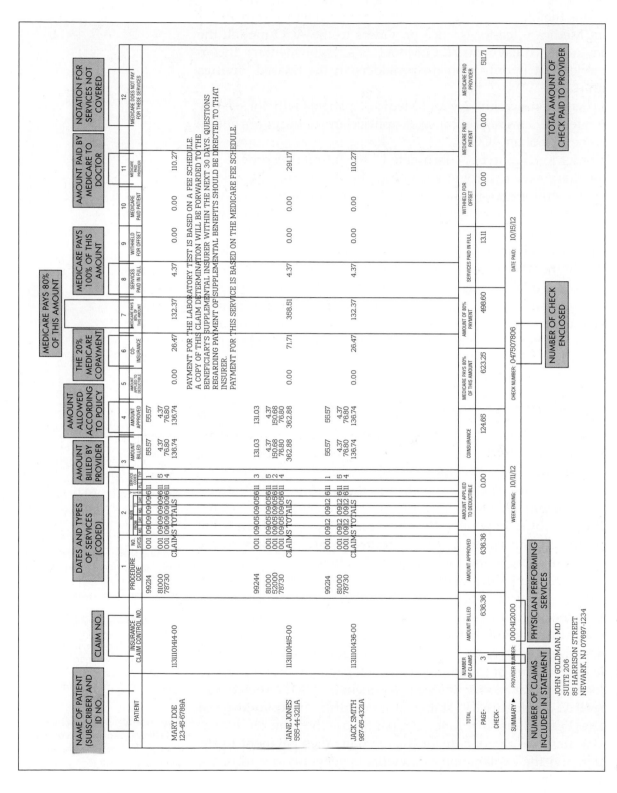

Figure 6.9 Remittance advice

billing class; there will be more than one patient included, typically, and many insurance companies include more information than is listed below:

- Provider's name and National Provider Identification (NPI) number
- Patient's name
- Claim number
- Medical record number
- Date(s) of service
- Claim status (open, denied, more information needed, paid, etc.)
- Electronic Transaction Number (if RA and payment have been sent via electronic means)
- Service detail
  - Each CPT code billed (as submitted on the claim form)
  - Amount charged for each code
  - Allowed amount (amount the insurance carrier has agreed to pay) for each code
  - Co-pay paid by patient
  - Adjusted amount (difference between what was charged and the allowed amount)

- Recap of charges and payments include
  - Total reported charges amount
  - Charges not covered amount
  - Charges denied amount
  - Covered charge amount

   Go to http://connect.mcgraw-hill.com to complete this exercise. **EXERCISE 6.4**

Investigate an Unpaid Insurance Claim

A patient, Mark E. Shaw, calls the billing office because he has received an EOB from his insurance company that his office visit of September 25, 2013, was not covered, and therefore the charges are his responsibility to pay. He contacted his insurance company and was told that the diagnosis submitted is for history of kidney stones (Z87.442) and is not covered. He recalls that his office visit on September 25 was for a follow-up of his diabetes mellitus. He asks the biller to check the account. The biller finds that indeed, the documentation on his record shows that his chief complaint was for follow-up of diabetes, which should be a first listed diagnosis on the claim for September 25. This exercise will take you through looking up the diagnosis code(s) that were filed on the insurance claim for the September 25 visit and correcting the first listed diagnosis to read E11.9, diabetes mellitus, type 2.

1. Click Search for Patient.
2. Type "Shaw" in the *Last Name field.
3. Click Search.
4. Click Select.
5. Click Patient Charts.
6. Click Close.

(continued)

7. Click Progress Note.
8. Click View Superbill Summary.
9. Click the radio button next to the diabetes mellitus diagnosis code.
10. Click the up arrow key.
11. Click the up arrow again.
12. Click OK.
13. Click Save.

A corrected claim may now be sent to the insurance company.

 You have completed Exercise 6.4

6.8 Managing Accounts Receivable in PrimeSUITE

The management of patient accounts, from charging patients for services to tracking accounts receivable and collections, begins by setting up the parameters of each insurance carrier and each plan within the insurance. The plan refers to the extent of coverage offered. For instance, 400 patients in your office may have Blue Cross/Blue Shield insurance, but for those 400 patients, there may be more than 20 plans. Plans differ regarding:

- Co-pay requirement—Some plans require a co-pay, others do not, and the dollar amounts vary by plan. Let's look at an example: Neil Holt is an engineer for Johnsontown Analytics, and his insurance is McGraw-Hill Prime. He is responsible for a $20 co-pay, and he is responsible for 20% of all outpatient service charges. Lisa Haver also works for Johnsontown Analytics, and she too has McGraw-Hill insurance, but she works at a different location in a different state, and her plan requires a $25 co-pay, plus 20% of all outpatient services.

- Extent of coverage and whether or not services are covered at all—for example, Neil Holt's plan may cover outpatient mental health services, while Lisa Haver's does not.

- Rules regarding filing of claims—may differ from plan to plan, and they certainly differ from insurance company to insurance company.

Because of these differences, it is imperative that the medical office or hospital use a system that efficiently applies the various policies to the correct patients.

When a medical office purchases any type of software, in this case PM software, an administrative staff member (the office manager, office administrator, or business manager) works with an installation specialist from the software company to build libraries that are used to perform functions within the different applications (accounts receivable, patient chart, etc.).

Common libraries include:

- Insurance company library—includes all of the insurance companies and the individual plans that are represented by the patients in the practice. These can be created, edited, or deleted within PrimeSUITE.

- ICD-10-CM, CPT, and HCPCS Level 2 code tables—must be maintained every year to account for additions, deletions, and amendments to codes. In order to get paid in a timely manner, only active, valid codes can be submitted; otherwise the claim will be rejected.
- Fee schedule—listed by CPT code and done for Medicare, group insurance, and by individual contracts for managed care plans. The charge for each service is documented in a fee schedule.
- Reports—in particular, aging reports (length of time a claim has remained unpaid) are set up to allow for timely tracking and follow-up of claims.
- Alerts—reminders to the office staff related to the billing functions. Some examples are co-pay alert, write-off, and overdue balance, just to name a few. Alerts assist the staff in collections processes in particular.

Using PM software to accomplish the filing of, follow-up, and collection of claims also allows electronic remittance of claims as well as electronic receipt of payment from insurance carriers. The healthcare professional can see at a glance exactly what is happening with a claim or claims at any given time in the process. Collections procedures are also streamlined using PM software. Many offices use an outside collections agency to collect overdue balances. With the use of PM software, a report of accounts ready for collections is sent electronically, the office is able to see the status of the account, and paid claims are sent to the office, often electronically.

Greater billing accuracy is an advantage of using PM software, and there is less chance of lost charges. Each time a patient is seen, and the care provider documents the progress note in PrimeSUITE and orders tests that are done on-site, she is prompted to select the ICD-10 code and the CPT codes that correspond to the diagnosis and procedures.

The face-to-face time between a patient and the care provider is charged with a CPT code known as an **Evaluation and Management (E&M)** code. It is generated based on documentation made by the care provider. The E&M code is dependent on whether the patient is new to the practice (not seen within the past three years) or an established patient (seen within the last three years); the level of history (including chief complaint and review of systems); the level of physical exam performed; and the depth of medical decision-making necessary.

Two examples of E&M codes are:

99213 An office visit for an established patient, 20 years old, who was seen for exercise-induced asthma.

99203 Initial office visit for a 30-year-old patient who has recently been complaining of rectal bleeding.

In your CPT coding class, you will learn the intricacies of assigning E&M codes, but at this point it is important to know that E&M codes are CPT codes that reflect the professional services rendered to a patient.

Evaluation and Management (E&M) The CPT codes used to capture the face-to-face time between a patient and the care provider; takes into consideration the extent of the history, extent of the physical exam, and the level of medical decision-making required.

Enter Documentation to Alter E&M Coding Level

The level of E&M code, and therefore the amount charged for the face-to-face time of a visit, is tied to the extent of history, review of systems, and physical exam documented as structured data in PrimeSUITE. In this exercise, you will change the level of E&M code by editing documentation in the medical record of Ashley Murray.

1. Click E&M.
2. Click Calculate.
3. Click PE.
4. Click Chest to add it to the Physical Exam.
5. Click T (template).
6. Click Use Template Text.
7. Click T (template).
8. Click Use Template Text.
9. Click Skin to add it to the Physical Exam.
10. Click T (template).
11. Click In–Office Proc. Results.
12. Click Add Inter-Office Procedure.
13. Click Rapid Strep.
14. Click OK.
15. Click E&M.
16. Click Calculate.

 You have completed Exercise 6.5

Once the claim has been filed and payment has been sent to the office (either by mail, direct deposit into the practice's account, or sent electronically), the payment is posted to the patient's record for that particular date of service.

We will now follow the steps to post a payment using PrimeSUITE.

Post an Insurance Payment to an Account

In our scenario, Dr. Ingram's office has received an RA, which includes payment to cover the claim for Mark Robinski for date of service September 13, 2013. There are two charges for the September 13th account. They are CPT code 99214, which is an Evaluation and Management code for the face-to-face time he spent with the doctor, and code 82951, which is for a glucose tolerance test. The total amount of the remittance for Mark Robinski is $100. Seventy-five dollars of the $100 is for the services under the 99214 code. Twenty-five dollars of it is for the services billed under code 82951. We will be working in the A/R Management module under the insurance transactions function. The objective is to mark the services as paid, based on the amount of money received.

Follow these steps to complete the exercise on your own once you have watched the demonstration and tried the steps with helpful prompts in practice mode. Use the information provided in the scenario to complete the information.

1. Click Search for Patient.
2. Type "Robinski" in the *Last Name field.
3. Click Search.
4. Click Select.
5. Click Insurance Transactions.
6. Click the Amount field for the 99214 charge.
7. Type "$75.00".
8. Click the Amount field for the 82951 charge.
9. Type "$25.00".
10. Click Save.
11. Click OK.

✓ **You have completed Exercise 6.6**

The Medical Billing Process is shown in Figure 6.10. Some steps may be repeated two or three times, but the goal is payment of the claim.

Medical Billing Cycle

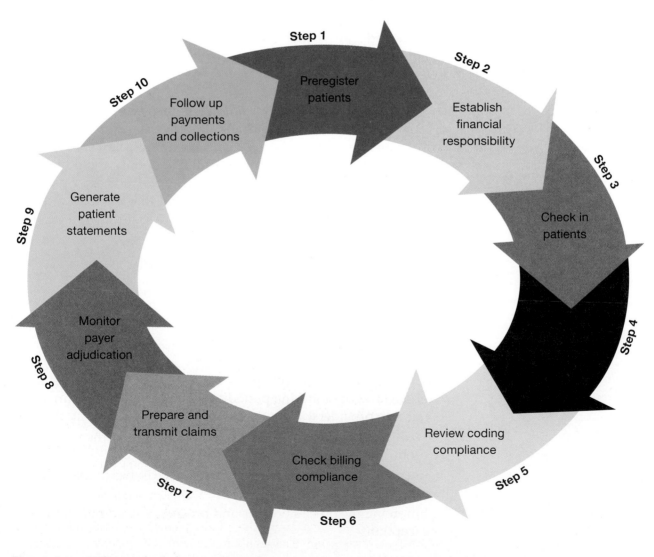

Figure 6.10   Billing and reimbursement cycle

Medicare, Medicaid, TRICARE, Worker's Compensation, group health insurance, and managed care plans are all examples of types of insurance coverage. Each has rules and regulations related to the coding, billing, and collection of healthcare claims. Intentionally not following those rules and regulations can result in allegations of fraud, or at the very least, **abuse**. Abusive coding and billing practices are inconsistent with typical coding and billing practice. Being found guilty of either can result in monetary fines or in the worst-case scenario a sanction from any one or more of the above insurance plans. If a care provider is sanctioned from Medicare, that means he/she is forbidden to accept Medicare patients into his or her practice. If the practice is an internal medicine practice, Medicare enrollees most likely make up a good percentage of the patient population in the practice. Needless to say, being sanctioned from Medicare will impact his/her practice to the point where it may put the provider out of business.

The Qui Tam Online Network, found at http://www .quitamonline.com/fraud.html lists common forms of Medicare fraud. Qui Tam means that a private individual has "blown the whistle" on suspected fraud.

Managed care plans that find a care provider or practice engaging in fraudulent activity may drop that office from their preferred provider list, resulting in a negative impact to the practice's income.

For federal programs, the Office of Inspector General (OIG) investigates suspected cases of fraud. In order to defend the practice in the event of a visit from the OIG, a **compliance plan** should be in place in every medical office and hospital. Not only should it be in place, it should also be followed. If the OIG does audit your practice, showing that you have a compliance plan and that it is followed will be an advantage; having one and *not* following it may not be. The requirements of a compliance plan are:

- Conducting audits and monitoring work performed by the office staff
- Developing and implementing standards of practice to be followed by office staff (including care providers) that are uniformly and consistently applied
- Appointment of a compliance officer
- Training new staff immediately after hire on office policies and procedures and offering periodic in-services to all staff (including care providers)
- Fixing any problems that are found, investigating the reason for problems, and retraining staff as necessary
- Encouraging staff to bring any compliance issues to the office administration
- Enforcing the office's policies and procedures and not making exceptions

Abuse Coding and billing that is inconsistent with typical coding and billing practices.

Compliance plan A formal, written document which describes how the hospital or physician's practice ensures rules, regulations, and standards are being adhered to.

Having, following, and referencing a practice's written policies, procedures, and compliance plan will assure sound fiscal practices within a practice or facility, and may be a sound defense should the practice ever be involved in fraud or abuse allegations.

APPLYING YOUR SKILLS

Accountable care organizations are part of the largest healthcare reimbursement reform in years. You have been given basic information about ACOs. Now, research on your own to find the following answers:

1. The Centers for Medicare and Medicaid Services (CMS) is responsible for ACOs. List and describe four participation requirements.
2. Why will it be so important to accurately code diagnoses and procedures as it relates to ACOs?
3. Do an Internet search of accountable care organizations and describe an ACO that you find.

chapter 6 **summary**

LEARNING OUTCOME	CONCEPTS FOR REVIEW
6.1 Illustrate the need for a claims management process. Pages 110–112	– Though in business to provide patient care, a medical office is still a business. – Written policies are necessary to run the office effectively and efficiently. – Use of PM software improves efficiency. – A patient account for a visit begins when the appointment is made. – Insurance verification should be completed—either before the day of the visit or when the patient arrives (prior to is preferred). – Patient check-out occurs once the visit is complete.

6.2 List the information contained in an encounter form (Superbill). Pages 112–114	– A Superbill is otherwise known as an encounter form and includes at least:
	  • Name and address of medical practice
	  • NPI number
	  • Patient's name
	  • Patients charge number
	  • Date and time of visit
	  • CPT codes
	  • Diagnosis narrative by care provider
	  • ICD-10-CM diagnosis codes
	– It can be hard-copy or electronic.
	– The information on the Superbill transfers to the CMS-1500 claim form.
	– It includes some identifying information about the encounter as well as the diagnosis and procedure codes using ICD-10 and CPT code sets.

6.3 Apply procedures to update a patient's account in PrimeSUITE. Pages 114–117	– Co-payment may be collected at the time of check-in or check-out, depending on office policy. – Financial alerts appear when the patient is checked into PrimeSUITE at the time of arrival. The insurance plan entered in the system determines which, if any, alerts appear. – Once paid, the co-pay is immediately posted in PrimeSUITE. – Charges start to accrue once the patient is taken to the examining room and is seen by a healthcare professional. – Insurance status may be looked up at any time.
6.4 Demonstrate ICD-10-CM/PCS and CPT codes in PrimeSUITE. Pages 117–120	– The provider's assessment is otherwise known as the diagnosis (or diagnoses, plural). – Services rendered may be diagnostic (x-rays, lab tests) or therapeutic (sutures, cleansing of a wound, injections). – Diagnoses are coded using the ICD-10-CM code set and are used in both hospital and outpatient (physicians' offices) settings. – The first listed diagnosis is the one most closely related to the reason the patient was seen. – Any conditions that were diagnosed, treated, or required more nursing or provider attention should be documented. – Procedures are coded using CPT in the physician's office.

(continued)

LEARNING OUTCOME	CONCEPTS FOR REVIEW
	– Procedures are coded using ICD-10-CM in the hospital setting. – HCPCS level 2 codes are used to code equipment or supplies. – Coding is done for statistical and reimbursement purposes.
6.5 Examine the correlation between documentation and code assignment. Pages 121–122	– All services and procedures performed must be medically necessary. – The diagnoses support the medical necessity for the procedure(s) and service(s). – Performing services that aren't medically necessary and billing for them is considered fraud.
6.6 Describe Accountable Care Organizations. Pages 122–123	– A new reimbursement model for Medicare patients. – Came about through the Affordable Care Act (ACA). – Goal is high-quality care, patient satisfaction, decreased redundancy of services, and coordination of care. – Voluntary partnership between physicians, hospitals, and other healthcare providers. – Two current models: Medicare Shared Savings and Advance Payment. – Dependent on measurable outcomes through reporting based on ICD-10, CPT, and HCPCS codes as well as the ability to share patient information between and among members of the ACO.
6.7 Describe the information contained in a remittance advice or explanation of benefits. Pages 123–126	– Accounts receivable—money paid to the office by insurance carriers. – Transactions—documentation of all money paid and applying it to the correct patient's balances. – Remittance advice (RA), also referred to as an explanation of benefits (EOB), accompanies the payment and explains the claims to which the payments apply. – The subscriber is the person who is covered under the group insurance plan.
6.8 Apply procedures to manage accounts receivable in PrimeSUITE. Pages 126–130	– Efficiency and effectiveness of managing the financial aspects start with accurately setting up the parameters of each insurance carrier and the plans within each in the PM software. – The type of plan a patient has determines the extent of coverage and the co-pay requirements. – Each insurance carrier (and the plans within) has rules and regulations regarding filing of claims. – Libraries are built within the PM software for each insurance carrier.
6.9 Demonstrate the need for a compliance plan. Pages 130–131	– All offices should have written policies and procedures for all processes in the office, but in particular for the financial aspects. – All policies should be complied with uniformly and consistently. – Each insurance carrier also has rules and regulations that must be followed. – Not following the rules and regulations may constitute fraud or abuse. – The Office of Inspector General enforces the rules and regulations set forth by any federal insurance plans.

(continued)

Copyright © 2015 The McGraw-Hill Companies

- The office should have a compliance plan to assure all rules and regulations are being followed. The plan should include:
  - conducting internal audits of work performed
  - developing standards of practice
  - appointment of a compliance officer
  - training of new personnel; updates for experienced personnel
  - correcting any known problems; retraining staff as necessary
  - encouraging open communication from staff regarding compliance issues
  - enforce all policies and procedures

chapter review

MATCHING QUESTIONS

Match the terms on the left with the definitions on the right.

_____ 1. **[LO 6.5]** fraud

_____ 2. **[LO 6.7]** transaction

_____ 3. **[LO 6.1]** managed care plan

_____ 4. **[LO 6.7]** accounts receivable

_____ 5. **[LO 6.8]** Evaluation and Management codes

_____ 6. **[LO 6.1]** fee schedule

_____ 7. **[LO 6.7]** subscriber

_____ 8. **[LO 6.9]** compliance plan

_____ 9. **[LO 6.3]** co-payment

_____ 10. **[LO 6.7]** explanation of benefits

a. list of how much is charged per service by CPT code

b. document sent from an insurance company to a subscriber outlining payment decisions

c. portion of a bill that is usually the responsibility of the patient; typically collected upon check-in

d. the primary individual covered under an insurance plan

e. formal, written guidelines that describe how a healthcare office intends to follow established rules and regulations

f. actions, such as posting payments or processing claims, done in a Practice Management system to update patient accounts

g. codes representing the face-to-face time spent with a provider

h. process of receiving and posting payments for medical claims

i. an act of deception which takes advantage of another person or entity

j. form of insurance that monitors patients, care, and performance to ensure quality

MULTIPLE–CHOICE QUESTIONS

Select the letter that best completes the statement or answers the question:

1. **[LO 6.2]** The information contained in the encounter form is eventually transferred to the _____ form for submission.
   a. claim
   b. encounter form (Superbill)
   c. insurance
   d. registration

 Enhance your learning by completing these exercises and more at http://**connect.mcgraw-hill.com**!

2. **[LO 6.5]** Only services deemed medically _____ can be billed to insurance.
   a. necessary
   b. progressive
   c. restorative
   d. useful

3. **[LO 6.4]** What does the "CM" stand for in ICD coding?
   a. Care management
   b. Clinical modification
   c. Code management
   d. Coding methodology

4. **[LO 6.8]** The amount of a patient's co-pay may vary by:
   a. care provider.
   b. insurance plan.
   c. office location.
   d. visit type.

5. **[LO 6.3]** Charges begin to accrue once the _____.
   a. appointment is made
   b. patient checks in at the reception area
   c. MA or care provider interacts with patient
   d. claim has been filed

6. **[LO 6.7]** A remittance advice is typically given to a/an _____, whereas an explanation of benefits is typically given to a/an _____.
   a. patient; provider
   b. provider; patient
   c. insurance company; patient
   d. provider; insurance company

7. **[LO 6.2]** In PrimeSUITE, a red "X" on a Superbill Summary indicates:
   a. an absent diagnosis.
   b. an invalid code assignment.
   c. a charge line will not be posted.
   d. a charge is ready.

8. **[LO 6.9]** To avoid negative consequences, a compliance plan should be _____ in every hospital and medical office.
   a. discussed
   b. followed
   c. used as a guide
   d. written

9. **[LO 6.8]** The _____ is usually the person to set up information libraries within Practice Management software programs.
   a. care provider
   b. healthcare professional
   c. medical assistant
   d. office manager

10. **[LO 6.5]** Who is the only person authorized to make a diagnosis?
    a. Care provider
    b. Healthcare professional
    c. Medical assistant
    d. Office manager

11. **[LO 6.3]** To check if a claim has been paid, which menu will the healthcare professional look at?
    a. Accounts payable
    b. Accounts receivable
    c. Claims processing
    d. Claim updates

12. **[LO 6.6]** Which of the following is true of the advance payment ACO model?
    a. It is based on fee-for-service.
    b. It is an incentive model.
    c. It is the largest Accountable Care Organization.
    d. It requires participation by hospitals and medical vendors.

13. **[LO 6.1]** Depending on the terms of a patient's insurance coverage, the balance remaining after insurance has paid may be:
    a. written off as paid in full.
    b. removed from the master index.
    c. sent to collections.
    d. written off as paid in full or sent to collections.

14. **[LO 6.1]** Expected methods of payment are discussed when a patient:
    a. checks in.
    b. is seen by the provider.
    c. is discharged.
    d. makes an appointment.

SHORT ANSWER QUESTIONS

1. **[LO 6.1]** List four ways Practice Management software improves claim management.

2. **[LO 6.7]** Contrast accounts receivable with accounts payable.

3. **[LO 6.8]** What is the difference between an insurance provider [carrier] and an insurance plan?

4. **[LO 6.2]** List at least five items that are typically included on a hard-copy Superbill.

5. **[LO 6.3]** What is an alert?

6. **[LO 6.5]** How have EHRs improved the face-to-face time between patients and care providers?

 Enhance your learning by completing these exercises and more at http://connect.mcgraw-hill.com!

7. **[LO 6.2]** Explain how the icons available in Practice Management software make claim management easier and more accurate.

8. **[LO 6.6]** Summarize the goal of Accountable Care Organizations in one or two sentences.

9. **[LO 6.5]** Explain *fraud* in terms of the healthcare profession.

10. **[LO 6.3]** List three reasons why you might need to check the status of an insurance claim.

11. **[LO 6.8]** What is an aging report?

12. **[LO 6.7]** What four items are included in the recap of charges and payments found on an EOB?

13. **[LO 6.4]** List the three types of codes that are used, and give an example of how each is used.

14. **[LO 6.4]** Discuss at least three benefits of moving to ICD-10.

15. **[LO 6.9]** What is the difference between fraud and abuse?

APPLYING YOUR KNOWLEDGE

1. **[LO 6.3]** Discuss why many healthcare practices refuse to see patients who do not pay their co-pays at the time of their visit.

2. **[LOs 6.5, 6.9]** Research two recent cases of medical/insurance fraud (use the Qui Tam website as a starting point) and discuss the outcome of each case. Provide specifics about your sources [Internet, medical journals, textbooks, etc.].

3. **[LOs 6.2, 6.4, 6.5]** If the ICD-9 code sets are updated and revised each year, why is it necessary to completely overhaul the system to ICD-10?

4. **[LOs 6.1, 6.8]** Why might an office need to use a collections agency to pursue overdue accounts?

5. **[LO 6.7]** Why is there so much information contained on an RA or EOB form?

6. **[LOs 6.4, 6.5, 6.9]** Anna Devlan is a healthcare professional. Recently she posted some patient claims; when performing the coding process, Anna could not find a code that exactly matched the diagnosis made by the care provider. So she found the closest match and coded that. Did Anna commit fraud and/or abuse? Explain your answer.

7. **[LO 6.6]** Paul Donovan, a Medicare patient, suffers from Crohn's disease and rheumatoid arthritis. Recently, he presented to County Hospital complaining of hip pain. How will the interoperability offered under Accountable Care Organization models impact Mr. Donovan's care?

Privacy, Security, Confidentiality, and Legal Issues

PrimeSUITE

Learning Outcomes

At the end of this chapter, the student should be able to:

7.1 Identify the HIPAA privacy and security standards.

7.2 Evaluate an EHR system for HIPAA compliance.

7.3 Describe the role of certification in EHR implementation.

7.4 Apply procedures to set up security measures in PrimeSUITE.

7.5 Follow proper procedures to access sensitive or restricted-access records.

7.6 Apply procedures to ensure data integrity.

7.7 Apply procedures to release health information using PrimeSUITE.

7.8 Account for data disclosures using PrimeSUITE.

7.9 Exchange information with outside healthcare providers for continuity of care using PrimeSUITE.

7.10 Outline the content of compliance plans.

7.11 Appraise the importance of disaster recovery planning.

Key Terms

Access report
Accounting of disclosures
American Health Information Management Association (AHIMA)
Audit trail
Blog
Breach of confidentiality
Computer virus
Confidentiality
Covered entity
Data integrity
Disaster recovery plan
Directory information
Encryption

Firewall
Hardware
Healthcare Information and Management Systems Society (HIMSS)
Malware
Minimum necessary information
National Alliance for Health Information Technology (NAHIT)
Notice of Privacy Practices
Password
Privacy
Social media
User rights

What You Need to Know and Why You Need to Know It

No matter what type of healthcare professional you become—a nurse, medical assistant, health information manager, coder, biller, registration clerk, receptionist, or care provider—you will come in contact with patients' health information. In healthcare, and particularly with electronic healthcare, privacy and security are on everyone's minds—the patients', the providers', the media's, and the government's. There is concern that computer hackers and personnel who work in healthcare facilities will gain access to records that they have no legitimate need to access. The concern is justified, but even in a paper system, frequent privacy breaches have occurred. It is just as easy for a healthcare professional to look in a patient's chart at the nurses' station as it is to sit down at a computer that is left open to a patient's record and read it. In this chapter we will discuss laws that protect privacy and security as well as methods to lessen the chances of privacy breaches occurring. It is the responsibility of all healthcare professionals and care providers to maintain patient privacy and confidentiality and to access the health information only on a need-to-know basis.

7.1 The HIPAA Privacy and Security Standards

You were introduced to HIPAA earlier, but to recap, HIPAA was passed in 1996. It contains several rules, though for our purposes, we will be concentrating on the privacy and security rules. In addition, in 2009, the Health Information Technology for Economic and Clinical Health Act (HITECH) went a step further, making the original privacy and security rules under HIPAA more stringent. HITECH also gives more power to federal and state government authorities to enforce the privacy and security rules.

On March 26, 2013, the Omnibus Final Rule to the HITECH Act went into effect, with compliance required in September 2013. Changes include more enhancements to protecting patient privacy, additions to individual patient rights, and strengthening of the government's ability to enforce the law. HIPAA was expanded to give more control over any covered entity's business associates—for example, external coding consultants or software service providers. The Notice of Privacy Practices has been expanded and the maximum penalty for violation of the law was increased to $1.5 million per violation. Related to HITECH, the breach notification standards have been enhanced. Examples of the enhancement in patient rights include the requirement that providers who utilize electronic health records must provide patients with their record in electronic form, when requested. In addition, patients who are paying for their services in cash may instruct the provider not to bill their insurance and not to divulge any information about the services to the patient's health insurance carrier.

The intent of both is to ensure that protected health information (PHI) is kept private and secure. They give patients the right to determine who sees their health information, but still gives **covered entities** (a healthcare provider, a clearinghouse, or a health insurance plan) the leeway to access PHI needed to care for patients, collect payment for services rendered, and operate a business. Protected

for your information **fyi**

More information about the changes to HIPAA and HITECH may be found at www.hhs.gov/news/press/2013pres/01/20130117b.html.

Covered entity Any healthcare entity that captures or utilizes health information. These include healthcare plans (insurance companies), clearinghouses that process healthcare claims, individual physicians and physician practices, any type of therapist (mental health, physical, speech, occupational), dentists, hospital staffs, ambulatory facilities, nursing homes, home health agencies, pharmacies, and employers.

health information is any piece of information that identifies a patient—it includes a patient's name, DOB, address, email address, and telephone number; patient's employer; any relatives' names; social security number; medical record number; account numbers tied to the patient's account; fingerprints; any photographs of the patient; and any characteristics about the patient that would automatically disclose his or her identity (for instance, "the governor of the largest state in the United States").

In addition, PHI includes the medical information that is tied to the person, including diagnosis, test results, treatments, and prognosis; documentation by the care provider and other healthcare professionals; and billing information.

HIPAA states (and HITECH enhances) that only persons who have a need to know may have access to a patient's PHI. And, to take it a step further, they are only entitled to access to the **minimum necessary information** required to do their jobs. An example would be a covered entity such as a health insurance company that is working on a claim for a patient who underwent coronary artery bypass three months ago. Unless they can prove otherwise, the minimum necessary information they need is the supporting documentation related to the bypass surgery. The fact that the patient delivered a child in 1980 has nothing to do with the bypass surgery, and therefore they do not need access to those records.

There are many ways that facilities protect the **privacy** and **confidentiality** of their patients. Privacy is the right to be left alone; in other words, no one should infringe upon a patient's time or personal space while being treated. Confidentiality is keeping a secret; in healthcare, it means keeping information about a patient to oneself. Patients have the right to expect that their medical information is going to be kept confidential. Written policies and ongoing education of staff are two very important aspects of complying with the HIPAA and HITECH rules.

Privacy and confidentiality policies should address, at a minimum:

- Release (disclosure) of information to outside sources only upon written authorization of the patient/legal representative. Release to inside sources (access) is only on a need-to-know basis. The policy should also address any exceptions, for instance to an insurance company, to public health officials in cases of mandatory reporting (infectious diseases, for example), and to licensing and accrediting agencies.

- Release of **directory information** without a written authorization. Directory information includes the fact that the patient is in the hospital (or is being treated at an ambulatory facility) and his or her room number.

- Written guidelines and examples of what is considered minimum necessary information.

- Faxing of documentation—information that can and cannot be faxed and also the protocol to be followed should information be faxed to the wrong location!

Minimum necessary information As required by the Health Insurance Portability and Accountability Act (HIPAA), releasing the minimum information to satisfy the reason the information is needed or the minimum necessary to perform a job function.

Privacy The right to be left alone; the right to expect that one's personal space is respected while undergoing healthcare.

Confidentiality The patient's right to expect that his/her health information will not be released to any person or entity without the patient/guardian's written authorization or as required by law or regulation.

Directory information The fact that a patient is an inpatient (or being treated as an outpatient) as well as his/her location within the facility.

- Computer access and lockdown—policy requires staff to lock their computers down (sign out) if they are going to be away from their desk for any length of time.
- Password sharing—makes it a disciplinary offense to share one's password with another.
- Computer screens—should be kept out of view of the public or anyone else who might have access to areas with computers.
- Shredding any hard-copy documents (where applicable) rather than just discarding them.

- Signing by patients of a **Notice of Privacy Practices** so that they are aware of how their personal health information will be used. The Notice of Privacy Practices must be in writing, signed by the patient, and informs the patient how his or her health information will be used, reasons it may be released, notice that he or she may view or have copies of the health record and may request amendments to it, and the procedure for filing a complaint with the Department of Health and Human Services. For an example of a Notice of Privacy Practices document, visit www.mhhe.com/greenway2e.
- Requirement that all staff (including care providers) sign a document committing themselves to keeping private and confidential the information that is written, spoken, or overheard about any and all patients.

An example of a shredding policy statement in an office that no longer keeps hard-copy records (a "paperless environment") is:

The electronic health record is the legal health record at Greensburg Medical Center. Printed copies should only be made when there is a need to refer to the printed document rather than the computerized image. Once the printed document is no longer needed, it is to be placed in one of the marked shred bins immediately. Shred bins are located in the business office and in the secure area of the front office. The only exception to this policy is the printed copies made for patients' requests, or that are to be mailed by the Release of Information Specialist.

In addition to the policies noted above, security-specific policies should address:

- Password Protection—Every computer user must have a unique code or **password** that is known (and used) only by the user. Passwords should not be something that can be easily discerned; for instance, the user's birthdate, spouse's name, child's name, phone number, etc., would not be secure passwords. Instead, the password should be a combination of numbers and letters, at least six digits in length, and the system should be set up to prompt users to change their password at least every 90 days. Individual offices and facilities will set policies regarding their password configuration requirements.
- Appointment of a security and/or privacy officer—someone in the facility must be named as privacy and security officer, though these may be two different individuals. The privacy/security officer is ultimately responsible for setting, monitoring, updating, investigating, and enforcing all privacy and security policies.

- Log-in attempts—the system set-up should include automatic lock-out when a user attempts to log in a certain number of times (usually three) with the wrong password. The policy and procedure should also address how to regain access.

- Protection from **computer viruses** and **malware**. This should include the facility's policy on downloading music or other attachments that may carry viruses and malware. A virus is a "deviant program, stored on a computer floppy disk, hard drive, or CD, that can cause unexpected and often undesirable effects, such as destroying or corrupting data. Malware comes in the form of worms, viruses, and Trojan horses, all of which attack computer programs" (Williams and Sawyer).

- Security audits—a policy should be set and carried out that requires random security audits to monitor access to patients' records. Often, this may be done on a rotating basis so that all staff members (including providers) are audited periodically, or it may be done based on a random selection of patients in the database. Of course, the investigation of any rumored or known breaches should include a security audit.

- Off-site access—with the use of current technology, many PMs and EHRs can be accessed via the Internet. Policies must dictate who can access remotely as well as what information can be viewed and/or edited remotely.

- Printing policies—the more information is printed from the EHR or PM software, the greater chance there is of unauthorized disclosure. Print only when absolutely necessary.

- Detailed policies and procedures that address privacy or security incidents. Disciplinary action should be addressed in this policy as well.

- Staff education—requirement that all staff (including care providers) participate in continuing education opportunities to reinforce the laws governing privacy and security.

- Email—it is a part of everyday life, not just in our personal lives but in our work lives as well. Anything written in an email is protected information. However, it is not a secure means of communication, and the facility should adopt policies related to the sending and receiving of email messages, including what, if any, patient-related information can be sent via email. Like faxes, emails can go to the wrong individual, constituting a privacy breach. There must be a policy regarding patient-related emails or emails to or from patients—are they a part of the patient's health record, and if so, how will the email become part of the record? Emails should be **encrypted**, which means the words are scrambled and can only be read if the receiver has a special code to decipher it, but encrypting still does not ensure total security. Encryption applies to any information that is electronically transmitted.

Firewalls should also be used to deter access to the system by unauthorized individuals. Williams and Sawyer define a firewall as

Computer virus A deviant program, stored on a computer floppy disk, hard drive, or CD, that can cause unexpected and often undesirable effects, such as destroying or corrupting data.

Malware Include examples such as worms, viruses, and Trojan horses, all of which attack computer programs.

for your information (fyi)

Use caution when authoring or responding to any email concerning a patient in the clinical applications of PrimeSUITE since the email will become a permanent part of the patient's EHR.

Encryption A security method in which words are scrambled and can only be read if the receiver has a special code to decipher the scrambled message.

Firewall A system of hardware and/or software that protects a computer or a network from intruders by filtering activity over the network.

"a system of hardware and/or software that protects a computer or a network from intruders."

Hardware also has to be protected, and policies must be written to govern the security of hardware devices. Hardware includes desktop computers, laptop computers, hand-held devices, and the like. These devices are always at risk for loss or theft. But to protect the information on a device, follow these simple rules:

- Always lock down the device and require a password to log on.
- Never store the passwords to any of your hardware devices or sites on the computer.
- Back up files onto a CD, external hard drive, or flash drive.
- Encrypt PHI if policy allows health records to be stored on it.
- Use the portable devices in a secure area—using one in the cafeteria and walking away to freshen your coffee is not secure.
- Wipe the hard drive of any computers that are taken out of use before recycling them or placing them in the trash.

Privacy and security need to be kept in mind at all times in any healthcare facility or practice. Not doing so, even unintentionally, may result in hefty fines. The new fines, as a result of the Omnibus Final Rule, are:

Category of Violation	Fine per Violation	Total Violation When Breach Involved the Same Provision within the Same Calendar Year
Unknowing (unintentional)	$100–50,000	$1,500,000
Reasonable cause	$1,000–50,000	$1,500,000
Willful neglect (corrected)	$10,000–50,000	$1,500,000
Willful neglected (not corrected)	Minimum of $50,000	$1,500,000

Healthcare organizations using an EHR must meet the HIPAA standards of privacy and confidentiality. In addition, states may have even more stringent rules. The American Recovery and Reinvestment Act of 2009 (ARRA), through HITECH, made the rules regarding privacy and security of electronic systems more stringent yet. Accounting of disclosures is one area that will affect hospitals and practices alike. Facilities must be able to provide a patient with a listing of disclosures, if requested; this is known as **accounting of disclosures**. Also, facilities with an EHR must be able to provide a patient with a listing of people who had access to their protected health information. This is known as an **access report**. The access report must contain the name of the individuals who accessed that person's record, and also the names of persons who do not work at the facility who had access to the record. For instance, a hospital may grant a local nursing home admissions department the right to view the health record of a patient who is being considered for nursing home placement. This is required to

Hardware The tangible items that are used in automation (e.g., the processing unit, screen, keyboard, mouse, laptops, hand-held devices).

Accounting of disclosures Providing the patient, upon request, with a listing of all disclosures of his/her health information, both internally and externally.

Access report A report of all persons (within the facility) who have had access to a patient's protected health information.

assess whether or not the nursing home has the facilities needed to care for that patient, and is part of the continuum of care; thus, it is a necessary release. The hospital would note, in the access report, that the patient's PHI was released to a certain nursing home, but would not be able to supply the names of the individual(s) who accessed it at the nursing home.

7.2 Evaluating an EHR System for HIPAA Compliance

According to the Office of the National Coordinator for Health Information Technology (ONC) website, "Health information technology (health IT) makes it possible for health care providers to better manage patient care through secure use and sharing of health information." Health IT includes the use of electronic health records (EHRs) instead of paper medical records to maintain people's health information.

To better manage patient care using electronic means, however, it is necessary to comply with certain regulations. The HIPAA rules that address electronic health information are listed in Table 7.1.

Regarding passwords, though longer passwords are more secure than shorter ones, the most secure passwords include a combination of letters (upper and lower case), symbols, and numbers. The password "summerday" is more secure than "summer," for example, yet "summer18$#" is even more secure. Healthcare organizations set their own policies regarding the length and configuration of passwords.

TABLE 7.1	Functionality of an EHR as required by HIPAA regulations
Functionality	**Meaning**
Password Protection	Passwords must be assigned to all users of an electronic health record system and the passwords must meet certain criteria: length, properties, expiration intervals, and number of log-in attempts before lockout.
User Identification	Each user must have a unique identifier to log in. Often consists of the person's first initial and last name. Allows for tracking and reporting of activity within the system by the user.
Access Rights	Policies are written and adhered to regarding access to functionality within the EHR that is dependent on the person's (or position's) need to know.
Accounting of Disclosures	Upon authorized request, an accounting of all disclosures from a patient's health record, going back a minimum of 6 years from the date of request, must be provided. The patient's health record must also be made available to the patient, or to an outside entity at the patient's request.
Security/ Backup/ Storage	A backup of the EHR database must be kept in a secure location, and restoration of the backup database must be possible at any given time. Other security requirements include controlled access to the database, use of passwords to access the database, use of firewalls, antivirus programs, etc.

continued

Functionality	Meaning
Auditing	The ability to run reports by user or by patient, that specify the menu, module, or function accessed; the date and time of the access; whether the information was viewed, edited, or deleted; and the user ID of the individual staff member.
Code Sets	The EHR must use ICD-10 codes, CPT codes, and HCPCS codes to store and transmit information.

It may be the office administrator who starts the search for EHR software and keeps in mind the requirements of a compliant system. Other individuals who should also be involved in researching, selecting, and implementing the EHR include a representative of care providers, a member of the front office (reception) staff, a clinical staff representative, health information staff, coding/billing staff, and an information technology (IT) professional who is an expert in the technological aspects of the software and hardware, networking, and interoperability of systems. This group should always keep in mind:

- The required components of a compliant EHR
- The needs of the office or facility
- The intended budget for acquiring a system as well as yearly budget requirements
- Staff and training needs
- The intent of the EHR—is it to interface with the existing PM system, or will an entirely new system that accomplishes both be purchased?
- The time line—what is the target date for implementation?

7.3 The Role of Certification in EHR Implementation

There are many agencies that certify EHR software. Both the information technology (IT) and the health information technology (HIT) aspects of an EHR system must be taken into consideration, and during the process of assessing various systems and vendors, looking at certified EHR systems is a good place to start.

Through HITECH, the ONC was given authority to establish a certification program for EHRs. The ONC, through consultation with the Director of the National Institute of Standards and Technology, recognizes programs for this voluntary certification if they are in compliance with certification criteria (DHHS: Proposed Establishment).

The **Healthcare Information and Management Systems Society (HIMSS)** is an independent, nonprofit organization with the mission "To lead healthcare transformation through the effective use of health information technology" (HIMSS: About HIMSS). HIMSS and the **American Health Information Management Association (AHIMA)** are professional associations that are highly

Healthcare Information and Management Systems Society (HIMSS) An association of health informatics and information professionals formed to promote a better understanding of healthcare informatics and management systems.

American Health Information Management Association (AHIMA) A professional association for the field of health information management.

respected in the fields of Information Technology (IT) and Health Information Management (HIM). Each has myriad sources, references, guides, best practices, and practice briefs for use in the selection and implementation of an EHR, and both organizations highly value certification.

In 2004, the American Health Information Management Association (AHIMA), the Healthcare Information and Management Systems Society (HIMSS), and the **National Alliance for Health Information Technology (NAHIT)** organized the Certification Commission for Health Information Technology (CCHIT). Its mission is to create a nongovernment, nonprofit organization that would certify EHR software, and it was called the Certification Commission.

The mission of CCHIT, as found on its website, is to ". . . accelerate the adoption of robust, interoperable health information technology" (Certification Commission). CCHIT is an independent, nonprofit organization that certifies EHR systems.

Other certifying agencies include InfoGard, Drummond Group, Inc., and ICSA Labs, to name just a few. The ONC-certified Health IT Product List can be found at http://onc-chpl.force.com/ehrcert/.

Selecting a product that is certified is good business practice and will save the office administration much of the legwork necessary to ensure selection of a product that not only meets the needs of the organization, but has already been tested and proven to meet regulatory requirements.

It is worth a student's time to view this listing, select one or more products, and view the ONC criteria that have been met by each.

National Alliance for Health Information Technology (NAHIT) An association formed to promote the use of health information technology (health IT).

7.4 Applying Security Measures

Assigning passwords, allowing access to only the functions that are necessary to perform a job, and following the other policies outlined in Section 7.1 all play a role in assuring the privacy, confidentiality, and security of the health information stored in your facility's PM and EHR systems.

The next two exercises apply basic security measures in PrimeSUITE. These functions will usually be set up by the office administrator or manager.

Adding Users to PrimeSUITE

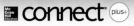

Go to http://connect.mcgraw-hill.com to complete this exercise.

HIM   EHR   PM   EXERCISE   7.1

Add a New Clinical User and Assign a Password

In this scenario, the office manager has just hired a new MA, Patric Olson, and he is going to set Patric up as a user in PrimeSUITE. Certain information is needed from Patric before the office manager begins the setup process. You will notice that the password "greenway" is used in the initial

(continued)

setup of Patric Olson. In the examples used throughout the worktext, the default password is "greenway." In an actual work setting, this default password would be changed to a password of the user's choice that meets the practice's password requirements.

Field	Value
Full name	Olson, Patric
Username	polson
Email	polson@greenwaymedical.com
Sex	Male
Telephone number	770-555-1234
DOB	07/08/1960
Soc. Security No.	123-45-1234

Follow these steps to complete the exercise on your own once you have watched the demonstration and tried the steps with helpful prompts in practice mode. Use the information provided in the scenario to complete the information.

1. Click User Administration.
2. Click Add New.
3. Type "polson" in the Username:* field.
4. Click the Email: field.
5. Type "polson@greenwaymedical.com".
6. Click the SSN: field.
7. Type "123-45-1234".
8. Click the First Name:* field.
9. Type "Patric".
10. Click the Last Name:* field.
11. Type "Olson".
12. Click the Contact Number: field.
13. Type "770-555-1234".
14. Click the Date of Birth: field.
15. Type "07/08/1960".
16. Click the Sex:* drop-down menu.
17. Click Male.
18. Click the Must Change Password At Next Login check box.
19. Click Save.
20. Type "******" in the *New Password field.
21. Click the *Confirm Password field.
22. Type "******".
23. Click OK.
24. Click OK.

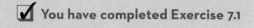 **You have completed Exercise 7.1**

Set Up a Care Provider

In our next scenario, there is also a new care provider starting this week, Lynette Dean, M.D. The office manager will set her up in the system, assigning a user ID and user rights.

The information necessary before beginning the setup process is:

Field	Value
Full name	Dean, Lynette
Sex	Female
Credentials	MD
NPI number	1234567891
State Medical License number	345678
DEA Number	GA456789
On staff at Greensburg Medical Center	Yes
Provides billable services from Greensburg Medical Center	Yes
Assigned User ID	Idean

Follow these steps to complete the exercise on your own once you have watched the demonstration and tried the steps with helpful prompts in practice mode. Use the information provided in the scenario to complete the information.

1. Click Care Providers.
2. Click the *Last Name field.
3. Type "Dean".
4. Click the *First Name field.
5. Type "Lynette".
6. Click the Sex drop-down menu.
7. Click Female.
8. Click the *Credentials drop-down menu.
9. Click MD to select it.
10. Click the National Provider Identifier field.
11. Type "1234567891".
12. Click the State License Number field.
13. Type "345678".
14. Click the DEA Number field.
15. Type "GA456789".
16. Click On Staff?
17. Click Billable?
18. Click the Set User ID icon.
19. Type "Idean" in the *UserName field.
20. Click Search.
21. Click Lynette.
22. Click Select.
23. Click Save.

 You have completed Exercise 7.2

Setting User Rights for Staff

User rights The limitations of one's access to the functionality of the software as defined by their job description or position within the organization.

We will take security functions a step further by adding **user rights**. Log-on rights simply mean that one is assigned a log-in and password to allow access to the computer software, in our case, Prime-SUITE. The user is then assigned user rights, which are privileges that limit access to only the functionality of the software needed by that individual. The position held and job description of each staff member (including care providers) dictate what privileges each person has.

EXERCISE 7.3   Go to http://connect.mcgraw-hill.com to complete this exercise.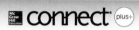

Assign User Rights to an MA

In the scenario that follows, John Greenway is an office manager. He will be setting up the user rights for Patric Olson, an MA who is new to the office. We will start by setting up Chart rights from the action bar on the left side of the screen. Chart rights have to do with viewing, adding, editing, or changing documentation within patients' charts. For instance, Patric will be able to access the Patient Chart page of every patient. He will have access to a very extensive allergy module, which will include setting up a patient's allergy shot schedule, dosage calculations, and similar applications. Of course, *he will do this based only on the physician's orders.* Patric will be able to delete vital signs from a Facesheet; reasons for this may be that the vitals were incorrectly typed into the Facesheet, or were put on the wrong patient's chart, or that the healthcare professional who entered the blood pressure, for example, did not get an accurate reading. *These privileges are very sensitive and are <u>only</u> given to appropriate staff members with the expertise and position within the practice to warrant such rights.* But even deleted, the original documentation is not lost forever—hidden is actually a better description for it—there is an *audit trail* that shows the original documentation, and then the corrected version. The topic of data integrity and versions of documentation will be covered in more detail later in this chapter.

Custom views of the Facesheet can be set up in many EHR software packages, PrimeSUITE included. The information displayed is consistent, but the way it looks on the screen is different. Some MAs or nurses are granted the right to sign off on lab results; *that right is determined by office policy (and may vary by care provider) as well as level of knowledge of the individual.* An example would be a standard blood test, such as a CBC, that is completely within normal limits on an established patient; the care provider may feel that an experienced MA or nurse is qualified to sign off on those results without sending them through for review by the care provider. The same applies to some prescriptions. The care provider may give a verbal order to an MA or nurse for a prescription renewal to be called in to the patient's pharmacy or refilled by ePrescription. For example, Robyn Berkeley is a long-time patient of Dr. Rodriguez. She has a long-standing prescription for metronidazole for treatment of her rosacea, and she has run out; the MA gives Dr. Rodriguez the request, and he then authorizes her to send through a refill via ePrescirbe. The MA is able to access and print (or electronically transmit) the prescription renewal with Dr. Rodriguez's digital signature.

User rights for all registration functions are also set up; if the healthcare professional works in the reception and registration areas, she would

(continued)

have user rights to any routine daily functions including registering a patient for the first time, editing demographic information, scheduling an appointment, checking a patient in or out, viewing alert flags, and so on.

System rights affect just that—the overall system. The rights you will see in this exercise include importing documents that do not originate within PrimeSUITE and accessing patient tracking.

Follow these steps to complete the exercise on your own once you've watched the demonstration and tried the steps with helpful prompts in practice mode. Use the information provided in the scenario to complete the information.

1. Click User Rights.
2. Click Current User.
3. Click Patric Olson.
4. Click Chart.
5. Click Chart.
6. Click Access the Patient Charts Page.
7. Click Allergy Module-Can modify serum sheet status.
8. Click Allergy Module-Override EP rules.
9. Click Facesheet-Delete vitals.
10. Click Facesheet-Manage problem list custom views.
11. Click Lab Flowsheet-Initial a lab or revoke initials.
12. Click Orders-Add to order favorite list.
13. Click Orders-Edit/delete from orders favorite list.
14. Click Prescriptions-Access ePrescribe.
15. Click OK.
16. Click Prescriptions-Can edit medication alert override.
17. Click OK.
18. Click Prescriptions-If a digital signature other than this user's is saved with a prescription, allow printing of the signature.
19. Click OK.
20. Click Save.
21. Click Registration.
22. Click View Patient or Person Registration Information.
23. Click Modify Patient or Person Registration Information.
24. Click View Patient List.
25. Click Check-In patients.
26. Click Undo Check-Out.
27. Click View and Modify Chart Patient Flags.
28. Click View Clinical Alerts Flags.
29. Click Save.
30. Click System.
31. Click Document Import.
32. Click Access Document Import.
33. Click Save.
34. Click Patient Tracking.
35. Click Access Patient Tracking.
36. Click Save.
37. Click Close.

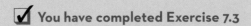 **You have completed Exercise 7.3**

Setting User Rights for a Manager

Go to http://connect.mcgraw-hill.com
to complete this exercise.   connect plus+

Assign User Rights to an Office Manager

Office managers or administrators have increased functionality such as setting up files in accounts receivable management, chart configuration and administration, registration screens, research (clinical trial) functionality, reporting, scheduling, and overall system configuration. As you go through the exercise that follows, in which you will assign rights to Diane Baxter, take a look at the entire list of rights that are assigned. The research category pertains to participation in clinical trials that are run by the Food and Drug Administration.

Follow these steps to complete the exercise on your own once you have watched the demonstration and tried the steps with helpful prompts in practice mode.

1. Click User Rights.
2. Click Current User.
3. Click Diane Baxter.
4. Click A/R Management.
5. Click Select All.
6. Click Save.
7. Click Chart.
8. Click Chart Admin.
9. Click Select All.
10. Click Save.
11. Click Research.
12. Click Select All.
13. Click Save.
14. Click Registration.
15. Click Select All.
16. Click Save.
17. Click Reporting.
18. Click Select All.
19. Click Save.
20. Click Scheduling.
21. Click Select All.
22. Click Save.
23. Click System.
24. Click Select All.
25. Click Save.
26. Click Close.

 You have completed Exercise 7.4

Setting Up a Group

connect plus+ Go to http://connect.mcgraw-hill.com to complete this exercise.

(HIM) (EHR) (PM)   EXERCISE   7.5

Create a Group

In the previous exercises, we have been working with just one staff member. In this exercise we will set up an entire group within PrimeSUITE. Setting up groups, such as all medical assistants, all receptionists, all care providers, etc., allows the office administrator to give rights by group rather than having to set up each person individually. Of course, if some of the users within the group have higher-level rights, then their profile can be modified by adding rights individually.

In Exercise 7.5 we will be working within the Group Administration module of the Systems Menu. Essentially, a group is formed and the individual staff members are moved into it, and finally the group is named. Or, a group may already exist and staff members are moved into it. The other advantage of groups is that if an email needs to be sent to an entire group, for instance, the health records staff, then just one email needs to be sent rather than to each staff member. An example would be that the health records staff is required to attend an in-service meeting on HITECH regulations at 2:00 p.m. on August 5. Just one message can be sent to the entire group notifying them of this in-service meeting.

Follow these steps to complete the exercise on your own once you've watched the demonstration and tried the steps with helpful prompts in practice mode.

1. Click Group Administration.
2. Click Allison Tubiak (atubiak).
3. Click the Move highlighted item to selected list arrow.
4. Click Jennifer Brady (jbrady).
5. Click the Move highlighted item to selected list arrow.
6. Click Jared Howerton (jared).
7. Click the Move highlighted item to selected list arrow.
8. Click Patric Olson (polson).
9. Click the Move highlighted item to selected list arrow.
10. Click Save Group.
11. Type "MedAssts" in the Save Security Group field.
12. Click Save.
13. Click Enable Messaging.
14. Click Save Group.

 You have completed Exercise 7.5

Set General Security

General security settings involve password maintenance. To complete the exercise, you will need the following information regarding Greensburg Medical Center's security policies:

Configuration Setting	Value
Password length	7 characters
Password change occurs	Every 90 days
Maximum inactivity before system automatically logs off	15 minutes
No. of days before password can be re-used	364 days
Log-in banner	Good Morning Greensburg!

Follow these steps to complete the exercise on your own once you have watched the demonstration and tried the steps with helpful prompts in practice mode. Use the information provided in the scenario to complete the information. There are already some values that appear in the exercise, so we will not be covering every setting.

1. Click System Configuration.
2. Double-click Min Password Chars field.
3. Type "7".
4. Double-click Days Password Valid field.
5. Type "90".
6. Double-click Inactivity Limit field.
7. Type "15".
8. Double-click Days Prevent Password Reuse text box.
9. Type "364".
10. Click Practice Defined Login Banner field.
11. Type "Good Morning Greensburg!".
12. Click Save.
13. Click OK.

☑ **You have completed Exercise 7.6**

Audit Trails

   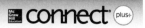
Run an Audit Trail Report

Audit trail A permanent record or accounting of accesses, additions, amendments, or deletions to a health record. Also a report which shows accesses by user to each function of the software.

In this exercise, an **audit trail** report will be run. This functionality helps to fulfill the HITECH requirement to provide an accounting of disclosures (or, in this case, accesses to a record), or it may be used to monitor activity of a certain staff member or activity in general in a particular area of the EHR software.

Our objective in this exercise is to view the Vitals History accesses over the past month by one of the staff members with the user ID of "greenway."

(continued)

Follow these steps to complete the exercise on your own once you have watched the demonstration and tried the steps with helpful prompts in practice mode.

1. Click Report Selection . . . F7.
2. Click System.
3. Click Audit Log Report.
4. Click the Report Type drop-down.
5. Click the Scroll bar.
6. Click Vitals History.
7. Click the User drop-down.
8. Type "g".
9. Click greenway.
10. Click the Date drop-down.
11. Click Month To Date.
12. Click Immediate View.
13. Click Print.
14. Click Print.

✓ You have completed Exercise 7.7

7.5   Handling Sensitive and Restricted Access

A health record contains not only pertinent clinical data, but also information about a patient that may be considered embarrassing or make a patient uncomfortable. Examples would be personal history data such as history of abortion, or having given up a child for adoption, or the fact that a minor patient is adopted. In these instances, a record may be marked as sensitive within PrimeSUITE or other EHR software so that extra care is taken when handling or releasing information.

Though all health information is confidential and is not released unless a proper authorization is on file, as required by law, or for continuity of care, some health information is such that a higher level of confidentiality is vital, even from staff within an office or hospital. Take, for instance, a patient who is well known to the office and in the community, with a diagnosis of a sexually transmitted disease. In this case, only the care provider and staff who absolutely have a need to know in order to process the record or insurance claim would have access to that record. Perhaps the sister-in-law of that patient is a receptionist in the office—it would not be prudent for her to handle that particular record. Or, consider another patient who is on an antidepressant, but does not want the record open to the entire staff because one of the medical assistants in the office is a friend of hers. In both of these examples, the record might be marked as "sensitive" within PrimeSUITE and access to those records may be limited to only a select few providers and staff within the practice; this is known as "restricted access" within PrimeSUITE. Many practices mark records of all of their staff (and often any family members) as restricted access, and only the office manager controls access to providers and other staff members who have a need to know as necessary.

Records of celebrities or other well-known individuals would also be considered sensitive and/or allow restricted access. A well-publicized case of a privacy breach involving George Clooney and his girlfriend occurred in 2007. The two were in a motorcycle accident and were taken to a New Jersey hospital. More than 20 staff members of that hospital were suspended for a month without pay due to accessing the pair's health records without a need to know and without authorization.

EXERCISE 7.8 PM EHR HIM

Go to http://connect.mcgraw-hill.com to complete this exercise.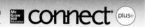

Mark a Record as Sensitive

Corinne Hess is a 17-year-old patient of Dr. Rodriguez who has been suffering from depression. The record contains information that is of a very personal nature and is going to be flagged as "sensitive."

Follow these instructions to mark the record as sensitive:

1.-48. Register Corinne as a new patient using the information on the registration form shown in Figure 7.1. (Hint: Use the *Search for Patient* and *Registration* functions to complete these steps; refer to exercise 3.2 for assistance with individual steps, as well as the steps in Connect Plus.)

49. Click **Save**.
50. Click **View/Edit Patient Flags**.
51. Click **Sensitive Chart**.
52. Click **Save**. (A key icon will appear on Corrinne's Facesheet.)

✔ **You have completed Exercise 7.8**

EXERCISE 7.9 PM EHR HIM

Go to http://connect.mcgraw-hill.com to complete this exercise.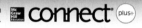

Mark a Record as Restricted Access

David Olivetti is the brother-in-law of Kaitlyn, a medical assistant at Greensburg Medical Center, and is good friends with Dr. Rodriguez. Dr. Ingram is his regular physician at Greensburg Medical Center. Because of the relationship with Kaitlyn and Dr. Rodriguez, David does not want either to have access to his EHR. In this exercise, David's record will be marked for restricted access.

1. Click Search for Patient.
2. Type "Olivetti" in the *Last Name field.
3. Click Search.
4. Click Select.
5. Click Patient Charts.
6. Click View/Edit Patient Flags.
7. Click Restricted Chart.
8. Click Save. (A padlock icon will appear on David Olivetti's Facesheet.)

✔ **You have completed Exercise 7.9**

Greensburg Medical Center
REGISTRATION FORM
(Please Print)

Today's date: *September 3, 2013*	Care Provider: **Dr. Rodriguez**

PATIENT INFORMATION

Patient's last name:	First:	Middle:	❑ Mr. ❑ Mrs.	❑ Miss ☒ Ms.	Marital status (circle one)
Hess	*Corinne*				(Single) / Mar / Div / Sep / Wid

Is this your legal name?	If not, what is your legal name?	(Former name):	Birth date:	Age:	Sex:
☒ Yes ❑ No			***05/06/1994***	19	❑ M ☒ F

Street address:	Social Security no.:	Home phone no.:
904 Wrigley Road	*887-66-2489*	*770-555-3450*

P. O. Box:	City:	State:	ZIP Code:
	Carrollton	*GA*	*30117*

Occupation:	Employer:	Employer phone no.:
Student		

Email address: *corinne@anywhere.com*	Cell phone: *770-555-8989*	

Race: *white*	Ethnicity: *American*	Primary language: *English*	Religion: *Protestant*

Next of kin: Jared Hess, father   Home phone: *770-555-1234*   Work phone: *770-555-5544*   Cell phone: *770-555-7881*

INSURANCE INFORMATION
(Presentation of Insurance Card is required at time of each visit)

Person responsible for bill:	Birth date:	Address (if different):	Home phone no.:
Jared Hess	*07/23/1968*	*Same*	*Same*

Is this person a patient here?   ☒ Yes   ❑ No

Occupation:	Employer:	Employer address:	Employer phone no.:
Teacher	*Carrollton Elementary*	*900 W. Norfolk Avenue*	*770-555-5000*

Is this patient covered by insurance?   ☒ Yes   ❑ No

Please indicate primary insurance	☒ McGraw-Hill Healthmark Insurance	❑ BlueCross/Shield	❑ [Insurance]	❑ [Insurance]	❑ [Insurance]

❑ [Insurance]	❑ Workers' Compensation	❑ Medicare	❑ Medicaid *(Please provide card)*	❑ Other

Subscriber's name:	Subscriber's S.S. no.:	Birth date:	Group no.:	Policy no.:	Co-payment:
Jared Hess	555-88-1456	*07/23/1968*	*1600*	*GAR512374*	$ 20.00

Patient's relationship to subscriber:	❑ Self	❑ Spouse	☒ Child	❑ Other	Effective Date: *01/06/1999*

Name of secondary insurance (if applicable):	Subscriber's name:	Group no.:	Policy no.:

Patient's relationship to subscriber:	❑ Self	❑ Spouse	☒ Child	❑ Other

IN CASE OF EMERGENCY

Name of local friend or relative (not living at same address):	Relationship to patient:	Home phone no.:	Work phone no.:
Amanda Jaxon	*Aunt*	*770-555-8954*	*770-555-1518*

The above information is true to the best of my knowledge. I authorize my insurance benefits be paid directly to the physician. I understand that I am financially responsible for any balance. I also authorize [Name of Practice] or insurance company to release any information required to process my claims.

Jared H. Hess	*09/03/2013*
Patient/Guardian signature	Date

Figure 7.1   Corinne Hess registration form

Data integrity refers to the accuracy, timeliness of collection, the consistency of definitions used to collect the data, and, in addition, there is an expectation that there has been no manipulation or tampering with the data once it has been collected and reported. To maintain **data integrity**, the healthcare facility must have strict policies regarding who may access data, the definition of a complete record, accuracy of data, consistent applications of data dictionary definitions, and the timeliness of data entry. Think of it this way: If a patient is seen on Wednesday, but the documentation in the health record is not entered until Friday, how accurate do you think it will be? Or, if one of the staff members instructs a patient to document his past surgical history, but to only include surgeries done under general anesthesia in the past five years, yet the office policy shows a data dictionary definition of surgery as *any* procedure the patient has had while under local, regional, or general anesthetic at any time in the past, then how consistent is the data? What about a healthcare professional who finds a blood pressure reading of 152/80 in a patient, yet enters it as 140/80 and knowingly leaves it as is, figuring it is "close enough." If you were a care provider using the information found in your EHR database, and you knew poor documentation practices were occurring, you wouldn't have much faith in using that data, would you? Or, if you were conducting a research study and knew that the data was flawed, how valid would the study be? In other words, any data found within the health record must be accurate, complete, and documented at the time of or as close to the time of occurrence as possible.

Data integrity Maintaining the accuracy and consistency of data.

Amending a Chart Entry

Integrity also applies to the addition, amendment, or omission of documentation that has already been recorded. Any alteration in the original documentation must be recoverable. With the use of paper records, if an entry in a health record was amended or corrected, it was obvious. See Figure 7.2 for an example of a proper chart correction. You can see readily that the entry was corrected; originally, it read that the patient had sustained a laceration to her right hand, when in fact, it was the left hand. A single line was drawn through the incorrect word, the correct word was inserted, and the correction was initialed and dated by the person who made the correction.

In an electronic record, original documentation that is found to be incorrect or incomplete may be hidden from view, and the amended information becomes part of the health record and is all that is viewable to the healthcare professional or care provider; however, that original hidden documentation can be recovered at any time. Our next exercise illustrates amendment of an entry in PrimeSUITE.

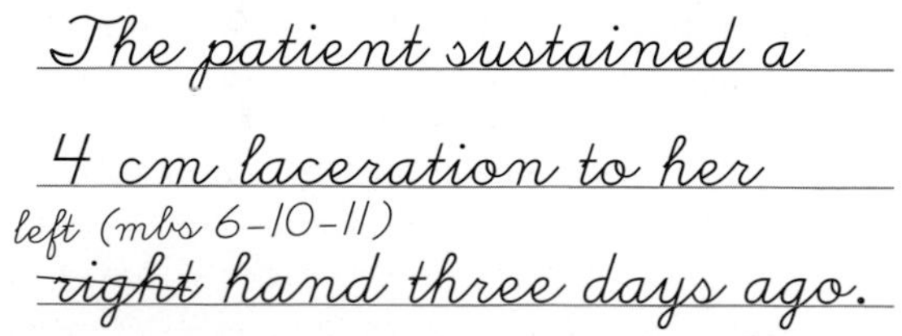

for your information **fyi**

The individual who made the original entry/error should be the person to make the correction in the health record.

The patient sustained a 4 cm laceration to her left (mbs 6-10-11) ~~right~~ *hand three days ago.*

Figure 7.2 Example of correction to paper documentation

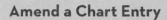

 Go to http://connect.mcgraw-hill.com
to complete this exercise.

Amend a Chart Entry

Juan Ortega's record contains an error in the progress note. The care provider documented the HPI of Juan Ortega's, but after she completed documenting and saved the note, she noticed a word was misspelled. She accesses the progress note of the chart and makes the correction. Notice, while going through the exercise, that in order to make the correction, the care provider must enter her password in order to change an entry. This additional step allows the care provider to think twice about amending the entry to be certain it is necessary and that the information she is about to add is correct. The original progress note with the error is known as version 1 and the corrected progress note as version 2.

Follow these steps to complete the exercise on your own once you've watched the demonstration and tried the steps with helpful prompts in practice mode.

1. Click Documents.
2. Click the Progress Note for August 29th.
3. Click Amend Document.
4. Click HPI.
5. Click Form.
6. Click the "who present" error.
7. Click who presents.
8. Click Close.
9. Click Save & Sign.

☑ **You have completed Exercise 7.10**

Hiding a Chart Entry

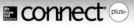

 Go to http://connect.mcgraw-hill.com
to complete this exercise.

Hide a Chart Entry

There are times when documentation is added to the wrong chart, or when misinformation is given or documented. In these cases, we would need to hide an entry. As noted in Exercise 7.10, though the entry is hidden, it is still retrievable at a later time. Our next exercise steps us through hiding an entry on Mark Robinski's chart. In this case, it is a progress note that was intended for another patient's chart. Typically, only certain staff members such as those who are in lead or administrative positions have this user right. This is not a procedure that is done often, nor is it done without a valid reason. Reasons might be that the note was put on the wrong patient's chart, or that the note pertains to that patient but not to that particular visit. Some software vendors use the term *deleting* rather than *hiding,* but regardless, the deleted/hidden entry will *always* be retrievable should the record be needed in a lawsuit, to verify some sort of inconsistency, or for insurance purposes.

(continued)

Follow these steps to complete the exercise on your own once you have watched the demonstration and tried the steps with helpful prompts in practice mode.

1. Click Documents.
2. Click Manage Chart Documents.
3. Click 09/13/2013.
4. Click Delete.
5. Click Yes.
6. Click Other.
7. Type "wrong patient" in the Other field.
8. Click OK.

✓ **You have completed Exercise 7.11**

Recovery of a Hidden Entry

 EXERCISE 7.12   Go to http://connect.mcgraw-hill.com to complete this exercise.

Recover a Hidden Chart Entry

Hiding a document does not mean that it is truly deleted forever. The original documentation can be retrieved by accessing the Documents Menu and then accessing Manage Chart Documents from the action bar.

Follow these steps to complete the exercise on your own once you have watched the demonstration and tried the steps with helpful prompts in practice mode.

1. Click Documents.
2. Click Manage Chart Documents.
3. Click View Deleted Docs.
4. Click 09/13/2013.
5. Click Undo Delete.
6. Click Yes.
7. Click Accidental Delete.
8. Click OK.

✓ **You have completed Exercise 7.12**

7.7 Apply Policies and Procedures to Release Health Information Using PrimeSUITE

Another requirement of meaningful use initiatives is to share health information with other healthcare professionals when necessary. For instance, Virginia Hill is a patient of Dr. Ingram's, and he is referring her to a specialist. It is important for the specialist to know her medical history and the reasoning for the referral; therefore, information is released electronically. This reason is known as continuity of care.

Many releases require a written authorization from the patient or legal representative. The specifics of release of information regulations will be covered in another course. For our purposes, we will be accounting for the disclosure. Release of information in the case of this referral would not require an authorization, nor would release of information to an insurance company for purposes of payment of the claim, nor release of information to public health agencies, as required by law. Written authorization is required for all releases of information to physicians' offices or hospitals that are not a result of a direct referral, attorneys, employers (if not a workers' compensation claim), spouse, children, and law enforcement agencies. Also, certain records such as those related to drug and alcohol abuse, mental health, and HIV/AIDS have more stringent release of information regulations; those will be discussed in great detail in another course.

Releasing information without a required authorization is known as a **breach of confidentiality**. Offices and healthcare facilities are required to report breaches, as was discussed earlier in this chapter, as part of the HITECH regulations. Not only is the office or facility held liable for any breaches, but individual staff members may be as well.

Breach of confidentiality Releasing information without a required, properly executed authorization or as restricted by law.

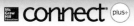

Go to http://connect.mcgraw-hill.com to complete this exercise.

EXERCISE 7.13

Compose a Correspondence Letter to Accompany the Release of a Patient's Immunization Record

Now, let's look at an exercise where a correspondence letter is accompanying the release of immunization records of a patient, Ian Mikeals, to a daycare center as requested by the child's mother.

Ian Mikeals has had the following vaccines: Hepatitis B, Pentacel (DTaP – IPV/Hib), PCV13, and ProQuad (MMRV).

Follow these steps to complete the exercise on your own once you've watched the demonstration and tried the steps with helpful prompts in practice mode. Use the information provided in the scenario to complete the information.

1. Click Search for Patient.
2. Type "Mikeals" in the *Last Name field.
3. Click Search.
4. Click Select.
5. Click Patient Charts.
6. Click Create Note.
7. Click Correspondence.
8. Click Select Template.
9. Click Notification of Release of Immunization Record.
10. Click WHICH VACCINES WERE GIVEN?
11. Click Hepatitis B.
12. Click Pentacel (DTaP - IPV / Hib).
13. Click Pneumococcal conjugate (PCV13).

(continued)

14. Click ProQuad (MMRV).
15. Click the Next arrow.
16. Click Sincerely.
17. Click Save & Sign.
18. Type "******" in the Password: field.
19. Click the green check mark.
20. Click Print/Fax Document.

✔️ **You have completed Exercise 7.13**

| 7.8 | **Accounting of Information Disclosures** |

An accounting of the releases is also necessary in order to comply with regulations. As noted above, most releases require a written authorization, but to comply with HITECH, *all* releases must be accounted for, whether the disclosure is to internal staff members or external requestors.

EXERCISE **7.14**
Go to http://connect.mcgraw-hill.com to complete this exercise.

Run a Report of Information Disclosures for a Particular Patient

In this scenario, the office manager needs to run a report of information disclosures (or, in this case, access) of the chart of a patient, Megan Hallertau, whose chart ID is 19927. She is particularly looking for disclosures (accesses) to one of the staff members, Bob Denney, who has a user ID of bdenney, that were made today.

Follow these steps to complete the exercise on your own once you have watched the demonstration and tried the steps with helpful prompts in practice mode. Use the information provided in the scenario to complete the information.

1. Click Report Selection . . . F7.
2. Click System.
3. Click Audit Log Report.
4. Click User: drop-down.
5. Type "b".
6. Click bdenney.
7. Click Patient ID: field.
8. Type "19927".
9. Click Component: drop-down.
10. Click Chart.
11. Click Immediate View.
12. Click Close.
13. Click Close Report.

✔️ **You have completed Exercise 7.14**

Communicating with other healthcare providers is another meaningful use requirement. It is known as Health Information Exchange (HIE). An advantage of utilizing an EHR is that patient care improves through the sharing of patient information at the point of care. With this functionality, care providers can access the findings of other physicians or test results immediately. Of course, this sharing is done through a secure environment, and there are regulations that address telecommunications and networking security as well. Secure email is one way that information can be shared between providers, the National Health Information Network (NHIN) Exchange is another, and there are state and private HIE programs as well. The State HIE Cooperative Agreement Program operates through use of ONC funding, and its purpose is to coordinate local HIEs or serve as the HIE for a given area.

for your information

Using a search engine, take the time to find your state's HIE on the Internet; each HIE has its own site and includes valuable information for care providers and staff.

 plus+ Go to http://connect.mcgraw-hill.com
to complete this exercise.   **HIM** **EHR**   **EXERCISE**   **7.15**

Exchange of Information for Continuity of Care

In this scenario, Ian Mikeals is a pediatric asthma patient of Dr. Ingram. Dr. Ingram is referring Ian to a pediatric asthma specialist.

Follow these steps to complete the exercise on your own once you've watched the demonstration and tried the steps with helpful prompts in practice mode.

1. Click Document Import.
2. Click Data Submission.
3. Click Referral Summary (XDS-MS).
4. Click the Reason for Referral field.
5. Type "asthma".
6. Click Preview.
7. Click Scroll down.
8. Click Print.

 You have completed Exercise 7.15

Exchange of Information Outside the Organization

There is another type of information exchange that has nothing to do with continuity of care, business purposes, or insurance purposes. It involves communicating *about* care via **social media**. Social media include Facebook, YouTube, Twitter, **blogs** (ongoing conversations about a topic that take place online), and the like. These outlets are used by patients to share their experience with a healthcare organization or to recount their journey through an illness; they can also be used by the organizations themselves as a means of marketing or public relations. Take a look at the Facebook page of Children's

Social media Interactive communication sites via the Internet. Examples are Facebook, YouTube, MySpace, and Twitter.

Blog Ongoing conversations about a topic that take place online via the Internet.

Hospital, Boston, for example, found at http://www.facebook .com/#!/ChildrensHospitalBoston?sk=info. Here you will find videos, testimonials, facts and figures about its patient population, and links to other related sites, as well as support groups and blogs, awards the organization has won, and a link to its social media policy, which is short, to the point and, in summary, states that while all comments are welcome, they should not be offensive, should be on-topic, and should not violate the privacy of patients or their family.

There is some risk in allowing patients to provide comments since not all of them will be positive, but by the same token, they are a vehicle to promote the institution, its accomplishments, and its services. They are also a service to the community by including needed information about the organization as well as links to related sites such as public health, educational sites, and support groups.

Employees of an organization also use social media (Facebook, Twitter, and LinkedIn, for example) and may contribute to blogs about their organization. Since what they say and how they say it can sometimes be misconstrued, it is imperative that healthcare organizations develop a policy to address the use of social media; and it should include this information:

- Circumstances under which an employee may access any social media site during work hours.
- Employees should maintain a positive tone in their posts, and be respectful of the organization and its staff when posting on an organization-sponsored site.
- The PHI of patients should *never* be posted (directly or implied).
- The identity of any patients (directly or implied) should *never* be posted.
- No copyrighted materials should be posted.
- No information about the organization may be posted, as this is the responsibility of the marketing or public relations department.
- Penalties or potential disciplinary action for failure to comply with the organization's social media policy.

The use of social media to share information about a particular person, which is set up and maintained by someone authorized by the patient with the objective of keeping family and friends updated on the patient's condition, is gaining popularity. One such site is Caring Bridge (www.caringbridge.org). What the patient or family cares to share on this site is under their control, but healthcare professionals who are or were involved in the patient's care need to be careful. A posting that you intend to be caring and helpful may be misinterpreted and perceived as intrusive by the family, so before posting, you should think twice about what you want to say and how you say it!

7.10 Compliance Plans

Think of all the regulations that affect healthcare—HIPAA, ARRA, HITECH, not to mention Medicare, Medicaid, and managed care plan requirements; it is a daunting task to ensure compliance with all of them. Having a formal compliance plan is key to surviving the regulatory maze. Think of a compliance plan as your office or facility's policies that ensure regulations are followed, and use it as a check-sheet to ensure that staff and care providers in your office or facility are following your own policies, which in turn ensure the following of rules and regulations. A compliance plan should include:

- A named compliance officer—a staff member who monitors new regulations, monitors existing ones, and is the "go-to" person, should an incident occur that is not in compliance.
- Written policies that cover, at a minimum:
  - Routine daily operations (registration, scheduling, human resources, etc.)
  - File backup
  - Computer access (both physical access as well as access to software and databases)
  - Release of patient information
  - Breach of confidentiality, including unauthorized disclosure
  - Security breaches, internal and external
  - Coding and billing (including anti-fraud and -abuse practices)

Policies should be kept in a location accessible to all office staff. All policies should also include the disciplinary process, should policies not be followed, intentionally or unintentionally.

An example of a Policy Statement regarding computer access and use of passwords may read:

Access to computer software, databases, and equipment shall be restricted to employees (including care providers) of Greensburg Medical Center. The extent to which access and rights are given is based on position description in order to carry out their job duties. Employees (including care providers) are required to keep their log-in user ID and password confidential; sharing with others is grounds for immediate disciplinary action, up to and including dismissal.

Reporting of compliance with meaningful use is also required; specific compliance strategies to conform with meaningful use will be covered later in this text.

The use of formal internal audits, which should be performed on every staff member (including care providers) on a periodic basis, not only allows the administrative staff to be proactive in finding and correcting problems, it also serves as a reminder and an educational tool for staff.

7.11 Safeguarding Your System and Disaster Recovery Planning

Protecting computer hardware and software is as important as protecting the information within the systems. Computer crime, unauthorized access to information, and natural disasters are all security concerns that must be addressed within any healthcare organization that processes or stores digital data.

Written policies as noted in Section 7.10 are deterrents at a very basic level, in particular, regarding controlling access. Restricting access in offices or areas where computers are present to employees only, turning computer screens away from public view, and shredding printed documents that include patient information are all examples. Encryption of data is necessary to deter unauthorized access to what is documented. Tracking the computer accesses of all employees on a periodic basis helps ensure that access is only on a need-to-know basis. Carefully screening job applicants and verifying previous employment are additional important screening mechanisms, since people are the greatest threat to computer security.

Backing up data on a daily basis is crucial. Backup can be made to online secondary storage, hard disk, optical disk, magnetic tape, and/or flash memory. A key component of backup is that the backed-up files should be stored at an off-site location. Should a fire or flood occur in your office, and the backup files are also damaged by the flood, they do little good.

Disaster recovery plan A written document that details an inventory of hardware and software, backup procedure, including location of backup files, the system used to alert users of the disaster, required security training for personnel, and procedure for restoring backup files.

Recent worldwide disasters have shown the need for having a **disaster recovery plan**. The plan must be written and staff must know what to do in the event of a disaster that affects the computer systems within the facility (Williams and Sawyer).

At a minimum, the plan should include:

- An accounting of all functions that are performed electronically within the office
- A listing of all computer hardware, software, and data related to each of those functions
- The specific location of the backup files and the format used for the backup
- Step-by-step procedures for restoring the backed-up data
- An alert system to notify personnel of the disaster
- Required security training for all personnel

Unfortunately, many facilities lack a disaster recovery plan and may not realize its importance until a data loss, security breach, or other disaster occurs. Not only should facilities have a plan, they should actually carry out the plan periodically as any other disaster plan would be practiced.

The importance of keeping *all* computerized functions safe, confidential, and secure cannot be overstated.

APPLYING YOUR SKILLS

Write a timeline and summary of the regulations that govern the collection, storage, and release of health information kept in an electronic format. Keeping in mind paper records versus electronic records, why was there a need for more stringent rules?

chapter 7 summary

LEARNING OUTCOME	CONCEPTS FOR REVIEW

7.1 Identify the HIPAA privacy and security standards. Pages 140–144	– HIPAA passed in 1996
	– Contains privacy and security rules, among others
	– HITECH made HIPAA rules more stringent and gave government authorities the power to enforce the privacy and security rules
	– Omnibus Final Rule to HITECH went into effect March 2013 with compliance required in September 2013
	– Enhancements were made to patient privacy and patient rights, strengthened enforcement of the law, and allowed more control over business associates
	– Fines for privacy breaches were increased
	– Providers using an EHR must provide patients with electronic copies of their records when requested
	– Patients paying by cash may instruct the provider not to bill their insurance and not to divulge any information regarding the treatment to the insurance company
	– The intent is to ensure protected health information (PHI) is private and secure
	– Covered entities include any healthcare facilities, health plans, clearinghouse, or other businesses that handle PHI
	– Only minimum necessary information may be released
	– Standards include:
	  • Define directory information
	  • Use of authorization to release PHI
	  • Enforce minimum necessary information release
	– Password configuration and protection
	– Appointment of a privacy and/or security officer
	– System configured to minimize number of log in attempts
	– Protection from viruses and malware
	– Use of security audits to monitor access
	– Policy to address remote access to the system
	– Policy on use and protection of hardware, particularly wireless devices
	– Written policy and procedures on breach notification
	– Staff education

7.2 Evaluate an EHR system for HIPAA compliance. Pages 145–146	**HIPAA Regulations and the EHR** – Password protection – Use of unique identifier for each user – Access to PHI only for those who have a need to know – Accounting of all disclosures (internal and external) – Security policy that addresses backup of data, storage, and restoration of backed-up data – Ability to audit by user or by patient who has accessed a record, and which area(s) of the record were viewed, edited, or deleted – Use of code sets—ICD-10-CM, CPT, and HCPCS to store and transmit information

(continued)

LEARNING OUTCOME	CONCEPTS FOR REVIEW
7.3 Describe the role of certification in EHR implementation. Pages 146–147	– CCHIT organized by AHIMA, HIMSS, and NAHIT in 2004 – Mission is to accelerate the use of an interoperable health information technology – Role is to certify EHR systems that meet all requirements of HIPAA and HITECH
7.4 Apply procedures to set up security measures in PrimeSUITE. Pages 147–155	– Add new clinical users – Assign password to new clinical users – Set up a care provider's user rights – Assign user rights to a healthcare professional (medical assistant) – Assign user rights to an office manager – Create a group – Set general system-wide security requirements – Run an audit trail report
7.5 Follow proper procedures to access sensitive or restricted-access records. Pages 155–157	– Sensitive information may or may not be clinical in nature, but is embarrassing in nature; therefore, the record is flagged – Restricted-access records are marked as such so that only select providers or staff may access them
7.6 Apply procedures to ensure data integrity. Pages 157–160	– The integrity of data can be ensured only if it is complete, accurate, consistent, timely, and has not been altered, destroyed, or accessed by unauthorized individuals – Strict organization-wide policies that are adhered to must be in place – Amendments and deletions to entries must be obvious, and the original format must remain – Amend a chart entry – Hide a chart entry – Recover a hidden chart entry
7.7 Apply procedures to release health information using PrimeSUITE. Pages 160–162	– Release of information is necessary for a multitude of reasons, including continuation of care – Authorization to release information may be required, and must be addressed in written organization policies – Must account for all disclosures to comply with HITECH – Compose correspondence and release immunization record using PrimeSUITE
7.8 Account for data disclosures using PrimeSUITE. Pages 162	– Internal and external disclosures of PHI must be accounted for – Run a report of information disclosures from a patient's chart
7.9 Exchange information with outside healthcare providers for continuity of care using PrimeSUITE. Pages 163–164	– Meaningful use standards require exchange of information between providers for smooth continuation of care – Sharing of electronic information must be through secure means – Exchange information for continuity of care using PrimeSUITE
7.10 Outline the content of compliance plans. Pages 164–165	– Healthcare organizations must have written compliance plans that address how the organization ensures compliance with all regulations governing operation of the organization as well as privacy, security, meaningful use, and general health information regulations – Written policies must be kept and available to all staff at all times
7.11 Appraise the importance of disaster recovery planning. Pages 165–166	– Contingency plan is equivalent to a back-up plan, should the system fail or a natural or other disaster occur – All potential security concerns should be addressed with a detailed backup plan – A written disaster recovery plan should be in effect

chapter review

MATCHING QUESTIONS

Match the terms on the left with the definitions on the right.

_____ 1. **[LO 7.4]** breach of confidentiality

_____ 2. **[LO 7.1]** confidentiality

_____ 3. **[LO 7.1]** hardware

_____ 4. **[LO 7.4]** audit trail

_____ 5. **[LO 7.1]** computer virus

_____ 6. **[LO 7.1]** covered entity

_____ 7. **[LO 7.1]** password

_____ 8. **[LO 7.11]** disaster recovery plan

_____ 9. **[LO 7.1]** directory information

_____ 10. **[LO 7.1]** encryption

a. person or group who has legal right to access protected health information by virtue of being a healthcare provider, clearinghouse, or health insurance plan

b. private, secure code that allows a user access to computer systems and software

c. security measure in which words are scrambled and can only be read if the receiving computer has the code to read the message

d. listing of patient information, such as hospital room number

e. documentation for addressing critical issues in the event of a crisis

f. permanent record of the changes made to various documents; available even after files are deleted

g. a break or failure of security measures that results in information being compromised

h. devices such as laptops, PDAs, and desktop computers that are at risk for theft

i. keeping information about a patient to oneself

j. deviant program, stored on a computer floppy disk, hard drive, or CD, that can destroy or corrupt data

MULTIPLE-CHOICE QUESTIONS

Select the letter that best completes the statement or answers the question:

1. **[LO 7.7]** In the event of a breach, who may be held responsible?
   a. Providers
   b. Office staff
   c. The facility
   d. All of these

2. **[LO 7.1]** Which of the following would be considered a covered entity?
   a. Healthcare provider
   b. Friend
   c. Significant other
   d. Teacher

3. **[LO 7.4]** Of the following, which factor contributes to the access rights allowed a user?
   a. Annual job performance
   b. Job description
   c. Level of education
   d. Number of patients seen

4. **[LO 7.11]** It is critical that backup files be stored:
   a. in paper form.
   b. offsite.
   c. onsite.
   d. with the originals.

5. **[LO 7.8]** HITECH regulations require that _____ information releases are accounted for.
   a. all
   b. external
   c. internal
   d. no

6. **[LO 7.2]** According to HIPAA regulations, healthcare providers must use _____ as opposed to written documentation to store and transmit information to insurance carriers.
   a. CPT codes
   b. ICD-10 codes
   c. HCPCS codes
   d. all of these

7. **[LO 7.3]** Meaningful use standards require offices to select an EHR that is:
   a. certified.
   b. comprehensive.
   c. fast.
   d. simple.

8. **[LO 7.7]** Releasing information without proper authorization is called a/an:
   a. breach of confidentiality.
   b. breach of trust.
   c. information breach.
   d. security breach.

9. **[LO 7.6]** When a document is amended or changed in an EHR, the original documentation is:
   a. deleted.
   b. hidden.
   c. printed.
   d. visible.

10. **[LO 7.10]** An office's compliance manual should be kept in a/an _____ location.
    a. accessible
    b. external
    c. electronic
    d. protected

11. **[LO 7.9]** The sharing of health information must be done in a _____ environment.
    a. healthcare
    b. private
    c. public
    d. secure

12. **[LO 7.4]** Under a care provider's order, medical assistants and nurses _____ allowed to send an ePrescription or call in a refill prescription to a pharmacy.
    a. are
    b. are not
    c. might be
    d. should not be

13. **[LO 7.1]** To help guard against security breaches, emails containing protected health information should be:
    a. deleted.
    b. encrypted.
    c. forbidden.
    d. sent.

14. **[LO 7.3]** The mission of CCHIT is to:
    a. actively promote the use of smartphones.
    b. ensure information security.
    c. increase the implementation of EHR systems.
    d. train facilities on HIPAA regulations.

SHORT ANSWER QUESTIONS

1. **[LO 7.2]** According to the ONC website, how does health information technology help care providers manage patient care better?

2. **[LO 7.7]** Define continuity of care.

3. **[LO 7.5]** If all health information is confidential, explain why it may still be necessary to mark some health records as "sensitive" or "restricted."

4. **[LO 7.6]** Why must a user enter her password in order to change a chart entry in PrimeSUITE?

 Enhance your learning by completing these exercises and more at http://connect.mcgraw-hill.com!

5. **[LO 7.10]** List at least six pieces of information that must be included in an office's compliance plan.

6. **[LO 7.11]** List the six pieces of information that form the minimum requirements of a disaster recovery plan.

7. **[LO 7.4]** List three responsibilities that fall into the office manager's or office administrator's job description.

8. **[LO 7.3]** What does it mean if an EHR system has been certified by the Office of the National Coordinator?

9. **[LO 7.1]** Explain what a security audit is, and list one example of when a security audit might need to take place.

10. **[LO 7.9]** Explain one advantage of using an EHR for communicating with other healthcare providers as discussed in the text.

11. **[LO 7.10]** What is the best way to ensure that your office is following all the different regulatory bodies governing healthcare?

12. **[LO 7.8]** Why must an office manager account for all information released, including those released internally?

13. **[LO 7.4]** Would a care provider and a medical assistant be assigned the same rights in PrimeSUITE? Why or why not?

14. **[LO 7.2]** List six things that an office's EHR team should keep in mind when rolling out a new system.

15. **[LO 7.11]** List three methods to safeguard computer hardware and software systems.

APPLYING YOUR KNOWLEDGE

1. **[LOs 7.1, 7.9]** Discuss two advantages and two disadvantages of using email to send information between providers.

2. **[LOs 7.1, 7.2, 7.4, 7.10, 7.11]** Discuss why many practices require users to change their passwords after a specified period, and why they do not allow users to reuse the same passwords over and over again.

3. **[LO 7.3]** Imagine that you are working in a small healthcare practice. Your supervisor has asked you to spearhead the adoption of an EHR program. Follow the link provided in the text to find the website listing certified EHRs. After browsing the site and looking at the sheer number of products listed, discuss some methods your healthcare office could use to choose the best EHR option.

4. **[LOs 7.6, 7.7]** Provide an example of both an internal and an external Breach of Confidentiality that might occur in a healthcare setting, and list a possible consequence of each breach. (For example, letting a temporary employee access a patient's chart with your username would be an internal breach; a consequence could be that a patient's health information is compromised when the temp accidentally sends the patient's chart information out in an accidental "reply all" email.)

5. **[LOs 7.1, 7.4, 7.6, 7.10, 7.11]** You are in the office cafeteria getting some water. One of your colleagues is at her desk, working on a laptop. She gets up to join you at the water cooler. As the two of you are talking, another staff member sits down in your colleague's chair and begins using the laptop to check her email. What is wrong with this scenario?

6. **[LOs 7.1, 7.2, 7.4, 7.6, 7.7, 7.9]** Paul Davies presents to County Hospital's ER with an arm injury. He refuses to talk about how he sustained the injury, and says he wants his medical records released to his sister, who will be coming to take him home. How would the objectives of an EHR make handling Mr. Davies's case easier?

7. **[LO 7.4]** Stephanie Byrd is a coder at Greensburg Medical Center. Her user ID is sbyrd. She recently got married, and wants her user ID changed to slopez, to reflect her married name. Stephanie is told by the office administrator that once a user ID is assigned, it cannot be changed. Why can't the user ID be changed?

 Enhance your learning by completing these exercises and more at http://connect.mcgraw-hill.com!

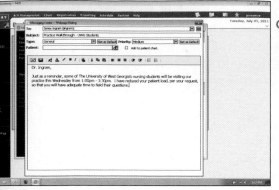

8

Management of Information and Communication

Learning Outcomes

At the end of this chapter, the student should be able to:

8.1 Use software as an internal communication tool.

8.2 Differentiate the steps used to import documents using scanning technology.

8.3 Build master files and templates using PrimeSUITE.

8.4 Create custom screens within PrimeSUITE.

8.5 Develop a task list within PrimeSUITE.

8.6 Set up system flags within PrimeSUITE.

Key Terms

Default values
Flags
Internet
Intranet
Live

Master file
Optical character recognition (OCR)
Resolution
Scanner
Templates

What You Need to Know and Why You Need to Know It

So far in this text, we have mainly looked at the collection of data, which in turn becomes information about a patient. In this chapter we will look at communicating that information. The information collected in a healthcare environment is shared with external sources such as other healthcare providers, public health agencies, Medicare, insurance companies, and professional organizations. The information included may be in the form of a summary of a patient's record, a report that answers a question, such as the local public health office asking how many cases of flu-related illnesses were seen during a given time period, or a piece of correspondence from one care provider to another. Additionally, the communication may be internal—within the facility. With PM and EHR software, communicating internally through use of an internal email system is efficient. Information is key to almost everything we do, personally and professionally, so having the information we need at our fingertips and communicating that information accurately and in a timely fashion are key to a well-run organization. Taking it a step further, patients who receive timely, accurate information and who experience good communication within the practice will have more confidence in the practice as a whole.

8.1 Internal Communications

The **Internet** is a series of networks that allows instant access to information from around the world. Internet sites may be private, requiring a user ID and password to gain access, or they may be public sites that are viewable by anyone. Within an organization, however, the **intranet** exists. An intranet is a secure environment or private internal network that is available only to a select group, e.g., the staff, within an organization. Examples of what might be shared on an intranet site include:

Internet A series of networks that allow instant access to information from around the world.

Intranet A secure environment or private internal network that is available only to a select group (e.g., the staff within an organization).

Facility's mission and value statements	Directory of staff and care providers	Compliance officer's name and contact information
Policies and procedures	FAQs	Forms, publications, newsletters
Organization charts	Office meeting minutes	Calendar of events
Link to the IT department	Calendar of upcoming events	Internal webmail link

The intranet is a one-stop-shop for staff and providers of a practice or other healthcare organization to gain access to all of the information needed to stay informed and a way to send and receive messages from colleagues. Of course, someone (usually a webmaster) has to keep the information up-to-date; otherwise, the outdated information is not information at all, and there is no benefit to having an intranet. When staff starts noticing that the site is not being kept current, they will stop accessing it and information will no longer be shared. If your current employer does have an intranet, take some time to really navigate it—look for the information stated above, and see if you can find other useful information there.

PrimeSUITE Tip PS

Any emails written from within the clinical areas of PrimeSuite will remain a permanent part of the patient's EHR.

The use of internal messaging improves communication within an office. It is particularly helpful in avoiding the "no one ever told me" syndrome. When internal email is used to communicate work-related information, and is not cluttered with personal communications, it is even more valuable. Many organizations have policies regarding use of the office email account, and though they may not mandate that it cannot be used as a personal means of communication, such use is most likely frowned upon and may lead to more stringent policies. Some offices use a priority rating on their work-related emails. This is particularly helpful to the care providers in sifting out what needs to be done immediately versus what can wait for a later time. High-priority messages would include patient care matters, medium priority would include changes in meeting dates or time-sensitive information, and low priority might be information such as lunch is ready in the lounge or FYI messages. When establishing rules for the priority system, everyone should at least be clear on what is and *is not* considered high priority.

EXERCISE 8.1

Go to http://connect.mcgraw-hill.com to complete this exercise.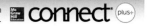

Send an Electronic Message Using PrimeSUITE Messaging

In this exercise we will look at carrying out an internal communication using PrimeSUITE. In the exercise that follows, Dr. Ingram is to attend an EMR meeting, but the date and time have been changed. In this instance, the message would only be sent to Dr. Ingram; if the message were for all of the care providers, then it would be sent using a group rather than typing in one name.

This function is accessible from the desktop screen.

Follow these steps to complete the exercise on your own once you have watched the demonstration and tried the steps with helpful prompts in practice mode. Use the information provided in the scenario to complete the information.

for your information fyi

You learned earlier in this text that the terms *electronic medical record (EMR)* and *electronic health record (EHR)* are often used interchangeably. At Greensburg Medical Center, EMR is the preferred terminology.

1. Click No Unread Messages.
2. Click Compose Message.
3. Type "jingram" in the To: field.
4. Click the Subject: field.
5. Type "EMR Meeting".
6. Click the Priority: drop-down.
7. Click Medium.
8. Type the salutation "Dr. Ingram," in the message field.
9. Press "Return".
10. Type "Just as a reminder, the EMR meeting this week has been moved to Thursday at 3:30 p.m." in the message field.
11. Click Send Message.
12. Click Close.

✓ **You have completed Exercise 8.1**

Communication involves many forms other than email messages. Reports, test results, or verifications of insurance coverage, just to name a few, are communicated many times throughout the day. These reports may be sent to the practice in digital or hard-copy format but in the end must be merged into the appropriate patient's record.

For example, Dr. Ingram sent Max Shaw to Memorial Hospital for a chest x-ray. The x-ray is completed and the report of the radiologist's findings is sent electronically to Greensburg Medical Center. It then needs to be merged (attached) to the patient's chart—the flow of this is depicted in Figure 8.1.

Not all documents can be sent electronically, however. Case in point—let's say a patient, David Malone, had his chest x-ray at Duffields Hospital, which does not have electronic capability yet. Instead, the report of the x-ray findings is in hard-copy form only. It can be faxed, mailed, or picked up from the hospital by a staff member. Since the goal of Greensburg Medical Center is a paperless office with a unit record for all patients, a hard-copy image would need to be manually scanned into the EHR once it arrives at the office (Figure 8.2).

When a hard-copy document needs to be scanned, the healthcare professional simply feeds the document through the scanner (or lays the document flat on a screen) (see Figure 8.3), follows the prompts that appear on the computer screen, and finally merges (attaches) the document with the proper patient's record within PrimeSUITE. The process of scanning is much like the process of making a photocopy. Just as a hard-copy document can be misfiled, so can a scanned image. Before a scanned image is attached to a patient's health record, the healthcare professional verifies that the correct patient and the

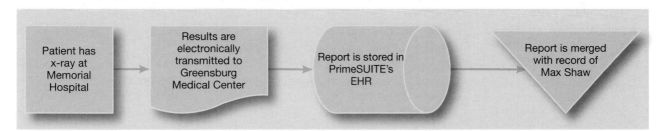

Figure 8.1 **Flow of report from hospital to merging with appropriate record in PrimeSUITE**

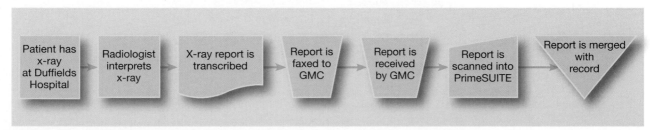

Figure 8.2 **Flow of faxed report from hospital to PrimeSUITE**

Figure 8.3 Scanner used to import a document

correct visit are selected. Also, the type of document (correspondence, authorization, history, or physical exam, for example) may be bar-coded so that the document is easily retrievable electronically.

Scanners digitize documents into a format that is readable by the computer. The scanning of documents utilizes **optical character recognition** technology to convert the document into a format that is computer readable. There are other scanning functions that you may be aware of and may not even realize it—in a grocery store, the cashier passes the bar code from a can of green beans across a small light source; he has just scanned the bar code so that the computer reads it as a 15.5-ounce can of green beans with a price of $1.25. In that case, the optical reader has read a bar code rather than words. This process not only results in a price for the item, it is also part of an inventory control system—the persons responsible for re-order now know that there is one less can of beans on the shelf!

Scanner A piece of equipment that digitizes documents into a format that is readable by a computer.

Optical character recognition (OCR) Technology that converts a document into a format that is computer readable—that is, into an electronic file.

EXERCISE 8.2   Go to http://connect.mcgraw-hill.com to complete this exercise.

Scan an Insurance Card into a Patient's Record

In the scenario that follows, Jessie Hamilton's insurance card is scanned using a desktop scanner at the time he checks in. Once it is scanned, the document is merged (attached) with Jessie's chart in PrimeSUITE. If your doctor's office is automated, the next time you arrive for an appointment and present your insurance card, watch this process. In all, it only takes a minute. In the exercise that follows, you are asked to enter the **resolution**, that is, the quality of the image as it will appear in the record. Obviously, in a legal record, the highest resolution would be selected.

Follow these steps to complete the exercise on your own once you have watched the demonstration and tried the steps with helpful prompts in practice mode. Use the information provided in the scenario to complete the information.

Resolution The quality of a scanned image as it will appear in the record. The higher the resolution, the crisper the image.

1. Click Document Import.
2. Type "Hamilton" in the *Last Name field.
3. Click Search.
4. Click Select.
5. Click Quick Scan using existing scanner settings.
6. Press Click to move all pages to Selected list.
7. Click the Select Document Type drop-down.
8. Click Insurance Card.
9. Click Save Resolution.
10. Click Quality (High).
11. Click Save.

 You have completed Exercise 8.2

Care providers and all healthcare professionals are extremely busy. Their first concern is the patient, not documentation. So, to make documenting easier and faster, **master files** (datasets that provide structure and are the building blocks for parts of the chart notes) and **templates** (preformatted documents built into the PM and EHR systems) are used. If you think back to the exercises where a patient's history or review of systems were entered, you saw many master files. Figure 8.4 is an example of a master file for selecting conditions in a patient's past medical history.

At Greensburg Medical Center, before the EHR went **live**, members of the staff built these master files with input from care providers. Master files list common conditions and diagnoses that patients at Greensburg Medical Center have had. Diagnoses can be added to an individual's record, or to the master file itself. Other master files in PrimeSUITE include PE, ROS, orders, diagnosis favorites, and HPI.

Building templates within the system is an administrative task that is done prior to going live, but they can be edited as necessary. Templates are preformatted documents that allow screenshots to be built, letters to be written, and progress notes to appear out of individual selections from master files. Care providers may prefer their documentation to look a certain way, so a practice that has five care providers may have five templates for written progress notes.

Master files   Datasets that provide structure and are the building blocks for parts of chart notes within an EHR.

Templates   Preformatted documents built into practice management and electronic health record systems.

Live   The point at which computer software or systems are put into real-time use within a practice or hospital.

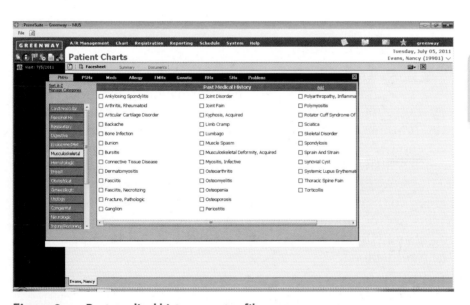

Figure 8.4   Past medical history master file

for your information

Master files or templates are structured data and therefore are used in the calculation of E&M codes electronically.

Go to http://connect.mcgraw-hill.com to complete this exercise.

HIM   EHR   PM

EXERCISE   8.3

Build a Master File in PrimeSUITE

To build a master file in PrimeSUITE, the Desktop will be accessed and then Review of Systems Admin will be selected from the Chart menu. In the exercise that follows, we will build the master file for Review of Systems

(continued)

Default value A value that automatically appears in a field each time it appears on a screen (e.g., the current date in a date field, the local area code in a home phone number field).

(ROS). The end product will be indicative of what this care provider wants as the **default values** (the value that automatically appears in a field) on the ROS screen and appears each time he sees a patient. For instance, the care provider wants the default value for weight loss to be a negative response; in other words, if a patient is asked if she has experienced unexplained weight loss, most of the time the answer will be no; therefore, this response will show as (-) weight loss on the ROS screen.

Setting up these default values is done from the System Set-Up module on the Chart menu.

Follow these steps to complete the exercise on your own once you have watched the demonstration and tried the steps with helpful prompts in practice mode.

1. Click Review of Systems Admin.
2. Click Constitutional.
3. Click fatigue.
4. Click weight loss.
5. Click Genitourinary.
6. Click urgency.
7. Click frequency.
8. Click dysuria.
9. Click Save.

☑ **You have completed Exercise 8.3**

8.4   Customization

Care providers, registration staff, medical assistants, nurses, therapists, billers, and coders all use the information in the PM and EHR software. But not all of the users "see" things the same way. The way information and subsets of information display in relation to one another on a computer screen is often most effective when the user is satisfied with how the information appears. Many PM and EHR software packages include flexibility to allow customization of screen configurations, and PrimeSUITE is no exception. Care providers and healthcare professionals in general will be more accepting of an EHR if they know they have some say in the appearance of the information.

EXERCISE   8.4

Go to http://connect.mcgraw-hill.com to complete this exercise.

Customize a Facesheet Screen

We will now look at a couple of exercises where customization is possible. The first task is to customize a Facesheet screen. In this scenario, the healthcare professional is going to customize a Facesheet. He starts by entering the User Settings Admin within the System Setup module that is in the Chart menu. Watch as he chooses the elements that will show on the Facesheet, and then how he changes the order in which they appear.

Follow these steps to complete the exercise on your own once you have watched the demonstration and tried the steps with helpful prompts in practice mode.

1. Click User Settings Admin.
2. Click the Facesheet & History tab.
3. Click History Sections.
4. Click Facesheet Sections.
5. Click Save.
6. Click Patient Charts.
7. Click Customize Facesheet.
8. Click Reason for Visit.
9. Click Allergy List.
10. Click Clinical Alerts.
11. Click Confidential.
12. Click Flowsheets.
13. Click Medication List.
14. Click Orders Tracking History.
15. Click Past Surgical History.
16. Click Problem List.
17. Click Task List.
18. Click Visit History.
19. Click Vital Signs.
20. Click anywhere left of the Customize Facesheet menu to close it.
21. Drag Medication List and drop on Confidential.

In addition to the Facesheet, the desktop can also be customized to meet the individual user's preferences.

 You have completed Exercise 8.4

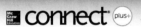  Go to http://connect.mcgraw-hill.com to complete this exercise.   **EXERCISE 8.5**

Customize a Clinical Desktop

Watch as this user sets up the Desktop (the first screen that appears when a user logs on) to meet her needs and preferences.

Follow these steps to complete the exercise on your own once you have watched the demonstration and tried the steps with helpful prompts in practice mode.

1. Click Customize Desktop.
2. Click Patient List.
3. Click Use Clinician Desktop.
4. Click Show Orders Tracking.
5. Click Show Unsigned Documents List check box.
6. Click Show Task List check box.
7. Click the Last Viewed Section First drop-down.
8. Click Patient List.
9. Click Save.

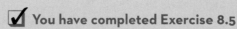 **You have completed Exercise 8.5**

With all the requirements we deal with in healthcare, having help with organizational skills is certainly an advantage! In PrimeSUITE, there is a functionality called a Task List or Tasks, where a care provider or other healthcare professional assigns tasks to another staff member or to an entire group. For instance, Dianna Pike, a care provider, wants a particular report to be run by the office administrator, Jon Viria. The request is simply put into Jon's task list so that he is aware that he has a task that needs to be completed. Or, if it is a task to be completed by an entire group, for instance, the health information department staff, the task—completion of a computerized in-service—can be assigned to the group rather than to each individual, saving the office administrator much time and ensuring that everyone gets the *same* message!

Some examples of tasks include:

- Calling patients to change appointments due to the change in a provider's vacation dates
- Registering for an upcoming seminar
- Calling a patient regarding the need for a follow-up laboratory test
- Making reservations for the office holiday party

As you can see, the tasks may not be clinical in nature; they can be anything that needs to be done by an individual or individuals in the practice.

EXERCISE 8.6   Go to http://connect.mcgraw-hill.com to complete this exercise.

Create a Task for the Receptionist

In the scenario that follows, a task is set up for Charlotte Baker to schedule a training session on ePrescribing. The message is "Charlotte, will you please contact Greenway and arrange a training session covering ePrescribe? I would like to have this done between October 1 and November 30. Thanks!" (without the quotes).

This function also allows the user to select the priority of the task—high, medium, or low. Practice policy may dictate what circumstances dictate each, and whether prioritization is used at all.

Follow these steps to complete the exercise on your own once you have watched the demonstration and tried the steps with helpful prompts in practice mode. Use the information provided in the scenario to complete the information.

1. Click Tasks.
2. Click Add New Task.
3. Click Type:.
4. Click General Task.
5. Click Send To:.
6. Click the Scroll bar.

7. Click Baker, Charlotte (cbaker).
8. Click OK.
9. Click Subject:.
10. Type "eRX training".
11. Click Due Date.
12. Click 25.
13. Click the Status: drop-down.
14. Click New.
15. Click Add Comment:.
16. Type the required message in the Comment field.
17. Click OK.
18. Click Save & Return.
19. Click Close.

☑ **You have completed Exercise 8.6**

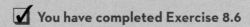

8.6 Using Software as a Reminder

If you work in healthcare you have a lot to remember, as you have already seen. It would be next to impossible to remember every situation about every patient. Using the functionality of PM or EHR software, including PrimeSUITE, makes keeping on top of everything easier, though, by including alerts or reminders in a patient's chart, through a series of flag alerts (reminders), or icons, each of which has a particular meaning.

Flags can be added in the system and can be used for any and all patients.

Flags A message that appears on a screen in written form or as an icon to serve as a reminder to staff and care providers.

Examples of common flags include:

- Frequently cancels appointments
- Phone number on file is no longer in service
- Confidentiality messages (such as do not leave message on home phone)
- Co-pay required (and can include amount)
- Patient is noncompliant
- Account in collections
- Do not charge late fee
- Payment plan set up
- Allergic to penicillin (can have several different medications)
- Environmental allergy to _____
- Sensitive information contained in chart
- Clinical alerts

  - Bone density scan due
  - Diabetic patient
  - Requires patient education
  - Pap smear due

A flag can be set up in the system for just about anything the office sees a need for. A word of caution though; do not set up so many flags that it is difficult to remember their meaning, or so that the alert becomes the rule rather than the exception and therefore is ignored!

Assign a Flag to a Patient's Chart

In this exercise, you will set up a system flag for a patient. In this case, Jessie Hamilton is allergic to bee stings, so the healthcare professional will add that flag to Jessie's chart.

Follow these steps to complete the exercise on your own once you have watched the demonstration and tried the steps with helpful prompts in practice mode. Use the information provided in the scenario to complete the information.

1. Click Search for Patient.
2. Type "Hamilton" in the *Last Name field.
3. Click Search.
4. Click Select.
5. Click View/Edit Patient Flags.
6. Click Allergic to Bee Stings.
7. Click Save.

So as you can see, computerization of the practice management and health record functions has many other benefits to care providers and staff than just maintenance of the information they collect. The use of software streamlines the processes and increases efficiency as well.

 You have completed Exercise 8.7

APPLYING YOUR SKILLS

Virginia Park called Dr. Hilliard today. He was looking at her medical history in her EHR, and then sent an email to his nurse from within the history section of PrimeSUITE. The body of the email read:

"Jane, Ms. Park has called five times with the same questions. I'm tired of her calling me. Please take care of this—I have better things to do than to deal with a hypochondriac."

Could this become an issue for Dr. Hilliard? Defend your answer.

chapter 8 **summary**

LEARNING OUTCOME	CONCEPTS FOR REVIEW
8.1 Use software as an internal communication tool. Pages 175–176	– Difference between Internet and intranet – Examples of information commonly shared on an intranet – Send a message using PrimeSUITE
8.2 Differentiate the steps used to import documents using scanning technology. Pages 177–178	– Reports within a chart are a type of communication – Documents may be imported from within PrimeSUITE or from an external source – Scanning a document involves a process of feeding (or laying flat) the document in the scanner, then attaching the document to the appropriate patient's chart – Scanning digitizes documentation into readable format – Optical character recognition (OCR) allows scanned images to be edited – Scan an insurance card and import it into the record of Jessie Hamilton
8.3 Build master files and templates using PrimeSUITE. Pages 179–180	– A master file is a listing of possible choices, e.g., a list of allergies, list of conditions, list of surgeries – Templates allow for building an end product such as a progress note, a piece of correspondence, or a screen view – Build a master file for an ROS
8.4 Create custom screens within PrimeSUITE. Pages 180–181	– Allow flexibility and personalization for individual users – Design a Facesheet view for a user
8.5 Develop a task list within PrimeSUITE. Pages 182–183	– Tasks are reminders that a job has been assigned – Can be made by any user – Can be a task set for a single user or a group – Assign a task to a user in PrimeSUITE
8.6 Set up system flags within PrimeSUITE. Pages 183–184	– Flags are alerts or reminders – Use them sparingly; otherwise, they no longer point out the exception to the rule, but rather become the rule – Set up a flag on a patient's record in PrimeSUITE

MATCHING QUESTIONS

Match the terms on the left with the definitions on the right.

_____ 1. **[LO 8.6]** flag

_____ 2. **[LO 8.3]** default value

_____ 3. **[LO 8.3]** master file

_____ 4. **[LO 8.3]** templates

_____ 5. **[LO 8.1]** intranet

_____ 6. **[LO 8.3]** live

_____ 7. **[LO 8.2]** scanner

_____ 8. **[LO 8.2]** optical character recognition (OCR)

a. secure internal environment available only to a select group

b. device that digitizes documents into a format readable by computers

c. an alert or reminder that appears in a patient's chart

d. dataset that provides structure and is the building block for parts of the chart notes

e. software that allows a saved document to be edited

f. using something in real time

g. preassigned value that appears in a field automatically

h. preformatted documents built into an EHR or PM system

MULTIPLE-CHOICE QUESTIONS

Select the letter that best completes the statement or answers the question:

1. **[LO 8.1]** The Internet is _____ and an intranet is _____.
   a. public; private
   b. private; public
   c. private; private
   d. public; public

2. **[LO 8.2]** A hard-copy document is attached to a patient's electronic chart by:
   a. copying.
   b. emailing.
   c. scanning.
   d. shredding.

3. **[LO 8.3]** Using templates makes it easier for care providers to focus on their first priority, which is:
   a. documentation.
   b. patient care.
   c. office staff.
   d. training.

4. **[LO 8.4]** PrimeSUITE allows each user to _____ certain features to their liking.
   a. access
   b. customize
   c. delete
   d. revise

5. **[LO 8.1]** A facility needs to make sure that the information on their intranet does not become:
   a. outdated.
   b. overused.
   c. private.
   d. secure.

6. **[LO 8.6]** It is _____ to have too many flags set up in PrimeSUITE.
   a. impossible
   b. possible
   c. necessary
   d. difficult

7. **[LO 8.3]** The Review of Systems menu choices are in PrimeSUITE is an example of a/an:
   a. index.
   b. master file.
   c. real-time menu.
   d. template.

8. **[LO 8.5]** A healthcare professional may assign work to another user with PrimeSUITE's _____ functionality.
   a. assignment
   b. groups
   c. tasks
   d. workload

9. **[LO 8.6]** Jane Howard often misses appointments; an alert is set to appear on her record; this alert is known as a/an _____ in PrimeSUITE.
   a. Flag
   b. Avatar
   c. Decal
   d. Symbol

10. **[LO 8.4]** Which of the following PrimeSUITE functions may be customized by a user?
   a. Access rights
   b. Insurance policies
   c. Patient information
   d. Screen layout

 Enhance your learning by completing these exercises and more at http://connect.mcgraw-hill.com!

SHORT ANSWER QUESTIONS

1. **[LO 8.1]** List four things that might be found on an organization's intranet.

2. **[LO 8.3]** Could one medical office have more than one template for a referral letter? Explain.

3. **[LO 8.1]** What will happen if an office's intranet is not kept current?

4. **[LO 8.3]** List four advantages of using master files and templates in a healthcare office.

5. **[LO 8.6]** List at least eight common flags used in PrimeSUITE.

6. **[LO 8.6]** Why might it be good to have a "Sensitive information contained in chart" alert pop-up when users access specific patient charts?

7. **[LO 8.5]** Explain how using the Task List function in PrimeSUITE helps to organize work.

8. **[LO 8.4]** Why might healthcare professionals be more accepting of an EHR if they are able to customize it in some way?

APPLYING YOUR KNOWLEDGE

1. **[LO 8.4]** How might a care provider "see" the information display in PrimeSUITE in the same way a patient registration staff member would?

2. **[LOs 8.1, 8.2, 8.6]** As office manager, what are some ways for you to ensure that staff members remember to attach hard-copy documents to the patient charts they are working on?

3. **[LO 8.3]** Discuss two advantages and any potential disadvantages to using templates for communication documents.

4. **[LOs 8.5, 8.6]** You are the office manager for a small practice. Since your office recently implemented an EHR system, you would like to have a staff training session to set forth guidelines and best practices for using system flags. Explain how you would use PrimeSUITE to assist you in your task, and come up with four talking points about proper use of flags and alerts.

5. **[LOs 8.3, 8.4]** Dr. Stewart hired a new associate, Dr. Reynolds, about six months ago. Dr. Reynolds has been trying without success to use PrimeSUITE efficiently. Though he likes the template method of documenting, he has found that much of what he prefers to document is not part of the existing templates, and he has to type by free-hand a lot of that data. He feels he is not paying as much attention to his patients as he should be during the visit because he is typing, and he is also concerned that his E&M code levels are lower than they should be. He comes to you, the office manager, to vent his frustrations. What, if anything, can be done to make his use of Prime-SUITE more effective and efficient? Would any of this have an impact on Dr. Reynolds's E&M code levels?

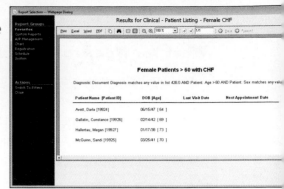

Decision and Compliance Support: Utilizing the Database

Learning | Outcomes

At the end of this chapter, the student should be able to:

9.1 Describe the uses of the dashboard in PrimeSUITE to meet meaningful use standards.

9.2 Explain how data and information are used in decision support.

9.3 Set up system reports using PrimeSUITE.

9.4 Set up custom reports using PrimeSUITE.

9.5 Illustrate uses for an index.

9.6 Describe uses for a registry.

9.7 Explain how data gathered in PrimeSUITE is used in the credentialing process.

Key | Terms

Aggregate

Benchmarking

Center for Medicare and Medicaid Services (CMS)

Certified Electronic Health Record Technology (CEHRT)

Core objectives

Credentialing

Custom report

Dashboard

Detail report

Drug formulary

Healthcare Integrity and Protection Data Bank (HIPDB)

Index

In-network

Menu objectives

National Practitioner Data Bank (NPDB)

Physician Quality Reporting Initiative (PQRI)

Query

Registry

Summary report

Variable

What You Need to Know and Why You Need to Know It

Running reports, supplying information to agencies, and ensuring compliance with meaningful use, licensing agencies, Medicare/Medicaid rules, managed care plans, and accrediting agencies are all responsibilities of administrative personnel. This person may be an MA who is an office manager, a health information professional, or a healthcare administrator. Participation in the meaningful use incentive program, in particular, will require submission of data that shows compliance with the standards in order to receive incentive grants. In this chapter, we will cover PrimeSUITE functionality that allows us to prove compliance with meaningful use, licensing agency, insurance providers, and state and federal reporting requirements.

9.1   Using the Dashboard in PrimeSUITE to Meet Meaningful Use Standards

Center for Medicare and Medicaid Services (CMS) An agency of the Department of Health and Human Services and responsible for administering the Medicare and Medicaid programs.

Core objectives Basic functions or collection of data that should be completed on a patient's visit or hospitalization.

In order for eligible professionals and hospitals to receive stimulus money, as part of HITECH legislation they must successfully show meaningful use of electronic health data. In other words, eligible professionals and hospitals that implement (or upgrade) certified electronic health record systems and comply with the core and menu objectives (covered below) will be eligible for monetary grants. The **Center for Medicare and Medicaid Services (CMS)** administers the program. The Stage 1 **core objectives** that show meaningful use of electronic health information include those listed in Table 9.1. For 2011, meeting the 15 core objectives is required.

TABLE 9.1	Medicare Core Objectives, 2011, Stage 1
Core Objective	**Explanation**
Use of computerized physician order entry (CPOE)	Medication orders made by care providers are done electronically rather than in writing in a paper record
Drug-drug and drug-allergy checks	An alert system exists, based on the medications and allergies entered for a patient, for potential drug to drug, or drug to allergy effects
ePrescribing	Care providers place prescriptions electronically rather than by paper
Recording of patient demographic information	The following demographics must be collected on all records: – Preferred language – Gender – Race – Ethnicity – Date of birth
Recording of a problem list	A listing of all current and active diagnoses for which the patient is being treated must be maintained

Core Objective	Explanation
Recording of a medication list	A listing of all current and active medications being taken by the patient; if the patient is on no medications, the record must reflect that as well
Recording of a medication allergy list	A listing of medication(s) to which the patient is allergic
Recording of vital signs	On each visit, the following must be recorded: — Height — Weight — Blood pressure — Body Mass Index (BMI) — Maintenance of a growth chart (for children 2–20 years, including BMI)
Recording of smoking status	For patients 13 years of age and older, smoking status must be recorded
Clinical decision support functionality	At least one clinical decision support rule must be Implemented. Example: A patient with a fasting blood sugar above 120 mg/dL may trigger an alert for diabetes mellitus, type 2
Reporting clinical quality measures	Each provider must specify the Reporting Numerators, Denominators, and Exclusions for each quality measure reported
Ability to exchange key clinical information between/among care providers	The capability to share among care providers such information as problem list, medication list, allergies, and diagnostic test results
Ability to provide an electronic copy of health information	Patients must be provided with electronic health information upon request; includes test results, problem list, medication list, and medication allergies
Ability to provide clinical summaries	For each office visit, a clinical summary should be provided to each patient
Privacy and security provisions	The software in use meets or exceeds standards set forth by the ONC Meaningful Use standards and includes technical specifications that ensure the privacy and confidentiality of information found in the database

For hospitals, the core objectives include all of those listed in the table *except* ePrescribing.

The 2011 **menu objectives** for Medicare include those listed in Table 9.2. Of the 10 listed, 5 needed to be met.

Menu objectives Additional functions that allow for greater use of EHR functionality.

Menu objectives are additional functions that allow for greater use of EHR functionality, for instance running statistical reports, registries, or lists; checking for drug interactions; and providing patients with educational materials about their illness.

TABLE 9.2	Medicare Menu Objectives, 2011, Stage 1
Menu Objective	**Explanation**
Drug-Formulary Checks	The office or hospital has access to at least one internal or external **drug formulary** (a list of provider-preferred generic and brand-name drugs covered under various insurance plans)
Lab Test Results Documented in the EHR	Results of laboratory tests ordered must be entered into the patient's EHR rather than being filed in paper format; results may be entered electronically through electronic data interchange, scanned into the record via manual scanning methods, or manually keyed in to the record from the paper results
Keeping of Patient Lists	The ability to generate a list of patients with a specific condition in order to satisfy quality improvement initiatives, reduce disparities, for research, or for outreach to patients with that diagnosis
Patient Reminders Generated	The ability to send reminder letters (or electronic reminders) for preventive and/or follow-up care
Timely Electronic Access	The ability to provide patients with their electronic record within four business days of the information being available in electronic form
Patient Education	Access to educational resources using EHR technology and providing the resources to patients, if appropriate
Medication Reconciliation	Documentation of medications the patient is taking as prescribed by other care providers
Summary of Care	The care provider submits a summary of care to physicians or an other healthcare facility that is assessing the patient or taking over the care of the patient
Immunization Registries	The capability to submit electronic data to immunization registries or other immunization information systems in accordance with applicable law
Syndromatic Surveillance	The capability to submit electronic data to public health agencies in accordance with applicable law

See Figure 9.1 for a Clinical Visit Summary given to a patient at the conclusion of the visit, which would satisfy the Summary of Care objective.

Hospitals had to incorporate 5 of the 10 menu objectives listed in Table 9.2 to be eligible for incentive grants in 2011.

Medicaid-eligible providers (physicians, dentists, nurse midwives, nurse practitioners, or physicians' assistants in rural health clinics), with some restrictions based on percentage of patients who are covered by Medicaid, will qualify for the full stimulus amount in the first year if a practice shows they have adopted, upgraded, or implemented EHR.

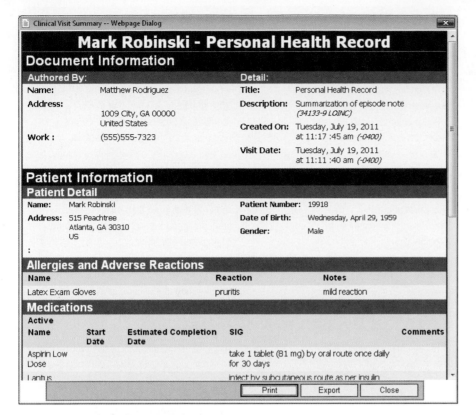

Figure 9.1   Clinical visit summary

Eligible professionals (EPs) and hospitals (including critical access hospitals, or CAHs) must meet Stage 1 meaningful use of electronic health data before progressing to Stage 2. The final rule for Stage 2 was published on September 4, 2012, but the earliest date Stage 2 requirements will be effective is in fiscal year 2014 (October 1, 2013 to September 30, 2014).

Table 9.3 illustrates the EP Core Objectives for Stage 2 as excerpted from the CMS Stage 1 vs. Stage 2 Comparison Table. All 17 are required to meet Stage 2 meaningful use.

The following Stage 1 core objectives were incorporated elsewhere in Stage 2 and therefore there was no need to list as separate objectives:

- Implement drug-drug and drug-allergy interaction checks
- Maintain an up-to-date problem list of current and active diagnoses
- Maintain active medication list
- Maintain active medication allergy list
- Report clinical quality measures (CQMs) to CMS or the states
- Capability to exchange key clinical information (e.g., problem list, medication list, medication allergies, diagnostic test results), among providers of care and patient-authorized entities electronically
- Implement drug-formulary checks
- Provide patients with timely electronic access to their health information (including lab results, problem list, medication lists, medication allergies) within four business days of the information being available to the EP

for your information **fyi**

The full comparison of Stage 1 to Stage 2 for eligible professionals can be found at http://www.cms.gov/Regulations-and-Guidance/Legislation/EHRIncentivePrograms/Downloads/Stage1vsStage2CompTablesforEP.pdf and the full comparison for eligible hospitals and CAHs can be found at http://www.cms.gov/Regulations-and-Guidance/Legislation/EHRIncentivePrograms/Downloads/Stage1vsStage2CompTablesfor Hospitals.pdf

TABLE 9.3   **Eligible Professional (EP) Core Objectives: Stage 2 Meaningful Use**

Stage 2 Explanation	Comparison to Stage 1
CPOE to be used for medication, laboratory, and radiology orders directly entered by any licensed healthcare professional who can enter orders into the medical record per state, local, and professional guidelines	Stage 1 addressed medications only, and at least 30% of unique patients had to have medication(s) ordered using CPOE Stage 2 requires more than 60% of medication, 30% of laboratory, and 30% of radiology orders created by the EP during the EHR reporting period are recorded using CPOE
Generate and transmit permissible prescriptions electronically (eRx)	Stage 1 required that more than 40% of permissible prescriptions written by an EP were transmitted electronically Stage 2 requires more than 50% of all permissible prescriptions written by the EP to be compared to at least one drug formulary and transmitted electronically using Certified EHR Technology
EHR must show evidence that the following demographics be included in the EHR of each patient: • Gender • Preferred language • Race • Ethnicity • Date of birth	Stage 1 required more than 50% of unique patients' EHR show evidence of collection of the demographics collected in structured format Stage 2 requires more than 80% of unique patients have the demographics collected in structured format
The following vital signs must be recorded: • Height • Weight • Blood pressure • Calculate and display BMI • Plot and display growth charts for children 2–20 years, including BMI	Stage 1 required more than 50% of all unique patients age 2 and over to show evidence of blood pressure, height, and weight recorded as structured data Stage 2 requires more than 80% of unique patients have blood pressure (for patients age 3 and over only) and height and weight (for all ages) recorded as structured data
The smoking status of patients 13 years of age and older must be recorded as structured data	Stage 1 required more than 50% of patients 13 years old or older have smoking status recorded as structured data Stage 2 requires more than 80% of patients 13 years old or older have smoking status recorded as structured data
Use clinical decision support to improve performance on high priority health conditions	Stage 1 required the EP to implement one clinical decision support rule Stage 2 requires: 1. Implement 5 clinical decision support interventions related to 4 or more clinical quality measures, if applicable, at a relevant point in patient care for the entire EHR reporting period 2. The EP or hospital EHR has functionality for drug-drug and drug-allergy interaction checks in place for the entire EHR reporting period

Stage 2 Explanation	Comparison to Stage 1
Provide patients the ability to view online, download, and transmit their health information within four business days of the information being available to the provider	Stage 1 required that more than 50% of all patients who request an electronic copy of their health information are provided it within 3 business days Stage 2 requires more than 50% of patients seen during the EHR reporting period are provided timely (available to the patient within 4 business days after the information is available to the provider) online access to their health information And, more than 5% of all patients seen during the EHR reporting period (or their authorized representative) view, download, or transmit to a third party their health information
Provide clinical summaries for patients for each office visit	Stage 1 required that clinical summaries were provided to patients for more than 50% of all office visits within 3 business days Stage 2 requires that clinical summaries are provided to patients within one business day for more than 50% of office visits
Protect electronic health information created or maintained by the Certified EHR Technology through the implementation of appropriate technical capabilities	Stage 1 required EPs to conduct or review a security risk analysis and implement security updates as necessary and correct identified security deficiencies as part of its risk management process Stage 2 requires an EP to conduct or review a security risk analysis, including addressing the encryption/security of data at rest and implement security updates as necessary and correct identified security deficiencies as part of its risk management process
Incorporate clinical lab test results into Certified EHR Technology as structured data	Stage 1 required more than 40% of all clinical lab test results ordered by the EP during the EHR reporting period whose results were either in a positive/negative or numerical format be included in the EHR as structured data Stage 2 requires more than 55% of all clinical lab test results ordered during the EHR reporting period whose results are either in a positive/negative or numerical format be included in the EHR as structured data
Generate lists of patients by specific conditions to use for quality improvement, reduction of disparities, research, or outreach	Stage 1 required an EP to generate at least one report listing patients of the provider with a specific condition The Stage 1 requirement remained the same in Stage 2
Use clinically relevant information to identify patients who should receive reminders for preventive/follow-up care	Stage 1 required more than 20% of all unique patients 65 years or older or 5 years old or younger were sent an appropriate reminder during the EHR reporting period Stage 2 requires the use of EHR technology to identify and provide reminders for preventive/follow-up care for more than 10% of patients with two or more office visits in the last 2 years

continued

Certified Electronic Health Record Technology (CEHRT)
A complement to Meaningful Use Stage 2; certification by the Office of the National Coordinator (ONC) of EHR software which meets certain standards.

Stage 2 Explanation	Comparison to Stage 1
Use certified EHR technology to identify patient-specific education resources and provide those resources to the patient if appropriate	Stage 1 required more than 10% of all patients seen by the EP are provided patient-specific education resources Stage 2 requires patient-specific education resources identified by **Certified Electronic Health Record Technology (CEHRT)** are provided to patients for more than 10% of all unique patients with office visits seen by the EP during the EHR reporting period
The EP who receives a patient from another setting of care or provider of care or believes an encounter is relevant should perform medication reconciliation	Stage 1 required that the EP perform medication reconciliation for more than 50% of transitions of care in which the patient is transitioned into the care of the EP The Stage 1 requirement remained the same in Stage 2.

The EP who transitions a patient to another setting of care or provider of care or refers a patient to another provider of care should provide a summary of care record for each transition of care or referral	Stage 1 required that the EP who transitioned or referred their patient to another setting of care or provider of care provided a summary of care record for more than 50% of transitions of care and referrals
	
	Stage 2 requires:
	  1. the EP who transitions or refers a patient to another setting of care or provider of care to provide a summary of care record for more than 50% of transitions of care and referrals;
	  2. the EP who transitions or refers a patient to another setting of care or provider of care to provide a summary of care record either (a) electronically transmitted to a recipient using CEHRT, or (b) where the recipient receives the summary of care record via exchange facilitated by an organization that is a NwHIN Exchange participant or is validated through an ONC-established governance mechanism to facilitate exchange for 10% of transitions and referrals;
	  3. the EP who transitions or refers a patient to another setting of care or provider of care must either (a) conduct one or more successful electronic exchanges of a summary of care record with a recipient using technology that was designed by a different EHR developer than the sender's, or (b) conduct one or more successful tests with the CMS-designated test EHR during the EHR reporting period

continued

Stage 2 Explanation	Comparison to Stage 1
Capability to submit electronic data to immunization registries or Immunization information systems and actual submission except where prohibited and in accordance with applicable law and practice	Stage 1 required the performance of at least one test of certified EHR technology's capacity to submit electronic data to immunization registries Stage 2 requires successful ongoing submission of electronic immunization data from Certified EHR Technology to an immunization registry or immunization information system for the entire EHR reporting period
Use secure electronic messaging to communicate with patients on relevant health information	This objective did not exist in Stage 1 Stage 2 requires the capability for a secure message to be sent using the electronic messaging function of CEHRT by more than 5% of unique patients seen during the EHR reporting period

Hospitals (including CAHs) have similar core objectives, as listed above for eligible professionals. The requirement to generate and transmit permissible prescriptions electronically is a menu objective rather than a core objective in hospitals. Also, the requirement to receive reminders for preventive/follow-up care does not apply to hospitals. The demographics objectives for hospitals include those listed for eligible professionals and also includes date and preliminary cause of death in the event of mortality in the eligible hospital or critical access hospital. Eligible hospitals are required to submit electronic syndromic surveillance data to public health agencies and actual submission except where prohibited and in accordance with applicable law and practice. Also in core objectives, eligible hospitals must have the electronic means to automatically track medications from order to administration using assistive technologies in conjunction with an electronic medication administration record (eMAR). In the paper system, that was known as the medication administration record (MAR).

Table 9.4 recaps the menu objectives for Stage 2 as they apply to eligible professionals. EPs are required to comply with three of the six menu objectives to qualify for meaningful use.

Eligible hospitals (including CAHs) desiring to meet Stage 2 menu objectives must also meet three of six possible objectives, which include:

- Record whether a patient 65 years old or older has an advance directive
- Record electronic notes in patient records
- Imaging results consisting of the image itself and any explanation or other accompanying information are accessible through CEHRT
- Record patient family health history as structured data
- Generate and transmit permissible discharge prescriptions electronically (eRx)
- Provide structured electronic lab results to ambulatory providers and transmit permissible discharge prescriptions electronically (eRx)

Stage 2 Explanation	Comparison to Stage 1
Capability to submit electronic syndromic surveillance data to public health agencies and actual submission except where prohibited and in accordance with applicable law and practice	Stage 1 required at least one test of certified EHR technology's capacity to provide electronic syndromic surveillance data to public health agencies Stage 2 requires successful ongoing submission of electronic syndromic surveillance data from Certified EHR Technology to a public health agency for the entire EHR reporting period
Record electronic notes in patient records	Stage 1 did not include this menu objective Stage 2 requires an EP to enter at least one electronic progress note created, edited, and signed for more than 30% of unique patients
Imaging results consisting of the image itself and any explanation or other accompanying information are accessible through CEHRT	Stage 1 did not include this menu objective Stage 2 requires more than 10% of all scans and tests whose result is an image ordered by the EP for patients seen during the EHR reporting period are incorporated into or accessible through Certified EHR Technology
Record patient family health history as structured data	Stage 1 did not include this menu objective Stage 2 requires more than 20% of all unique patients seen by the EP during the EHR reporting period have a structured data entry for one or more first-degree relatives or an indication that family health history has been reviewed
Capability to identify and report cancer cases to a state cancer registry, except where prohibited, and in accordance with applicable law and practice	Stage 1 did not include this menu objective Stage 2 requires successful ongoing submission of cancer case information from Certified EHR Technology to a cancer registry for the entire EHR reporting period
Capability to identify and report specific cases to a specialized registry (other than a cancer registry), except where prohibited, and in accordance with applicable law and practice	Stage 1 did not include this menu objective Stage 2 requires successful ongoing submission of specific case information from Certified EHR Technology to a specialized registry for the entire EHR reporting period

As you read through the core and menu objectives, notice how often "structured data" is mentioned. These data elements must be chosen from libraries within the EHR system rather than in free text within the EHR notes.

Not only was more functionality added in Stage 2, but the measure thresholds were increased as well.

In Stage 2, the ability to share patient information with other providers and healthcare facilities is a major emphasis; after all, a prime reason for using electronic health records is the improvement of patient care and outcomes by sharing patient information between and among providers, hospitals, and other healthcare facilities. A 2012 study conducted by CapSite, a healthcare technology research firm, revealed that 71% of hospitals in the United States plan to join an HIE (CapSite, September 2012), and a 2013 study conducted by the same research firm found that 46% of U.S. physician groups plan to join an HIE (CapSite, June 2013).

View a Practice's Dashboard

In the scenario that follows, we are going to view the **dashboard** (a visual comparison of actual performance to required performance) of a particular physician, Dr. John Greenway. Notice that for each core and menu objective, the provider's performance is compared to the required performance. The office manager, health information professional, or other designated individual should keep close watch on the dashboard to ensure compliance with meaningful use requirements. He or she would then take appropriate action should the percentage of participation fall or should it be apparent that a care provider is in jeopardy of not meeting the threshold. Appropriate action would start with education of the care providers to ensure they all understand the importance of compliance with meaningful use and understand that not complying will put the practice in jeopardy for receiving stimulus funding.

Follow these steps to complete the exercise on your own once you have watched the demonstration and tried the steps with helpful prompts in practice mode.

1. Click MU Dashboard.
2. Click View.
3. Click Dashboard when you have finished reviewing the screen.

Take a few moments to review this dashboard. Notice that 15 of the 15 required core objectives were met. This means that this physician used the EHR in his practice to fulfill all of the core objectives. Let's look at one of the core objectives—keeping a medication list. The requirement is that more than 80% of all patients seen by the care provider need to have at least one entry (or documentation that the patient is not currently prescribed any medication) as a documented data item. Dr. Greenway met this requirement 96.9% of the time—he documented the medication(s) each patient is taking (or that they are not taking any) 96.9% of the time. For charting vital signs, Dr. Greenway met that objective in 96.1% of his patients, while the requirement for that objective is that for more than 50% of all patients (age 2 and over), records show documentation of the height, weight, and blood pressure recorded as structured data.

☑ **You have completed Exercise 9.1**

Dashboard A visual comparison of actual performance to required performance.

PrimeSUITE Tip PS

PrimeSUITE refers to the core objectives as core requirements.

9.2 Data and Information Used in Decision Support

According to the Health Information Management and Systems Society, "Clinical Decision Support (CDS) is defined broadly as a clinical system, application, or process that helps health professionals make clinical decisions to enhance patient care. Clinical knowledge of interest could range from simple facts and relationships to best practices for managing patients with specific disease states, new medical knowledge from clinical research, and other types of information" (HIMSS, 2011).

CDS includes reminders and alerts, diagnostic and therapeutic guidance, links to expert resources (CDC, Mayo Clinic, and clinical trials, for example), and results of best practices. Many EHR vendors link directly to one of these expert sites. The trigger that a clinical alert or support should be displayed comes from the data that has already been captured in the patient's record. This is where the data dictionary and structured data that we covered earlier apply. In the exercise that follows, the trigger for the alert flag will be the patient's age (calculated by the system), the CPT codes for colonoscopy, and whether or not one of those codes has been assigned to any visit for a patient over the past 5 years (derived from calculating five years prior to the date of the visit). Decision support, or clinical decision support, is a functionality of an EHR whose value cannot be overestimated. Use of CDS tools improves patient safety, decreases duplication of procedures, reduces the performance of unnecessary testing, and as a result reduces the cost of healthcare, while improving patient outcomes, efficiency of care, and provision of clinically relevant, evidence-based care. Clinical decision support tools are built into most EHRs, including PrimeSUITE.

Recall that meaningful use requires that at least five clinical decision support interventions related to four or more clinical quality measures be implemented during the entire reporting period. An alert that pops up to ask a patient if he or she has had a colonoscopy does not meet the requirement unless that alert appears based on certain information found in the EHR about *that* patient compared to evidence-based criteria that have been embedded in the EHR software. For instance, an alert for colonoscopy would appear when a patient is 50 years of age and older, and/or there is an entry in the patient's problem list showing a history of rectal bleeding, or a family history of colon cancer is documented in the history section of his chart, and no CPT procedure codes for colonoscopy have appeared in the patient's visit history in the past 5 years.

Of course, if a care provider has this functionality available through the practice's EHR software and does not use it, then it is not beneficial to the patient, to the care provider, to the practice, or to satisfy meaningful use standards. There are still care providers who view CDS systems as "cookbook medicine"—those who find it too time consuming or who are annoyed by the pop-up reminders. One incentive to encourage the use of a CDS is pay-for-performance programs available in certain managed-care plans. In other words, if the practice's fiscal position is improved by using CDS technology, then the care providers are more accepting of CDS systems.

EXERCISE **9.2**   Go to http://connect.mcgraw-hill.com to complete this exercise.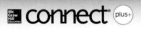

Build a Clinical Alert, Part A

In our next scenario, we are going to build a clinical alert in PrimeSUITE. This is a lengthy process for the alert we have chosen, so this will be done in two parts—Exercise 9.2 (Part A) and Exercise 9.3 (Part B).

We are going to build a clinical alert for all patients who are 50 years of age or older who have not had a colonoscopy in the past 5 years. To do this, we will use CPT codes for colonoscopy, of which there are eight. There are many CPT codes for colonoscopy because the codes differ based on the reason for doing the procedure as well as the extent of the procedure. (You will enter these codes in the order code fields in numerical order during the exercise.) The colonoscopy codes are:

45378	45382
45379	45383
45380	45384
45381	45385

These are called "filters," which will select (or exclude) patients from the database who do (or in this case do not) meet certain criteria. In this particular alert we will **query** the database for patients who are 50 years of age or older and who do not have one of the colonoscopy codes listed above attached to any of their visits for the past 5 years; once the alert is set up, their electronic record will then have the red ribbon icon attached to show that a colonoscopy is needed. To query means that we are going to search or "ask" the database for records that meet (or do not meet) the criteria noted in the filters. In our example we are querying the database for patients who are 50 years of age or older and who *do not* have one of the eight colonoscopy codes listed above attached to any of their visits over the past 5 years.

Follow these steps to complete the exercise on your own once you have watched the demonstration and tried the steps with helpful prompts in practice mode. Use the information provided in the scenario to complete the information.

1. Click Clinical Alerts.
2. Click in the Clinical Alert Description field.
3. Type "Pt due for colonoscopy."
4. Click Clinical Alert Filters.
5. In the "Include patients that meet All of the following criteria:" section, click the Field Name drop-down.
6. Click Scroll.
7. Click Patient: Age.
8. Click the Operator drop-down.
9. Click is greater than or equal to.
10. Click the Match Value field.
11. Type "50".
12. In the "Include the patients that have NOT had or do NOT meet all of the following criteria:" section, click the Field Name drop-down.
13. Click Scroll.
14. Click Order: Order Code.
15. Click the Operator drop-down.
16. Click matches any value in list.
17. Click Create Match List.
18. Type "45378" in the Order: Order Code field.
19. Click Add.
20. Type "45379".
21. Click Add.
22. Type "45380".
23. Click Add.
24. Type "45381".
25. Click Add.
26. Type "45382".
27. Click Add.
28. Type "45383".

(continued)

Query Searching a database for patients who meet certain criteria.

29. Click Add.
30. Type "45384".
31. Click Add.
32. Type "45385".
33. Click Add.
34. Click OK.

✓ **You have completed Exercise 9.2**

   EXERCISE 9.3 PM EHR HIM

Go to http://connect.mcgraw-hill.com to complete this exercise.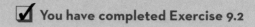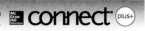

Build a Clinical Alert, Part B

In Part B we will continue adding filters, and you will need the following information:

The URL needed for the Clinical Alert URL is: http://www.cdc.gov/cancer/colorectal/basic_info/screening/guidelines.htm. This practice has chosen to use the Centers for Disease Control and Prevention (CDC) as the organization from which they base their expert advice.

This alert will be named "Colonoscopy Needed" (without the quotes).

Follow these steps to complete the exercise on your own once you have watched the demonstration and tried the steps with helpful prompts in practice mode. Use the information provided in the scenario to complete the information.

1. Click the Field Name drop-down.
2. Click Scroll.
3. Click Order: Order Date.
4. Click the Operator drop-down.
5. Click in the past.
6. Click #.
7. Click 5.
8. Click year(s).
9. Click OK.
10. Click OK.
11. Click Clinical Alert Flag.
12. Click Colonoscopy Needed.
13. Click OK.
14. Click the Clinical Alert URL field.
15. Enter the clinical alert URL.
16. Click Save.
17. Type "Colonoscopy Needed" in the Enter Alert Name field.
18. Click Save.
19. Click Garza, Alfredo Jose.

✓ **You have completed Exercise 9.3**

9.3 Use of Report-Writer for System Reports

PrimeSUITE and other PM/EMR software offer a multitude of standard reports that are set to run at certain times (end of month, for example) or on demand, as the information is needed. Some of the standard reports available in PrimeSUITE are:

- Payment analysis
- Procedure code analysis
- Provider revenue summary
- Patient balances
- Referring provider
- Appointment analysis report

The standard reports listed above and others in the reports library are necessary for efficient running of the office. Not keeping a close watch over revenue, balances, and constantly battling scheduling conflicts is not good business practice. Surprises in any of these areas can negatively impact the bottom line and cause unhappy staff, providers, and patients.

Running standard reports is as easy as a click of a button. It is always important to know the date ranges you want to include and if it is a report you run on a routine basis, you should always use the same parameters. In other words, if you run a report routinely that includes all of the care providers, do not make the mistake of running it next time with just a few of the providers; otherwise, you are not comparing apples to apples! Figure 9.2 shows the A/R Management Report Selection screen. This is the screen from which you would choose to run a Procedure Code Analysis Report, for example. This is a report that shows all procedures, and the volume of each, that are performed in the office. They are listed by CPT code. If you work for a dermatologist, the CPT code 42400, biopsy of salivary gland, should not appear on your Procedure Code Analysis Report, for example. If it does, then someone has made a coding error, since dermatologists typically do not excise salivary glands. If this does happen, then the affected account should be found and the code corrected. Another use for this type of report is cost justification. If one of the providers wants to purchase a newer model of a particular piece of equipment, and it will cost approximately $200,000, the managing partners in the

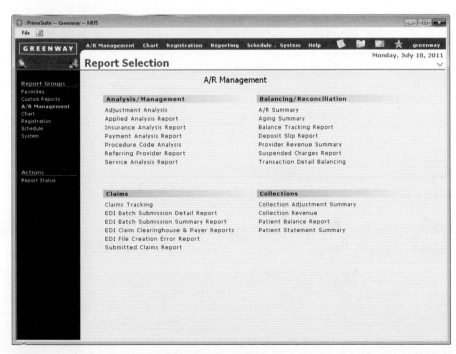

Figure 9.2 Report Selection screen

practice most likely would not approve the purchase if only a small number of procedures it will be used for are performed each year.

Major decisions, especially those that involve funding, should always be analyzed, and standard reports are a good starting point for the analysis. The findings from these reports give information—either baseline findings or changes over time. If information found in these reports is not analyzed, decisions will be made arbitrarily rather than based on facts.

Standard clinical reports are used as well. Examples include a listing of all active patients in the practice with a particular diagnosis, or a listing of all patients with an alert flag of smoker. You may want to run this type of report to answer a survey, where just the number of active smokers is requested. In this case, a **summary report** that includes only the total number (**aggregate**) of active smokers for a specific time period would be included rather than their name, address, etc. Reports that do include patient identifying information and list each case individually are known as **detail reports.**

Figure 9.3 depicts a Provider Revenue Summary report in PrimeSUITE.

Summary report A statistical report that includes totals rather than data for individual patients. Examples include a report of total patients seen during a particular time by gender; a report of the total number of patients seen in the office with E&M code 99214.

Aggregate The sum total; for instance, the sum total of patients between the ages of 60 and 100 in a practice.

Detail report Any report that includes patient indentifying information and lists each case individually rather than as totals.

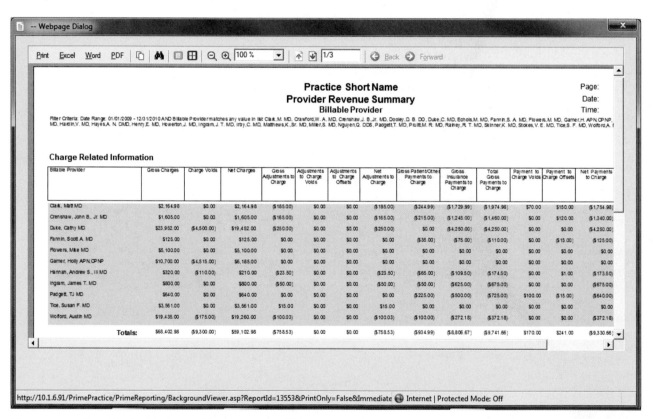

Figure 9.3 Provider Revenue Summary

EXERCISE 9.4 (PM) (EHR) (HIM) Go to http://connect.mcgraw-hill.com to complete this exercise. connect plus+

Run a Report of All Patients between the Ages of 60 and 80 Years Old

The first report we will run is a detail report of all patients in the practice between the ages of 60 and 80 years old. You may need to run this report because one of the managed care plans that your practice participates in has sent you a survey asking for the aggregate (sum total) of your patient population between the ages of 60 and 80, for example.

Follow these steps to complete the exercise on your own once you have watched the demonstration and tried the steps with helpful prompts in practice mode.

1. Click Report Selection. . . F7.
2. Click Custom Reports.
3. Click Patient Demographics.
4. Click Patients in the Practice 60-80.
5. Click Immediate.
6. Click Close.

☑ **You have completed Exercise 9.4**

9.4 Custom Report Writing

Custom reports are built to include **variables**. Variables are the factors that vary from one patient to the next (e.g., age, ZIP code, diagnosis code, procedure code). We select the variables in these reports that we want our patients to meet or not meet. In Exercise 9.4 there was only one variable—the patient's age—which had to be between 60 and 80 years. If we had wanted to narrow our search to patients between 60 and 80 years old who live in ZIP code 21122, then we would have to run a custom report in order to capture only those patients who live in the locality with a ZIP code of 21122 and are between 60 and 80 years old.

We often run these custom reports to answer inquiries from managed care agencies, federal or state departments of health, public health agencies, or accrediting agencies. We may even do so for a newspaper reporter or a student who just wants aggregate data about a particular diagnosis in order to write an article or write a research paper. A cardiology practice may take part in a study with other cardiology practices in town, and will run a custom report to compare their patient demographics to those of the other practices. When statistics concerning one practice or hospital are compared to the statistics of other practices or hospitals, this is referred to as **benchmarking**, which is the comparison of one set of statistics to the overall statistics (using the same variables).

Other custom report examples include:

- The number of patients treated in the practice with a particular diagnosis, for example, congestive heart failure sorted by care provider
- The number of patients treated in your practice who live in a particular ZIP code, are smokers, and have diabetes
- The number of patients in a practice who have Medicaid as their primary source of payment and are between the ages of 30 and 60 years.
- The number of patients who have allergies to penicillin, are Hispanic, and live in ZIP code 12345

Custom report Reports which are designed by the office or hospital rather than coming as part of a software package (standard reports).

Variable In relation to a statistical report, the factors that vary from one patient to the next. Examples include age, zip code, or diagnoses.

Benchmarking Comparison of one set of statistics to the overall statistics when the same variables are used for each.

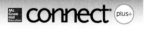
Build a Custom Report of All Patients with a Diagnosis of I50.9 Who Are Female and over the Age of 60, Part A

In this custom report, we are going to choose female patients *over* the age of 60 who have a diagnosis documented in their chart of congestive heart failure (CHF), which is ICD-10-CM code I50.9. (You will need to enter this code in the exercise.) There are other more specific CHF codes; however, for our purposes we will just look at the unspecified CHF cases. This exercise is split into two parts because of its length—Exercise 9.5 (Part A) and Exercise 9.6 (Part B).

Follow these steps to complete the exercise on your own once you have watched the demonstration and tried the steps with helpful prompts in practice mode.

1. Click Report Designer.
2. Click Clinical - Patient Listing.
3. Click Import.
4. Click Chart.
5. Click Clinical - Patient Listing.
6. Click Reports.
7. Click Patients with Diagnosis X (v2).
8. Click Start Import.
9. Click Clinical - Patient Listing.
10. Click Patients with Diagnosis X (v2).
11. Click Filter.
12. Click Current Report Filters.
13. Click Edit Match List.
14. Click Clear.
15. Type "I50.9" in the Diagnosis: Document Diagnosis field.
16. Click Add.
17. Click OK.

✓ **You have completed Exercise 9.5**

 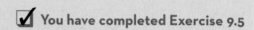
Build a Custom Report of All Patients with a Diagnosis of I50.9 Who Are Female and over the Age of 60, Part B

Now, continue on to Part B of building this custom report. The name of the report is Female patients > 60 with a diagnosis of CHF. The description is "A listing of female patients older than 60 years with a document diagnosis of I50.9" (without the quotes).

1. Click the Field Name drop-down.
2. Click Scroll.

3. Click Patient: Age.

4. Click the Operator drop-down.

5. Click is greater than.

6. Click the Match Value field.

7. Type "60".

8. Click the next Field Name drop-down.

9. Click Scroll.

10. Click Patient: Sex.

11. Click the next Operator drop-down.

12. Click matches any value in list.

13. Click Create Match List.

14. Click Female.

15. Click OK.

16. Click OK.

17. Click Properties.

18. Click the Name: field.

19. Type "Female patients > 60 with a diagnosis of CHF".

20. Click the Description: field.

21. Type "A listing of female patients older than 60 years with a documented diagnosis of I50.9".

22. Click Save.

23. Click Save.

24. Click Close.

✓ **You have completed Exercise 9.6**

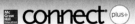 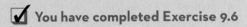

Go to http://connect.mcgraw-hill.com to complete this exercise.

EXERCISE 9.7

Build a Custom Report to Add a Flag to Multiple Records at One Time

In this custom report, we will show how easy it is to add a flag to many records at one time. In our scenario, we will add an exclamation point icon to the charts of all patients 13 years of age and older who do not have a smoking status on the registration page. Collection of this data is a Meaningful Use requirement.

Follow these steps to complete the exercise on your own once you have watched the demonstration and tried the steps with helpful prompts in practice mode.

1. Click Clinical Alerts.

2. Click the Clinical Alert Description field.

3. Type "Smoking Status Documentation".

4. Click Clinical Alert Filters.

5. Click the Field Name drop-down.

(continued)

6. Click Scroll.
7. Click Patient: Age.
8. Click the Operator drop-down.
9. Click is greater than or equal to.
10. Click the Match Value field.
11. Type "13".
12. On the lower half of the screen, click the Field Name drop-down.
13. Click Scroll.
14. Click History: SHx.
15. Click the Operator drop-down.
16. Click is equal to.
17. Click the Match Value field.
18. Type "unknown".
19. Click OK.
20. Click Clinical Alert Flag.
21. Click Smoking Status Unknown.
22. Click OK.
23. Click Save.
24. Type "Smoking Status Documentation".
25. Click Save.

The records of all patients 13 years of age and older who do not have a smoking status indicated will now have the smoking indicator icon attached to their record.

 You have completed Exercise 9.7

9.5 Uses of Indexes

Index A listing—for instance, a Diagnosis Index is a report that is sorted by diagnosis code and includes the total number of patients seen with that disease for a given period of time; a Master Patient Index (MPI) is a listing of all patients who have ever been seen in a hospital or a practice.

An **index** is a listing. Indexes are generally used to find basic information; a disease index is run and is sorted by ICD-10-CM diagnosis code and under each code lists each patient by name and health record number (dates of admission/discharge, attending physician, discharge disposition may also be included). Hospitals run the disease index to get a grasp of the types of patients being seen in the facility. This is also a good way to check for inaccuracies in coding. Another example would be a listing of all patients who are assigned to each care provider individually. In inpatient and outpatient settings, the Disease, Operation (procedure), and Physicians' Indexes are commonly run reports.

Managed care insurance plans often want to see the Physicians' Index or Diagnosis Index to get a profile of the type of patients treated by a practice before considering it for **in-network** status (meaning there is a contract between a managed care plan and the provider to offer services to members of the managed care plan at a prenegotiated rate). Another reason to see this index is to provide proof that a physician has cared for a certain number of patients when he or she is seeking board certification, such as a board-certified urologist, a board-certified obstetrician, etc. Disease indexes are also used for case finding for such entities as the cancer registry,

In-network Care providers who contract with a managed care plan to offer services to members of the managed care plan at a prenegotiated rate.

trauma registry, birth defect registries, and so on. Registries will be discussed in the next section.

A common index in a hospital setting is the Master Patient Index (MPI) (the listing of all patients seen in a hospital), which includes basic identifying information. Running the entire MPI may be done to look for missing information, to look for duplicate patients, or to look for names entered outside the practice's defined specifications (i.e., making sure that names are formatted according to data dictionary specifications).

9.6 Uses of Registries

Whereas an index is a listing of information, a **registry** is also a listing, but it is in chronological order. Examples in a hospital are admission and discharge registries, since they are run on a daily basis and include the names of all patients admitted and all patients discharged on a certain date. Another example is a birth registry—it is kept by date and time of birth, but it is sorted by the name of the newborn and also includes the name of the mother, the time of birth, and the name of the attending physician. And death registries, which are kept by date and time of death, include the patient's name, cause of death, and the signature of the person pronouncing the death, among other data elements.

Registry A listing that is filed in chronological order based on when something occurred. Examples include a birth registry, death registry, or cancer or trauma registry.

Cancer registries are required by law. These are registries of all patients diagnosed or treated for cancer. The registry of these patients is then sent to the state cancer registry where statewide statistics are compiled regarding the incidence of each type of cancer as well as survival rates by type of cancer within that state. The state registry is responsible for reporting to the Centers for Disease Control and Prevention (CDC). Hospitals, physicians' offices, outpatient radiation therapy facilities, and ambulatory care centers may keep and report a registry of cancer patients on a yearly basis. Take the time to look for the most commonly diagnosed cancers in the United States found at http://www.cdc.gov/cancer/dcpc/data/types.htm. Cancer registries will be covered in more detail in another course.

Trauma registries are one of the newer registries, created in the early 1990s; as the name implies, this is a registry of all patients diagnosed or treated with traumatic injuries, and includes fractures, burns, open wounds, and the like. The 2010 Annual Report of the American College of Surgeons' National Trauma Databank can be found at http://www.facs.org/trauma/ntdb/pdf/ntdbannualreport2010.pdf. It is interesting to page through the report; you will see the enormous amount of data reported by hospitals throughout the country. In Table 16 on page 29 of the report, you will see a breakdown by mechanism of injury (fall, burn, suffocation, transport vehicles, motor vehicle accidents, etc.). From there, the data gets more specific, for instance, incidence of falls by age or incidents by region of the country (Table 42, page 60). As you can see, the southern part of the country has the highest incidence of traumatic incidents at 34.76%. The Northeast has the lowest at 17.15%. State and local health and safety officials can then use this information to analyze reasons for a higher–than–average incidence (in the case of the South), or a lower–than–average incidence (as is the case in the Northeast).

Immunization registries are of particular importance to public health. Some private physician offices keep a registry of immunizations by patient; however, not all medical practices keep this registry; it may just be a public health department that does so. Some states require reporting of immunizations by law. For instance, a West Virginia state law requires all providers to report all immunizations they administer to children under age 18 within 2 weeks of administering the immunization.

Other registries include birth defect, diabetes, implant (any material implanted into the body), transplant, and HIV/AIDS registries. The requirements for these vary from state to state as well as by managed care plan or other third-party requirements, and for quality reporting purposes.

Prime SUITE, like most other EHR systems, makes the process of running an index or registry very fast. Its accuracy depends on whether the entry of the data was correct in the first place! This is another reason why accuracy is so important.

The Center for Medicare and Medicaid Services (CMS) receives registry information directly from PrimeSUITE. This information satisfies the **Physician Quality Reporting Initiative (PQRI)** measures. Participation in PQRI is voluntary and is a pay-for-performance incentive program. Participating care providers submit data on any of the 100 designated quality measures, which include diabetes, hypertension, stroke, and glaucoma, just to name a few. The full list is accessible at http://www.cms.gov/PQRS/Downloads/2011_PhysQualRptg_MeasuresList_033111.pdf. PQRS preceded the Accountable Care Organizations discussed in the chapter on financial management.

for your information

CMS is an agency of the Department of Health and Human Services that is responsible for developing and enforcing regulations that govern Medicare-related issues.

PrimeSUITE includes an option to receive an alert at the point of care if the information entered for a patient qualifies for one or more of the PQRI Measure Groups.

There are times when hospitals, medical practices, or other healthcare entities contribute to outside registries. Of note is the **National Practitioner Data Bank (NPDB)**, which came about as part of the Health Care Quality Improvement Act of 1986. This is a database of malpractice payments, revocation of privileges, licensure denial or suspension, denial of medical staff privileges, and the like. Reporting any of these adverse actions to the NPDB is required by law. Hospitals or offices considering granting privileges to or hiring of care providers, state boards of medical examiners or licensing boards, state boards of medicine, or the care providers themselves can query the databank when necessary. Healthcare entities that are considering granting privileges to a physician must query the NPDB during the hiring/privileging process.

Hospitals, care providers, and all other healthcare organizations must report adverse actions related to fraud and abuse to the **Healthcare Integrity and Protection Data Bank (HIPDB)**. Reporting to either the NPDB or the HIPDB can be done on one site rather than attempting to determine which specific data bank to report incidences to. More information about both of these can be found at http://www.npdb-hipdb.com/.

9.7 **The Credentialing Process**

Credentialing does not involve a database, nor does the process necessarily require the use of a database. It is mentioned here because information is captured and maintained for reporting purposes when a healthcare professional files for renewal of a medical license, applies for board certification (and continuing board certification), applies for hospital privileges (or maintaining such privileges), and reports to managed care entities.

Credentialing is the process of ensuring a care provider has the proper qualifications to practice medicine. In other words, if a physician claims to be a cardiac surgeon, then the practice or hospital must verify that he has the educational background and experience (medical residency) necessary to perform surgeries typically carried out by a cardiac surgeon. It must verify that he has shown verification that he is a qualified medical professional in that specialty. Also, it means that he is in compliance with specific policies (called bylaws) for that organization, and that he has purchased sufficient malpractice insurance coverage. Some insurance carriers will not reimburse providers who perform medical care for which they are not qualified. Further, some will not invite physicians to be participating providers in an insurance plan unless they are board-certified. Board certification involves successfully completing a test that is directly related to the specialty area, and which goes above and beyond state medical licensure. Physicians must be Medicare-credentialed in order to submit claims to Medicare for payment. When a medical practice hires a new care provider, information regarding education, experience, state license number, DEA number, NPI number, proof of malpractice insurance, and documentation of any pending or settled claims against the care provider are all on file, usually within the PM software. And, as noted above, the NPDB and HIPDB must also be queried prior to granting privileges, hiring, or including him as a participating provider by insurance carriers.

Credentialing The process of ensuring a care provider has the proper qualifications (education, experience, malpractice coverage) to practice medicine.

APPLYING YOUR SKILLS

In the chapter on reimbursement, we discussed a new outcome-based pay for a performance reimbursement method, the Accountable Care Organization (ACO). How will the concepts learned in this chapter apply to care professionals and hospitals who are part of an ACO?

chapter 9 **summary**

LEARNING OUTCOME	CONCEPTS FOR REVIEW
9.1 Describe the uses of the dashboard in PrimeSUITE to meet meaningful use Standards. Pages 190–199	– List meaningful use Stage 1 and 2 core objectives for providers and hospitals – List meaningful use Stage 1 and 2 menu objectives for providers and hospitals – Use the dashboard in PrimeSUITE to assess performance
9.2 Explain how data and information are used in decision support. Pages 199–202	– Define clinical decision support – Use improves patient safety, decreases duplication, reduces unnecessary testing, reduces cost of healthcare – Use improves patient outcomes, improves efficiency – Some care providers are not accepting of CDS technology
9.3 Set up system reports using PrimeSUITE. Pages 202–205	– Standard reports are commonly used by most medical practices – Standard reports are system built – Administrative as well as clinical standard reports are available – Differentiate between summary and detail reports
9.4 Set up custom reports using PrimeSUITE. Pages 205–208	– Custom reports are run based on specific parameters or variables – Custom reports are used when standard reports do not provide the level of detail necessary
9.5 Illustrate uses for an index. Pages 208–209	– Index is a list – Typically used to find all patients who meet certain criteria – Examples: Master Patient Index, Diagnosis Index, Procedure Index, Physician Index
9.6 Describe uses for a registry. Pages 209–211	– A listing of information in chronological order – Examples: birth registry, cancer registry, trauma registry, PQRI Measures registry – Submissions required by National Practitioner Data Bank (NPDB) – Submissions required by Healthcare Integrity and Protection Data Bank (HIPDB)

9.7 Explain how data gathered in PrimeSUITE is used in the credentialing process. Page 211	– Verification that care provider holds certain credentials
	– Included in the credentials are:
	  • education (undergrad as well as medical school)
	  • residency(ies) dates and institution(s)
	  • pending or settled malpractice cases
	  • proof of purchase of malpractice insurance

chapter **review**

MATCHING QUESTIONS

Match the terms on the left with the definitions on the right.

_____ 1. **[LO 9.1]** dashboard

_____ 2. **[LO 9.5]** in-network

_____ 3. **[LO 9.1]** meaningful use

_____ 4. **[LO 9.6]** CMS

_____ 5. **[LO 9.6]** registry

_____ 6. **[LO 9.5]** index

_____ 7. **[LO 9.2]** decision support

_____ 8. **[LO 9.1]** CEHRT

_____ 9. **[LO 9.3]** summary report

_____ 10. **[LO 9.1]** core objectives

_____ 11. **[LO 9.6]** PQRI measures group

_____ 12. **[LO 9.1]** drug formulary

_____ 13. **[LO 9.7]** credentialing

_____ 14. **[LO 9.1]** Stage 2

_____ 15. **[LO 9.3]** detail report

a. requires more than 80% of unique patients have the demographics collected in structured format

b. consolidated clinical data that removes any patient information in the printout

c. tool built into most EHRs that provides staff with results of research and best practices to enhance patient care

d. software used to capture health information which meets standards set by the Office of the National Coordinator

e. subgroup of common or similar conditions pulled from registry data

f. consolidated clinical data that includes specific, demographic, or patient identifying information in the printout

g. verification process that ensures a care provider is legally authorized through education and experience to practice medicine

h. care provider or practice that contracts with insurance companies to provide care to their subscribers at a reduced rate

i. feature of PrimeSUITE that allows a provider to visually track their fulfillment of core objectives

j. requirements that must be met for a professional to receive Medicare stimulus money to purchase or upgrade an EHR

k. benchmark tasks that demonstrate meaningful use of electronic health information

l. quality reporting measures are reported to this agency

m. a listing of specified information, such as all patients covered by one care provider

n. list of provider-preferred generic and brand-name drugs covered under various insurance plans

o. a chronologically ordered list used in calculating statistics and record-keeping

 Enhance your learning by completing these exercises and more at http://connect.mcgraw-hill.com!

MULTIPLE-CHOICE QUESTIONS

Select the letter that best completes the statement or answers the question:

1. **[LO 9.7]** A credentialing requirement is:
    a. being hired by a professional organization.
    b. gaining additional medical degrees.
    c. having malpractice insurance.
    d. knowing procedures outside of one's specialty.

2. **[LO 9.1]** In the CPOE standard, Stage 1 only addressed:
    a. laboratory orders.
    b. medication orders.
    c. radiology orders.
    d. transfer orders.

3. **[LO 9.2]** When an alert is created, specifying a detail such as "search for patients 30 years or older" is an example of using a/an:
    a. decision.
    b. filter.
    c. outlier.
    d. trend.

4. **[LO 9.5]** A healthcare professional will typically use an index to locate _____ information.
    a. basic
    b. encrypted
    c. statistical
    d. virtual

5. **[LO 9.1]** Healthcare facilities have _____ year[s] after the adoption of an EHR to prove meaningful use.
    a. 1
    b. 2
    c. 3
    d. 4

6. **[LO 9.3]** PrimeSUITE's reports can be used to:
    a. justify the cost of new equipment.
    b. perform quality checks.
    c. track care provider data.
    d. All of these.

7. **[LO 9.2]** Meaningful use requires that a practice not only implement at least one clinical support rule, but also:
    a. reduce alerts.
    b. prove use.
    c. track compliance.
    d. use evidence.

8. **[LO 9.4]** Custom reports have at least _____ variable(s) that is/are not available through a standard report.
   a. one
   b. two
   c. three
   d. four

9. **[LO 9.6]** You are reviewing a report which shows the patients born at Memorial Hospital from January 1, 2012 through December 31, 2012. The report is sorted by date and includes patient name, name of mother, time of birth, and name of obstetrician. Which type of report are you reviewing?
   a. Dashboard
   b. Index
   c. Registry
   d. Summary

10. **[LO 9.3]** PrimeSUITE's Referring Provider report is an example of a _____ report.
   a. clinical
   b. custom
   c. special
   d. standard

11. **[LO 9.5]** Care providers who contract with insurance carriers typically agree to a _____ rate of reimbursement for those services.
   a. higher
   b. lower
   c. special
   d. standard

12. **[LO 9.6]** Currently, participation in the Physician Quality Reporting Initiative is:
   a. discouraged.
   b. mandatory.
   c. standard.
   d. voluntary.

SHORT ANSWER QUESTIONS

1. **[LO 9.1]** What does it mean for a healthcare setting to report clinical quality measures?

2. **[LO 9.5]** Why might a hospital need to periodically run an entire Master Patient Index?

3. **[LO 9.3]** Contrast a summary report and a detail report.

4. **[LO 9.1]** Discuss the consequences (if any) if a provider does not achieve her core menu/objective percentages.

 Enhance your learning by completing these exercises and more at http://**connect.mcgraw-hill.com**!

5. **[LO 9.2]** Explain the purpose of using filters when running a report.

6. **[LO 9.7]** What information is included in a provider's credentials?

7. **[LO 9.4]** If you needed to run a report of all the patients in your practice who were diagnosed with asthma, were African American, and were under the age of 15, what type of report would you be running? Explain your answer.

8. **[LO 9.3]** What is a Procedure Code Analysis Report?

9. **[LO 9.2]** List the benefits of clinical decision support.

10. **[LO 9.6]** List three things a registry might be used for.

11. **[LO 9.1]** Discuss the difference between the Stage 1 and Stage 2 meaningful use requirements for providing patients the ability to view or transmit their health information.

APPLYING YOUR KNOWLEDGE

1. **[LO 9.1]** Why might hospitals be exempt from the ePrescribing core objective?

2. **[LOs 9.1, 9.3, 9.4, 9.5, 9.6]** As a healthcare professional, part of your job is answering patient questions. One day, a patient comes in very concerned. When you ask what's wrong, she says, "I read about this term called Syndromatic Surveillance, and it really worries me! I don't want the government keeping tabs on me when I'm sick!" What would you say to her to alleviate her fears?

3. **[LO 9.6]** Why are registries kept in chronological order?

4. **[LO 9.2]** How could PrimeSUITE assist a practice in the fight against cancer?

5. **[LOs 9.2, 9.3, 9.4, 9.6]** Imagine that the state you reside in recently passed a measure requiring that a report of all immunizations administered at your practice be submitted to the state office of public health. How would you go about fulfilling this request while maintaining patient confidentiality? How could your office use the data to improve patient care?

6. **[LO 9.7]** Dr. Smith is a new provider in your office. Currently, he does not have board certification. Is it imperative that he obtain this credential? Why or why not?

7. **[LO 9.1]** Discuss why the Stage 2 meaningful use requirements are more stringent than those for Stage 1.

10

Looking Ahead—The Future of Health Information and Informatics

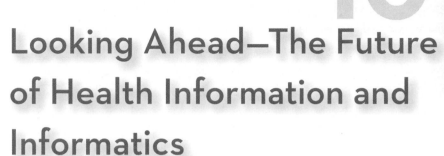

Learning Outcomes

At the end of this chapter, the student should be able to:

10.1 Compare Health Information Management to health informatics.

10.2 Discuss barriers to the adoption of electronic health records.

10.3 Describe three emerging technologies or models that are improving the care of patients through information technology.

10.4 Illustrate three mobile devices that will make the collection and sharing of health information more timely and efficient.

10.5 Describe how virtual private networks (VPNs) and cloud computing are advancing the use of EHRs.

Key Terms

Cloud computing
Decryption
Evidence-based medicine
Health Information Management
Health informatics
Local area network (LAN)
Patient-Centered Medical Home (PCMH)
Patient portal

Personal digital assistant (PDA)
Smartphone
Tablet computer
Telehealth
Telemedicine
Virtual private network (VPN)
Wide area network (WAN)
Wi-Fi

What You Need to Know and Why You Need to Know It

Technology is part of the healthcare world, whether you are a clinician or hold an administrative role. It was mentioned earlier that healthcare as a whole has been reluctant to embrace the digital age. That is not so when it comes to computerization of medical technology such as diagnostic and treatment procedures, however. Newer technologies are less invasive, require shorter recovery time, require less (or no) hospitalization, and are safer overall than previous procedures. Though we are far ahead in the use of medical technology for diagnostic and treatment purposes, we lag far behind other industries where computerization of *information* is concerned. In this final chapter we will explore some of the more common methods to access electronic records and will discuss newer (at least to healthcare) technologies that are in limited use, but gaining in momentum. As a healthcare professional, it is imperative that you stay abreast of emerging technologies. Even if you do not initially hold a position where you are involved in selection or implementation, you will definitely *use* technology in all of the positions you will hold throughout your career. And, since you have chosen healthcare as a profession, you have also chosen to become a lifelong learner—do not get too comfortable with how something is done today, as it will surely change in the blink of an eye!

Health Information Management A profession that encompasses services in planning, collecting, aggregating, analyzing, and disseminating individual patient and aggregate clinical data (in paper or electronic format).

10.1 Health Information versus Health Informatics

The American Health Information Management Association (AHIMA) Committee on Professional Development states the vision of **Health Information Management** as:

Health information management is the body of knowledge and practice that ensures the availability of health information to facilitate real-time healthcare delivery and critical health related decision-making for multiple purposes across diverse organizations, settings, and disciplines. (AHIMA)

The health information management professional's role in the provision of quality healthcare is to ensure the availability of complete, accurate, timely health information and the collection of data necessary to make healthcare decisions, whether related to a particular patient or the population as a whole.

Where health information management pertains to both paper and automated capture, retrieval, storage, and use of health information, **health informatics** is the management of automated health information in particular. Health information professionals whose work is geared more toward informatics focus on structure of data, interoperability, design of input and output tools, security controls, development of data dictionaries, workflow configuration in an automated environment, and classification systems and terminologies used in a computerized healthcare system.

In short, health informatics is the technological side of managing health information—the design, development, structure, implementation, integration, and management of the technical aspects of electronic record-keeping. HIM professionals have historically ensured accurate, complete, readily available health information for use by care providers, administrators, researchers, public health officials, and insurers. Their focus is the content of the record, as

Health informatics The management of automated health information; the technological side of managing health information—the design, development, structure, implementation, integration, and management of the technical aspects of electronic (automated) health record-keeping.

well as integration of systems, and the ability to share electronic information. They manage health information regardless of the media on which it is kept. The HIM professional and the IT professional within a facility have always worked very closely together to ensure that standards are met and information is available, yet private and secure. In health informatics there is a melding of the two disciplines—IT expertise with HIM expertise, and this may be one and the same person in many cases.

For years, Health Information Management programs at all levels have included coursework in information-related software as well as electronic record-keeping in their curriculums. Colleges and universities now include in-depth coverage of the electronic health record in their medical assisting, medical billing and coding, medical office management, and healthcare administration programs.

In a physician's office, as well as other outpatient facilities, there may not be degreed health information professionals per se, but there is an individual within the facility who should know the requirements of a legal electronic health record, documentation requirements, and privacy and security regulations. Software service providers also have support staff who are active participants in the installation and training of a PM or EHR system. They advise practices on using the software efficiently and effectively to ensure security and privacy of the information collected, and to ensure that documentation requirements are being met. If the practice does not have a full- or part-time technology position staffed, the office will contract with either a consultant or the software service provider's team.

Check Your Understanding

1. Between health information management and health informatics, which discipline is most closely associated with IT and which with information itself?
2. How could a practice management software service provider assist an office or facility that does not have a degreed HIM professional on staff?

10.2 Barriers to Adopting an Electronic Health Record

We started our journey through the electronic health record system by pointing out that there was a great deal of resistance to giving up paper records; this subject is worth revisiting before discussing even newer technologies that, though in use, are still the exception rather than the rule.

For years, care providers have been documenting the health records of patients by writing orders, progress notes, and chart notes, or by dictating History & Physicals (H&Ps), discharge summaries, operative reports, consultation reports, and correspondence. They are used to it; it is the way it has always been done. Providers know that if a laboratory test result is needed during a patient's visit, they need only flip to the laboratory tab of the patient's folder and it will be there (well, hopefully it will be). Paper and folders are inexpensive, relatively speaking. If it was impossible to complete the record at the time the patient was seen, the record would be sent to the health information department for completion at a later time, or if a patient was seen in the office and the provider needed to dictate the chart note, it was easy enough to take the record back to her private office to complete later. Many care providers see this paper system as being easier, and it may seem more efficient; however, the quality of documentation that is written or dictated days (or even weeks) after the care was provided is questionable, paper records are often illegible if they are handwritten, and if dictation and transcription are used there is lag time before the typed report is filed in the record. Additionally, from a security perspective, a paper record can easily be picked up by someone with no need to have or see it and, if a paper record gets lost, hours of staff time can be spent searching for it.

Implementing and maintaining an electronic record is expensive, that is true. But, the argument for patient safety, higher quality medical care, point of care documentation, faster results of diagnostic tests, and ability to both share information with other care providers when necessary and access a patient's chart from any location, not to mention access clinical decision support, should outweigh the "high cost" argument. Financial incentives through HITECH have been the driving force for many practices that have now decided to convert to a paperless (or almost paperless) system. Beginning in 2011, hospitals and physicians' practices that adopted and proved meaningful use of EHRs started receiving incentive payments. Those who hold out, thinking that the EHR will go away, will be penalized for not doing so by 2015.

Converting from a paper system to an electronic system can be a lengthy, sometimes chaotic process. It can no doubt cause loss of productivity for both staff and care providers. When procedures within the office that are seemingly efficient in the manual form are computerized, there are bound to be errors in conversion, steps that are overlooked, and general frustration for all involved. However, proper planning, heeding the advice of the software service provider's installation team, and accepting the fact that the conversion, training of staff, and use of the system will all take longer than expected should make the whole process more tolerable. It does take time and effort to convert to and use an electronic system, but the same can be said for any change in procedure in any profession.

Check Your Understanding

1. Healthcare facilities that do not adopt electronic record technology will begin facing penalties in the year _____.
2. Up to this point, what has been the driving force behind facilities adopting EHRs?

Patient Portals

Patients today are more interested and involved in their own health-care. They are taking a more active role, and thanks to the Internet, arrive at their appointments knowing what their care provider may ask and why, and what treatment options exist. They have a list of questions ready for the care provider, which allows for a more productive visit. **Patient portals** are another means to better, more meaningful communication with a care provider, and are a functionality of EHRs that satisfy meaningful use regulation. A patient portal is a method of accessing portions of one's own office health record. These portals are secure and can only be accessed with a user ID and password. In PrimeSUITE the portal is known as PrimePATIENT. Through it, the patient can:

Patient portals A method of accessing portions of one's own health information from the care provider's or hospital's electronic health record.

- Email the practice with questions or concerns regarding care
- Make appointments
- Complete history forms and authorizations online
- Request prescription refills
- Get results of tests

More information is available about PrimePATIENT at http://www.greenwaymedical.com/wp-content/uploads/2013/03/Greenway_PrimePATIENT.pdf

By using the secure portal, the office staff spends less time answering phone calls, calling patients back (or playing phone-tag), and entering data in the record; patients are more satisfied because their questions are answered more promptly, and they feel that they are more in control of their care. You may not realize that your care provider offers patient portals; if the office is automated, and an EHR is in use, ask about it!

Many insurance plans have similar options for their subscribers, including communicating with a nurse or care provider to answer questions about symptoms, treatment options, coverage, and the like. Take a few moments to look at the website for your health insurance—does it have patient portal capability?

Personal Health Records (PHRs)

The personal health record (PHR) is maintained and kept with the patient, and is a record of his or her past and current health information including drug allergies or reactions, immunization dates, past and present medical conditions, surgical procedures, family history, list of current medications, and insurance information. The PHR is not a legal record because it is just that—personal; there are no safeguards to ensure it is complete, it is not written by a medical professional, much of it may have been compiled from memory, and it does not meet the legal requirement of "being compiled during the normal course of business." However, it is a valuable tool when a patient seeks medical care, particularly if emergency care is required or if there has been a change in care providers. The PHR is only as good as the information in it—*all* of the information should be up-to-date and accurate. It also needs to be available when needed. If patients expect their PHR to be a useful document, family members should know where the PHR is kept, and it should be taken to office visits or to the emergency department when such visits occur. Patients may keep the PHR in a paper format or online (or may print it from the online portal). There are many options for doing so, including the PHR websites of many major insurance carriers and the AHIMA PHR website found at http://www.myphr.com/. Other free online PHRs include https://www.healthvault.com/ and Telemedical.com, just to name a few. The AHIMA website provides a full list. PHRs are not a new technology, but their use is becoming more prevalent.

Telemedicine

Telehealth Associated with preventive care, telehealth is the use of audiovisual equipment through which the patient and the care provider or healthcare professional can connect remotely.

Telemedicine The use of technology to remotely monitor a patient's vital signs and perform tests such as an EKG, or forward radiologic images.

Telehealth and **Telemedicine** are of great benefit to patients who do not have the means to travel to a doctor's appointment or who live in remote, medically underserved areas. Telehealth is more associated with preventive care. With the use of audiovisual equipment, the patient and the care provider or healthcare professional can connect through teleconferencing technology, allowing each to see and hear the other. Through telemedicine technology, a patient's blood pressure, heart rate, respiratory rate, EKG tracing, or medical imaging can be monitored remotely. Should the care provider find something that is not within normal limits, the patient would then need to seek on-site care (or emergency care dispatched). The imaging technology of Picture Archiving and Communications Systems (PACS), whereby radiologic images are viewed remotely, is one of the original uses of telemedicine.

Through the use of telemedicine there is cost savings to both the insurance carrier and the patient; patients who would not otherwise be able to make visits to their care providers now have better access to care, which in turn improves outcomes and in general is more convenient for patients, particularly those who do not have transportation or who live a distance away from their care provider.

Take time to investigate telemedicine further by reading the Institute of Medicine report *Telemedicine: A Guide to Assessing Telecommunications for Health Care* found at http://www.nap.edu/open book.php?record_id=5296&page=137.

Many Veterans Affairs Medical Centers provide telemedicine or telehealth to assist in the care of veterans. The Department of Veterans Affairs telehealth website can be found at http://www.telehealth .va.gov/index.asp.

Patient-Centered Medical Homes (PCMH)

Patient-Centered Medical Home (PCMH) A model that was developed to care for patients with chronic conditions by the American Academy of Family Practitioners, to encourage and facilitate a patient's (and family's) involvement in his or her own care.

Patient-Centered Medical Home (PCMH) is a model that was developed to care for patients with chronic conditions by the American Academy of Family Practitioners. The premise encourages and facilitates the patient's (and family's) involvement in his or her own care. It is mentioned in this chapter because it ties in with the concept of a patient-centric health model. The PCMH also encourages a primary care physician approach to patient care, which is also the premise of many managed care insurance plans that require a "gatekeeper" to reduce redundancy and overutilization of testing and services, and provide overall more efficient and effective healthcare.

The use of health information technology is paramount to the PCMH model because the use of quality measures, including registries, referral tracking, results tracking, medication alerts, performance measures, use of evidence-based medicine, an updated problem list and current medication list, are all part of the PCMH model—all of the elements that are requirements of meaningful use as well.

Evidence-Based Medicine

Meaningful use of data requires decision support capability as part of the EHR. This is also known as **evidence-based medicine** because the diagnostic and treatment protocols are based on proven research and best practices from physicians' experiences with patients and their response to treatment. Through evidence-based medicine, a patient's plan of care is based on current, proven practice. Alerts or reminders automatically appear in a patient's chart based on data captured about that patient. An example would be a female patient who has just passed her fortieth birthday. The FDA Office of Women's Health recommends a screening mammogram be performed at the age of 40 and every 1 to 2 years thereafter (FDA). Current EHR software makes it possible for physicians to be alerted to the latest diagnostic and treatment recommendations and modalities, which in turn improves efficiency, patient care, and clinical outcomes. It is clear why the use of evidence-based medicine is part of the meaningful use regulations.

Evidence-based medicine Diagnostic and treatment protocols that are based on proven research and documented best practices.

Check Your Understanding

1. What are the diagnostic and treatment protocols of evidence-based medicine based on?
2. Is a patient's personal health record a legal document? Explain your answer.
3. If a patient is being monitored using telemedicine, what would happen if an abnormal reading was found?
4. How might a PCMH make a patient's experience more positive?

10.4 Making the World of Health Informatics User-Friendly and Convenient

In order for an electronic health record system to be successful, the care providers need to be satisfied with the product. They typically look for portability, mobility, flexibility, and convenience—all qualities of products used in the 21st century and all requirements of the healthcare team if they are to work efficiently.

Portable devices allow for flexibility and portability. They are advantageous because they are convenient (the provider does not have to find a computer to use); are cost effective (the provider can use an inexpensive device and there is no need to rework because notes and procedure codes are entered at the point of care, which reduces the number of lost or missing charges); improve accuracy (the care provider does not have to jot down notes that would need to be transferred into the record at a later time); and, in general, create overall satisfaction since the information needed to care for patients is available at any time from any location. The connection to the EHR may be through a **local area network (LAN)** or **wide area network (WAN)**. LANs link computers and related devices that are physically close to one another such as within a building; WANs connect computer networks together that are not physically close (see Figure 10.1). And, of course, access can be via the Internet. The types of portable devices used include **personal digital assistants (PDAs)**; they are small enough to fit in one's hand, yet allow access to LANs, WANs, and the Internet and may also have phone capability. **Smartphones** are telephones that also allow Internet browsing as well as audio, video, and camera functionality; and **tablet computers** are larger than PDAs or Smartphones, yet smaller than a laptop computer—they too provide access to LANs, WANs, and the Internet. Though PDAs and tablets are used, smartphones have much of the same functionality, and carrying one device rather than two or more may be favored by many users.

Local area network (LAN) Links computers and related devices that are physically close to one another such as within a building.

Wide area network (WAN) Connects computer networks together that are not physically close.

Personal digital assistant (PDA) A mobile device that is small enough to fit in one's hand, yet allows access to local area networks (LANs), wide area networks (WANs), and the Internet; may also have telephone capability.

Smartphone Telephones that allow Internet browsing, audio, video, and camera functionality.

Tablet computer Computers that are larger than PDAs or smartphones, yet smaller than a laptop computer; allow access to local area networks (LANs), wide area networks (WANs), and the Internet.

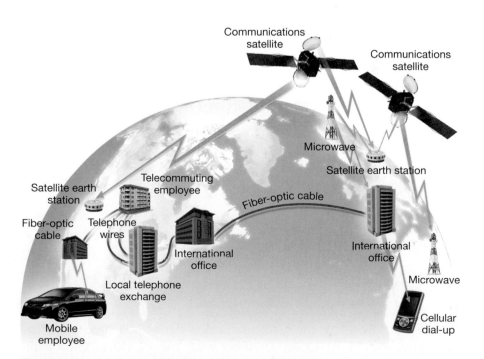

Figure 10.1   Depiction of a wide area network (WAN)

1. What are smartphones?
2. Describe three instances when access to an EHR on a mobile device would improve a care provider's efficiency or save time.

10.5 Virtual Private Networks—Advancing the Use of EHRs Remotely Yet Securely

To use mobile functionality, a wireless connection is necessary. This is known as **Wi-Fi**, which sends data via high radio frequency. Of course, utilizing mobile technology does require high levels of security. The use of a **virtual private network (VPN)** is one way to ensure the security of the information flowing between the mobile device and the EHR. A VPN uses the Internet as its path, but built into the VPN is software that encrypts (codes) the data being sent and interprets the data being received **(decryption)**. A VPN also verifies the identity of the user through his or her user ID and password, and only allows users access who have been granted permission to sign on to the network. A VPN is also used for employees who telecommute (work from home) and are dialing into the facility's computer system from their home computer or laptop. The use of a VPN provides for the secure environment to allow sharing of health information with users at remote locations. In addition to the VPN, a firewall is another security method (see Figure 10.2).

Wi-Fi Data exchange via high radio frequency.

Virtual private network (VPN) Software that encrypts (codes) the data being sent as well as interprets the data being received.

Decryption Interprets data being received in encrypted (scrambled) form.

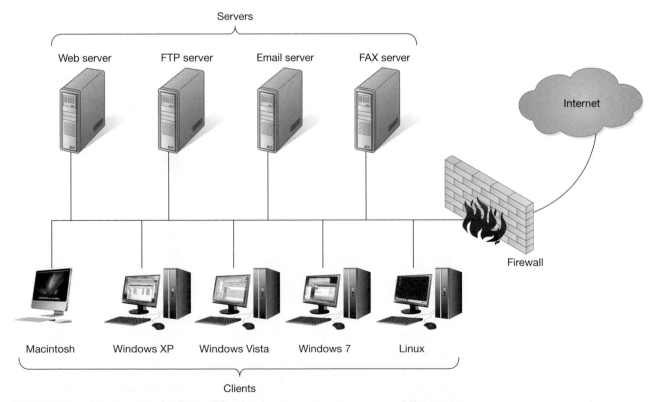

Figure 10.2   Placement of a firewall between computers, servers, and the Internet

Firewalls prevent unauthorized access into or out of the network through use of both hardware and software devices that filter activity over the network. Based on predefined rules, the firewall acts as a barrier—activity that passes the rules may continue in or out of the network; activity that does not pass the rules may not.

Security measures such as those noted above are necessary to exchange information on a small scale within or among related medical practices or hospitals, as well as between the Health Information Exchanges (HIEs) that are the vision of the Office of the National Coordinator (ONC).

Cloud Computing

Cloud computing The housing of data in a cloud environment, which is a commercially maintained site on the Internet.

In recent years, there has been a rise in systems that do not reside on a physical server that is owned, maintained, and operated by a hospital or medical practice. Rather, the data is housed in a cloud environment, which is a commercially maintained site on the Internet. In **cloud computing**, the cloud service provider is in control, rather than an Internet service provider. There is unlimited processing and storage capacity in a cloud environment. In a private cloud configuration, the storage space is solely for a single organization. It is scalable; the facility or office uses as much or as little storage space as needed, and thus pays for as much or as little as needed (Knorr). If there should be an equipment failure or damage of some sort, the database is not affected. Think of email services such as GMail® (Google) or Yahoo® or document storage services such as Google Docs, Evernote, or Dropbox; if a person loses his or her laptop or if a desktop computer is destroyed in a fire, emails and documents are not lost since the data is stored on Google's or Yahoo's server. The security of the data is ensured in cases such as these. There is no hardware cost (for servers) associated with data stored in the cloud, and the system is mobile, allowing care providers to utilize mobile devices to access records and receive important, time-sensitive notifications at any time.

The healthcare community may be slow to embrace cloud computing because there are still concerns about privacy, security, and a sense of loss of control by the facility or practice. There are quality concerns as well, which lead to thoughts of "who is minding the store." In addition, since cloud computing was virtually nonexistent when HIPAA originated, compliance questions remain (Cloud Computing Techie).

Pulling It All Together

The intent of this worktext has been to introduce students to the automation of health information with emphasis on those of you who have chosen to study Health Information Management, medical assisting, and medical billing and coding. Having chosen one of these professions, you will work closely with automated systems; many of you will be lucky enough to be involved in choosing a system from the very first steps, others will use the systems on a daily basis, and yet others will climb the ladder into implementation, training, and developing computer programs and systems that will enhance the automated exchange of information.

Medicine and healthcare are not static; changes occur daily. Those changes need to be communicated, implemented, and tracked to determine their impact on patient care. As a healthcare professional, you will not be observing from the sidelines; instead, you will be an active participant in improving quality healthcare through the availability of complete, accurate, and secure health information.

Check Your Understanding

1. How does a VPN verify a user's identity?
2. What role does encryption play in using VPNs?
3. Explain what is meant by the *scalability* of cloud computing.

APPLYING YOUR SKILLS

As a healthcare consumer, name 5 to 10 experiences you have personally had or have witnessed where any aspect of healthcare was electronic rather than manual.

chapter 10 **summary**

LEARNING OUTCOME	CONCEPTS FOR REVIEW
10.1 Compare Health Information Management to health informatics. Pages 218–219	– Define Health Information Management – Define health informatics – Role of HIM professional in each
10.2 Discuss barriers to the adoption of electronic health records. Pages 219–220	– Written records and dictation have been the norm – Paper and dictation are fairly inexpensive – Lengthy process to convert to electronic records – Training time is extensive – Loss of productivity – High frustration level
10.3 Describe three emerging technologies or models that are improving the care of patients through information technology. Pages 221–223	– Patient portals—means of communication between patient and medical practice – Personal health record—patient keeps own record of history, immunizations, allergies, surgeries, past conditions, and family history – Telemedicine—allows patient to be "seen" without leaving the home – Patient-Centered Medical Home (PCMH)—primary care physician is leader of a team that cares for the patient; patient is more involved than in traditional approach; use of technology inherent in the process – Evidence-based medicine—technology "researches" best practices and decision support to assure that patient is receiving most up-to-date diagnostic and treatment options
10.4 Illustrate three mobile devices that will make the collection and sharing of health information more timely and efficient. Pages 223–225	– Use of EHR can be more convenient by making it mobile; use of personal digital assistants (PDAs), smartphones, and tablet computers allow for portability – Wireless (Wi-Fi) connections are required to use portable devices

10.5 Describe how virtual private networks (VPNs) cloud computing are advancing the use of EHRs. Pages 225–227	– Though portability is necessary, so is security
	– Virtual private networks encrypt and interpret information that is sent and received via wireless networks
	– Use of firewalls as a security device
	– Cloud computing: commercially maintained storage site on the Internet
	  • Unlimited storage and processing capability
	  • Scalable (pay for as much or as little storage as used)
	  • Private cloud is for use by one organization
	  • Database not affected by equipment failure, power outages, or physical damage
	  • Security concerns and loss of facility control are concerns

chapter review

MATCHING QUESTIONS

Match the terms on the left with the definitions on the right.

_____ 1. **[LO 10.5]** decryption

_____ 2. **[LO 10.1]** Health Information Management

_____ 3. **[LO 10.3]** patient portal

_____ 4. **[LO 10.3]** evidence-based medicine

_____ 5. **[LO 10.3]** personal health record

_____ 6. **[LO 10.3]** telemedicine

_____ 7. **[LO 10.5]** VPN

_____ 8. **[LO 10.4]** Wi-Fi

_____ 9. **[LO 10.1]** health informatics

_____ 10. **[LO 10.5]** cloud computing

_____ 11. **[LO 10.4]** wide area network (WAN)

_____ 12. **[LO 10.3]** Picture Archiving and Communications Systems

a. clinical decision support based on research and best practices

b. one of the first telemedicine uses

c. link computers within the same company that are not located in close proximity

d. uncoding coded data to make it readable

e. high radio frequency wireless connection used by smartphones, PDAs, and other electronic devices

f. unlimited storage and processing capability

g. secure method of accessing individual health records and information through an EHR

h. secure Internet environment that encrypts data and allows remote access to health information

i. medical history maintained and kept by an individual patient

j. the monitoring or exchange of health information remotely

k. improving healthcare through working with data and ensuring that the best information is available for decision making

l. science that deals with health information, its structure, acquisition, and uses

MULTIPLE–CHOICE QUESTIONS

Select the letter that best completes the statement or answers the question:

1. **[LO 10.1]** Health informatics is basically the _____ part of managing health information.
   a. critical
   b. structural
   c. technological
   d. usable

 Enhance your learning by completing these exercises and more at http://**connect.mcgraw-hill.com**!

2. **[LO 10.4]** One benefit of accessing the EHR through mobile devices is a reduction in:
   a. cost.
   b. errors.
   c. satisfaction.
   d. both cost and errors.

3. **[LO 10.2]** Incentives are being offered to EHR adopters through _____ legislation.
   a. CCHIP
   b. HIPAA
   c. HITECH
   d. ONC

4. **[LO 10.3]** Care providers use _____ as a way to support their decisions and diagnoses.
   a. current medical trends
   b. evidence-based medicine
   c. meaningful use
   d. patient-centric care

5. **[LO 10.1]** Which of the following stakeholders are served by the Health Information Management profession?
   a. Patient care organizations
   b. Payers
   c. Research agencies
   d. All of these

6. **[LO 10.2]** According to the text, which of the following is a way to make the transition to EHRs easier?
   a. Allowing staff members to be frustrated and anxious about the change
   b. Following the advice and suggestions of the EHR service provider's installation team
   c. Providing immediate training so that ramp-up is quicker
   d. Saving money for EHR costs by eliminating staff

7. **[LO 10.3]** A PCMH focuses on _____ communication between patients and providers.
   a. decreased
   b. increased
   c. random
   d. structured

8. **[LO 10.1]** Of the following, which is an accurate statement?
   a. Eligible providers taking advantage of HITECH funds must have a credentialed or degreed health information professional on staff.
   b. In the event the eligible provider is unable to hire a credentialed or degreed health information professional on staff, he or she must use the services of a paid health information consultant.

c. Though not required, the expertise of a health information professional on staff, as a consultant or as offered by the service provider, is helpful.

d. The EHR software is already written to handle any health information–related issues; therefore, no additional input or services from a health information professional are necessary.

9. **[LO 10.4]** There must be a(n) _____ available in order for providers to use portable devices to access health information.
   a. computer terminal
   b. Internet hookup
   c. wireless connection
   d. wireless router

10. **[LO 10.3]** Who is responsible for maintaining a personal health record?
    a. HIM professional
    b. Patient
    c. Provider
    d. Medical staff

11. **[LO 10.2]** Penalties for facilities not adopting electronic health records will begin in _____.
    a. 2014
    b. 2015
    c. 2016
    d. 2017

12. **[LO 10.3]** Videoconferencing and remote vital sign monitoring are part of:
    a. patient-centric care.
    b. a patient portal.
    c. telemedicine.
    d. virtual health networks.

13. **[LO 10.5]** What does VPN stand for?
    a. Verifying Provider Network
    b. Verified Protocol Network
    c. Virtual Private Network
    d. Virtual Provider Network

14. **[LO 10.3]** Recent advances in healthcare rely increasingly on:
    a. change.
    b. precedent.
    c. technology.
    d. tradition.

Enhance your learning by completing these exercises and more at http://connect.mcgraw-hill.com!

SHORT ANSWER QUESTIONS

1. **[LO 10.1]** Explain the difference between health information and health informatics.

2. **[LO 10.3]** What are some advantages to a healthcare facility using the patient portal function?

3. **[LO 10.4]** What is meant by mobile device?

4. **[LO 10.5]** How does a VPN ensure data integrity and security?

5. **[LO 10.2]** Explain why many care providers view a paper-based system as easier than an electronic one.

6. **[LO 10.1]** What does an HIM professional do?

7. **[LO 10.2]** How can healthcare facilities make the adoption of EHRs as easy and painless as possible?

8. **[LO 10.4]** How do mobile applications reduce costs and errors?

9. **[LO 10.3]** Describe a Patient-Centered Medical Home (PCMH).

10. **[LO 10.5]** Explain what Wi-Fi is.

APPLYING YOUR KNOWLEDGE

1. **[LO 10.3]** After reading about the patient portal in your text, are there any disadvantages to using a system like PrimePATIENT? Justify your answer.

2. **[LO 10.2]** What is your opinion on the use of incentives to encourage healthcare facilities to adopt EHRs? Explain your answer.

3. **[LOs 10.4, 10.5]** You are a healthcare professional who has the ability to work from home on certain days. How would you go about accessing the work you need to do on a given day from your home?

4. **[LOs 10.1, 10.2, 10.3, 10.4, 10.5]** Your healthcare office is beginning to discuss adopting an EHR system, mobile accessibility, and other new capabilities such as telemedicine. Your supervisor has asked you to come up with some brief talking points for the staff discussing the new technologies, their advantages, and ways in which each staff member will be impacted by the new systems. Come up with a short outline for your presentation.

5. **[LO 10.5]** Justify why a physician's practice or hospital may choose cloud computing over onsite servers. Are there any drawbacks to using a cloud environment over traditional servers? Explain.

Greensburg Medical Center
REGISTRATION FORM
(Please Print)

Today's date: September 4, 2013	Care Provider: Dr. Rodriguez

PATIENT INFORMATION

Patient's last name:	First:	Middle:	❑ Mr. ❑ Miss	Marital status (circle one)
Lawrence	Jeannie	Elaine	❑ Ms. ☒ Mrs.	Single / (Mar) / Div / Sep / Wid

Is this your legal name?	If not, what is your legal name?	(Former name):	Birth date:	Age:	Sex:
☒ Yes ❑ No			07/02/1966	47	❑ M ☒ F

Street address:	Social Security no.:	Home phone no.:
4848 Castle Drive		770-555-8916

P. O. Box:	City:	State:	ZIP Code:
	Carrollton	GA	30117

Occupation:	Employer:	Employer phone no.:
Research and Design	Greenway Medical Tech	770-555-6666

Email address: jelawrence@greenwaymedical.com	Cell phone: 770-555-1419	

Race: white	Ethnicity: American	Primary language: English	Religion: Protestant

Other family members seen here: None	Preferred Communication: phone

INSURANCE INFORMATION
(Presentation of Insurance Card is required at time of each visit)

Person responsible for bill:	Birth date:	Address (if different):	Home phone no.:
self	07 /02/1966		same

Is this person a patient here?	☒ Yes ❑ No

Occupation:	Employer:	Employer address:	Employer phone no.:
Same as above	Same as above	121 Greenway Blvd	770-555-6666

Is this patient covered by insurance?	☒ Yes ❑ No

Please indicate primary insurance	☒ McGraw-Hill Healthmark Insurance	❑ BlueCross/Shield	❑ [Insurance]	❑ [Insurance]	❑ [Insurance]
☒ [Insurance]	❑ Workers' Compensation	❑ Medicare	❑ Medicaid (Please provide card)	❑ Other	

Subscriber's name:	Subscriber's S.S. no.:	Birth date:	Group no.:	Policy no.:	Co-payment:
Jeannie E. Lawrence		07/02/1966	6700	GAR5679191	$ 20.00

Patient's relationship to subscriber:	☒ Self	❑ Spouse	❑ Child	❑ Other	Effective Date: 07/01/2010

Name of secondary insurance (if applicable):	Subscriber's name:	Group no.:	Policy no.:
None			

Patient's relationship to subscriber:	❑ Self	❑ Spouse	❑ Child	❑ Other

IN CASE OF EMERGENCY

Name of local friend or relative (not living at same address):	Relationship to patient:	Home phone no.:	Work phone no.:
Gloria Heavner	Mother	770-555-7153	

The above information is true to the best of my knowledge. I authorize my insurance benefits be paid directly to the physician. I understand that I am financially responsible for any balance. I also authorize [Name of Practice] or insurance company to release any information required to process my claims.

Jeannie E. Lawrence	September 4, 2013
Patient/Guardian signature	Date

a

Abuse   Coding and billing that is inconsistent with typical coding and billing practices.

Access report   A report of all persons (within the facility) who have had access to a patient's protected health information.

Accountable Care Organization (ACO)   A reimbursement model where hospitals, physicians, other healthcare providers form partnerships whereby all are accountable for the quality of care, efficiency of medical services (to contain costs), and patient satisfaction. A pay for performance model of healthcare reimbursement.

Accounting of disclosures   Providing the patient, upon request, with a listing of all disclosures of his/her health information, both internally and externally.

Accounts payable   Monies being paid from the medical practice, for instance to pay for supplies, rent, utilities, payroll, etc.

Accounts receivable   Monies coming into a medical practice, for instance insurance payments or payments made by patients.

Administrative data   Identifying information, insurance-related information, authorizations, and business correspondence found in a patient's health record.

Affordable Care Act (ACA)   Signed into law in 2010, the ACA resulted in improved access to affordable healthcare coverage and protection from abusive practices by healthcare insurance companies. Gives consumers more control over their healthcare coverage and ties reimbursement to quality, patient satisfaction, and coordination of care.

Aggregate   The sum total; for instance, the sum total of patients between the ages of 60 and 100 in a practice.

American Health Information Management Association (AHIMA)   A professional association for the field of Health Information Management.

American Recovery and Reinvestment Act (ARRA)   Signed into law by President Obama on February 17, 2009; this economic "stimulus plan" includes provisions for the Health Information Technology for Economic and Clinical Health (HITECH) Act.

Application   Software that has a special purpose, such as word processing, spreadsheet, or for a particular industry such as practice management or electronic health record software.

Audit trail   A permanent record or accounting of accesses, additions, amendments, or deletions to a health record. Also a report which shows accesses by user to each function of the software.

b

Benchmarking   Comparison of one set of statistics to the overall statistics when the same variables are used for each.

Blog   Ongoing conversations about a topic that take place online via the Internet.

Breach of confidentiality   Releasing information without a required, properly executed authorization or as restricted by law.

c

Care provider   Term used to refer to physicians, physicians' assistants, dentists, psychologists, nurse practitioner, or midwife.

Center for Medicare and Medicaid Services (CMS)   An agency of the Department of Health and Human Services and responsible for administering the Medicare and Medicaid programs.

Certification Commission for Health Information Technology (CCHIT)   A nonprofit, nongovernmental agency whose purpose is to certify electronic health records for functionality, interoperability, and security.

Certified Electronic Health Record Technology (CEHRT)   A compliment to Meaningful Use Stage 2, certification by the Office of the National Coordinator (ONC) of EHR software which meets certain standards.

Chief complaint   The reason for which a patient has made an appointment (usually in his/her own words, for instance, "I have a sore throat.").

Clearinghouse   A service that processes data into a standardized billing format and checks for inconsistencies or other errors in the data.

Clinical decision support   Allows access to current treatment options for a disease, through electronic or remote methods. Alerts the care provider to possible medication interactions, gives treatment options based on results of clinical trials or research, alerts provider that a patient may have a particular diagnosis based on the data found in the patient's electronic record.

Clinical Documentation Architecture (CDA)   Developed by HL7, a document markup standard that specifies the structure and semantics of clinical documents such as discharge summary, operative report, etc.

Cloud computing   The housing of data in a cloud environment, which is a commercially maintained site on the Internet.

CMS-1500   The form used by physicians' offices to submit insurance claims.

Compliance plan　A formal, written document that describes how the hospital or physician's practice ensures rules, regulations, and standards are being adhered to.

Computerized physician order entry (CPOE)　Entering physician orders electronically rather than on paper. The order is transmitted directly to the appropriate department; for instance, an order for an x-ray would go directly to the radiology department, whereas an order for a CBC would go directly to the laboratory.

Computer virus　A deviant program, stored on a computer floppy disk, hard drive, or CD, that can cause unexpected and often undesirable effects, such as destroying or corrupting data.

Confidentiality　The patient's right to expect that his/her health information will not be released to any person or entity without the patient/guardian's written authorization or as required by law or regulation.

Continuity of Care Document (CCD)　A document exchange standard used to share patient summary information, such as in the case of a patient being referred from one healthcare provider to another.

Co-payment (co-pay)　The amount due from the patient at the time of the office visit; typically a requirement of managed care plans.

Core objectives　Basic functions or collection of data that should be completed on a patient's visit or hospitalization.

Covered entity　Any healthcare entity that captures or utilizes health information. These include healthcare plans (insurance companies), clearinghouses that process healthcare claims, individual physicians and physician practices, any type of therapist (mental health, physical, speech, occupational), dentists, hospital staffs, ambulatory facilities, nursing homes, home health agencies, pharmacies, and employers.

Credentialing　The process of ensuring a care provider has the proper qualifications (education, experience, malpractice coverage) to practice medicine.

Current Procedural Terminology (CPT)　Coding system used to convert narrative procedures and services into numeric form. CPT is used to code procedures and services in a physician's office; in a hospital setting, it is used for outpatient coding (emergency room, outpatient diagnostic testing, or ambulatory surgery, for example).

Custom report　Reports which are designed by the office or hospital rather than coming as part of a software package (standard reports).

d

Dashboard　A visual comparison of actual performance to required performance.

Data　A single, raw fact such as a patient's name, height, or weight. Often used interchangeably with information, though they are not synonymous terms.

Data dictionary　A document that specifies the format of each data field as well as a detailed explanation or definition for that field, which allows for consistency of data collection.

Data integrity　Maintaining the accuracy and consistency of data.

Decryption　Interprets data being received in encrypted (scrambled) form.

Deductible　The out-of-pocket payment amount that a policyholder must meet before insurance covers the service(s).

Default value　A value that automatically appears in a field each time it appears on a screen (e.g., the current date in a date field, the local area code in a home phone number field).

Demographic information　Administrative data that identifies the patient. Consists of name, date of birth, sex, and social security number (may vary by facility policy).

Detail report　Any report that includes patient identifying information and lists each case individually rather than as totals.

Directory information　The fact that a patient is an inpatient (or being treated as an outpatient) as well as his/her location within the facility.

Disaster recovery plan　A written document that details an inventory of hardware and software, backup procedure, including location of backup files, the system used to alert users of the disaster, required security training for personnel, and procedure for restoring backup files.

Discharge summary　A report completed by a care provider which summarizes a patient's stay in the hospital. It generally includes the final diagnoses, a summary of the patient's course in the hospital, any procedures performed, recap of diagnostic results, and discharge instructions.

Drug formulary　A list of provider-preferred generic and brand-name drugs covered under various insurance plans.

e

Electronic claims submission　Submitting insurance claims via wire to a clearinghouse or directly to the insurance carrier.

Electronic Health Record (EHR)　Comprehensive record of all health records for a patient, which is able to be shared electronically with other health providers as necessary.

Electronic Medical Record (EMR)　The legal patient record that is created within any healthcare facility (hospital, nursing home, ambulatory surgery facility, physician's office, etc.). The EMR is the data source for the electronic health record (EHR).

Encounter form (Superbill)　A document (paper or electronic) that is used in medical offices to capture the diagnoses and services or procedures performed and from which the CMS-1500 billing form is completed.

Encryption　A security method in which words are scrambled and can only be read if the receiver has a special code to decipher the scrambled message.

ePrescribing　Electronically transmitting prescriptions from care provider to pharmacy.

Evaluation and Management (E&M) The CPT codes used to capture the face-to-face time between a patient and the care provider; takes into consideration the extent of the history, extent of the physical exam, and the level of medical decision making required.

Evidence-based medicine Diagnostic and treatment protocols that are based on proven research and documented best practices.

Explanation of benefits (EOB) An explanation of the charges for services, the amount paid by the insurance company, and the amount due by the subscriber, which is sent to the subscriber (and also to the provider, in some instances).

f-g

Firewall A system of hardware and/or software that protects a computer or a network from intruders by filtering activity over the network.

Fee schedule The amount charged for services rendered in a physician's office by Current Procedural Terminology (CPT) code.

Flag A message that appears on a screen in written form or as an icon to serve as a reminder to staff and care providers.

Fraud Intentional deception, which in healthcare takes advantage of a patient, an insurance company, Medicare, or Medicaid.

h

Hardware The tangible items that are used in automation (e.g., the processing unit, screen, keyboard, mouse, laptops, hand-held devices).

Healthcare administrator A leadership position within a healthcare facility, including chief executive officer, chief operating officer, chief financial officer, chief information officer, or other higher level management positions. May also be referred to as healthcare manager or health systems manager.

Healthcare Common Procedure Coding System (HCPCS) Coding system required by Medicare and Medicaid to document services and procedures (Level 1, Current Procedural Terminology, CPT) and equipment, supplies, and transport (HCPCS Level 2).

Healthcare Information and Management Systems Society (HIMSS) An association of health informatics and information professionals formed to promote a better understanding of healthcare informatics and management systems.

Healthcare Integrity and Protection Data Bank (HIPDB) A database of adverse actions related to fraud and abuse.

Healthcare systems administrator A leadership position specifically responsible for the information technology (IT) functions within an organization or facility.

Health informatics The management of automated health information; the technological side of managing health information—the design, development, structure, implementation, integration, and management of the technical aspects of electronic (automated) health record-keeping.

Health information exchange (HIE) The movement or sharing of information between healthcare entities in a secure manner, and in keeping with nationally recognized standards.

Health Information Management A profession that encompasses services in planning, collecting, aggregating, analyzing, and disseminating individual patient and aggregate clinical data (in paper or electronic format).

Health Information Technology for Economic and Clinical Health (HITECH) Act A portion of the American Recovery and Reinvestment Act (ARRA) that is meant to increase the use of an electronic health record by hospitals and physicians through a monetary incentive program.

Health Insurance Portability and Accountability Act (HIPAA) Passed in 1996, this act includes regulations that afford people who leave their employment the ability to keep their insurance or obtain new health insurance even if they have a pre-existing medical condition. Also sets standards for storing, maintaining, and sharing electronic health information while ensuring its privacy and security.

Health Level Seven (HL7) A set of standards that makes sharing of data between or among healthcare entities possible.

History and Physical (H&P) A report completed by a care provider which includes the reason(s) the patient is being seen or admitted; the history of present illness; the pertinent past medical, surgical, social, and family histories; other current conditions/diseases the patient is being treated for; the report of a physical examination; working diagnoses; and plan of care.

History of present illness (HPI) The patient's description of current complaints such as when the symptoms started, the location of the condition, quality of the symptoms, severity of the symptoms, anything that makes the symptoms better or worse, and additional symptoms the patient is experiencing.

i-j-k

Index A listing—for instance, a Diagnosis Index is a report that is sorted by diagnosis code and includes the total number of patients seen with that disease for a given period of time; a Master Patient Index (MPI) is a listing of all patients who have ever been seen in a hospital or a practice.

Information Raw facts that, when viewed as a whole, have meaning. Example: a report of all patients treated at Memorial Medical Center with a primary diagnosis of streptococcal pharyngitis (strep throat), sorted by patients' age.

In-network Care providers who contract with a managed care plan to offer services to members of the managed care plan at a prenegotiated rate.

Institute of Medicine (IOM) An independent, nonprofit, nongovernmental organization that works to provide unbiased and authoritative advice to decision makers and the public.

Insurance plan   The medical insurance contract under which a patient is covered; the extent to which services are covered. Also referred to as "the plan."

Insurance verification   The process of contacting the insurance carrier and receiving validation of coverage for that patient, deductible status, and co-pay amount.

Interface   The ability of one computer system or component to accept or send data to another system without loss of integrity or meaning.

International Classification of Diseases-10th revision, Clinical Modification/Procedure Coding System (ICD-10-CM/PCS)   The classification system used to convert narrative diagnoses and procedures into numeric codes. Effective October 1, 2014, replaces ICD-9-CM.

Internet   A series of networks that allow instant access to information from around the world.

Interoperability   Through a single database, many different functions can take place and information can be shared.

Intranet   A secure environment or private internal network that is available only to a select group (e.g., the staff within an organization).

l

Library   In computer software, a listing or choice of entities, for instance, employers, insurance plans, ICD-10-CM codes, or CPT codes.

Live   The point at which computer software or systems are put into real-time use within a practice or hospital.

Local area network (LAN)   Links computers and related devices that are physically close to one another such as within a building.

m

Malware   Include examples such as worms, viruses, and Trojan horses, all of which attack computer programs.

Managed care plan   Insurance plans that promote quality, cost-effective healthcare through monitoring of patients, preventive care, and performance.

Master file   Datasets that provide structure and are the building blocks for parts of chart notes within an EHR.

Master Patient Index (MPI)/Patient List   A permanent listing of all patients who have received care in a hospital (inpatient or outpatient). In physicians' offices, more often referred to as Master Patient List or Patient List.

Meaningful use   Part of the requirements of the Health Information Technology for Economic and Clinical Health (HITECH) Act which is meant to increase the use of an electronic health record through monetary incentives provided the EHR is used in a meaningful way to improve patient care.

Medical necessity   The fact that there is a medical reason to perform a procedure or service. Documentation exists in the patient's record to show there are sufficient signs, symptoms, or history to warrant the services provided.

Medical record number   A unique number assigned to each patient seen by a facility or office.

Menu objectives   Additional functions that allow for greater use of EHR functionality.

Minimum necessary information   As required by the Health Insurance Portability and Accountability Act (HIPAA), releasing the minimum information to satisfy the reason the information is needed or the minimum necessary to perform a job function.

n

National Alliance for Health Information Technology (NAHIT)   An association formed to promote the use of health information technology (health IT).

National Health Information Network (NHIN)   A set of standards, services, and policies that enable the secure exchange of health information over the Internet.

National Practitioner Data Bank (NPDB)   Required by law, a database of malpractice payouts, revocation of privileges, licensure denial or suspension, denial of medical staff privileges, and similar actions.

National Provider Identifier (NPI)   A unique identifier that must be used on insurance claims to identify the care provider and/or group practice that rendered care to the patient.

Notice of Privacy Practices   A requirement of the Health Insurance Portability and Accountability Act (HIPAA) that patients are made aware (in writing) of their rights under HIPAA including the fact that the patient has the right to view/receive a copy of his/her own record, that amendment to the documentation may be requested, the ways in which their health information will be used and released to outside entities, and the procedure to file a complaint with the Department of Health and Human Services.

o

Office of the National Coordinator (ONC)   The principal federal entity charged with coordination, implementation, and use of health information technology and the electronic exchange of health information.

Optical character recognition (OCR)   Technology that converts a document into a format that is computer readable—that is, into an electronic file.

p

Password   A unique code, known only to the user, which is used to gain access to computer applications.

Past family history   Documentation of conditions and diseases found in immediate family members (e.g., diabetes mellitus, cancer, or heart disease).

Past medical history   Previous medical condition(s) for which the patient has been treated.

Past surgical history   Previous surgical procedure(s) the patient has undergone, the approximate date(s), name of surgeon, reason for procedure(s), and complications, if any.

Patient-Centered Medical Home (PCMH)   A model that was developed to care for patients with chronic conditions by the American Academy of Family Practitioners, to encourage and facilitate a patient's (and family's) involvement in his or her own care.

Patient portals   A method of accessing portions of one's own health information from the care provider's or hospital's electronic health record.

Personal digital assistant (PDA)   A mobile device that is small enough to fit in one's hand, yet allows access to local area networks (LANs), wide area networks (WANs), and the Internet; may also have telephone capability.

Personal health record (PHR)   A record, kept by the patient, that contains a person's health history, immunization status, current and past medications, allergies, and instructions given by a care provider; it often includes patient education materials as well.

Physical exam (PE)   An examination of the patient's body for signs of disease.

Physician Quality Reporting Initiative (PQRI)   A voluntary pay-for-performance incentive program. Participating care providers submit data on any of the 100 designated quality measures and receive monetary incentives for doing so.

Picture Archiving and Communications Systems (PACS)   Computerized system for enhanced viewing and sharing of images such as x-rays, scans, ultrasounds, and mammograms.

Point of care   Documentation, dictation, ordering of tests and procedures that occur at the same time the patient is being seen.

Practice Management   Software used in physicians' offices to gather data on every patient and perform administrative functions from the time an appointment is made through the time the bill for each visit is paid.

Privacy   The right to be left alone; the right to expect that one's personal space is respected while undergoing healthcare.

Problem list   A listing kept in the patient's health record of all current (active) and resolved medical conditions.

Protected health information (PHI)   Any piece of information that identifies a patient, including a patient's name, date of birth, address, email, telephone number, employer, relatives' names, social security number, medical record number, account numbers tied to the patient, fingerprints, photographs, and characteristics about the patient that would automatically disclose his or her identity. PHI also includes any clinical information about an identified patient.

q

Quality Reporting Document Architecture (QRDA)   Based on HL7's approved Clinical Documentation Architecture (CDA), QRDA is a data standard used for reporting quality measure data and that is EHR compatible across different health IT systems.

Query   Searching a database for patients who meet certain criteria.

r

Regional extension center   An organization that assists healthcare providers with the selection and implementation of electronic health record systems.

Regional Health Information Organization (RHIO)   Healthcare organizations in a geographic area that exchange health information with the goal of improving patient care, reducing duplication, and reducing unnecessary costs.

Registry   A listing that is filed in chronological order based on when something occurred. Examples include a birth registry, death registry, or cancer or trauma registry.

Remittance advice (RA)   A detailed accounting of the claims for which payment is being made by an insurance company. The remittance advice accompanies the payment from the insurance company.

Resolution   The quality of a scanned image as it will appear in the record. The higher the resolution, the crisper the image.

Review of systems (ROS)   A body system–by–body system inventory of any symptoms the patient is having or has had based on a series of questions asked by the care provider.

s

Scanner   A piece of equipment that digitizes documents into a format that is readable by a computer.

Scribe   An assistant who enters data either in writing or electronically into the health record as the care provider verbally dictates recent findings.

Shortcut key   Keys that link directly to a function rather than choosing from a menu.

Smartphone   Telephones that allow Internet browsing, audio, video, and camera functionality.

SOAP note   An acronym for the documentation used in a care provider's office to record the patient's symptoms, signs, assessment (diagnosis), and plan of care.

Social history   Lifestyle or social habits of the patient.

Social media   Interactive communication sites via the Internet. Examples are Facebook, YouTube, MySpace, and Twitter.

Speech (voice) recognition   Software that recognizes the words being said by the person dictating, and converts the speech to text.

Structured data   Data that fits a particular model or format, which can be tracked and may be part of a database. Examples include ICD-10-CM/PCS codes, CPT codes, a patient's temperature, or a patient's age.

Subscriber   The primary person covered by an insurance plan.

Summary report   A statistical report that includes totals rather than data for individual patients. Examples include a report of total patients seen during a particular time by gender; a report of the total number of patients seen in the office with E&M code 99214.

t

Tablet computer   Computers that are larger than PDAs or smartphones, yet smaller than a laptop computer; allow access to local area networks (LANs), wide area networks (WANs), and the Internet.

Telehealth   Associated with preventive care, telehealth is the use of audiovisual equipment through which the patient and the care provider or healthcare professional can connect remotely.

Telemedicine   The use of technology to remotely monitor a patient's vital signs and perform tests such as an EKG, or forward radiologic images.

Templates   Preformatted documents built into practice management and electronic health record systems.

Transactions   Posting of charges and the payment of claims in the Practice Management system to update patients' accounts.

u

UB-04   The form used to submit insurance claims for hospital patients.

Unstructured data   Data in the form of words or audio files that cannot be tracked. Examples include emails, written narratives, and audio files from speech recognition technology.

User rights   The limitations of one's access to the functionality of the software as defined by their job description or position within the organization.

v

Variable   In relation to a statistical report, the factors that vary from one patient to the next. Examples include age, zip code, or diagnoses.

Virtual private network (VPN)   Software that encrypts (codes) the data being sent as well as interprets the data being received.

Vital signs   Measurements taken (temperature, heart rate, respiratory rate, blood pressure, height and weight, and sometimes body mass index) to determine the status of basic body system functions.

Voice recognition technology   Software that recognizes the words being said by the person dictating and converts speech to text; differs from speech recognition because voice recognition "learns" the voice of the dictator and is therefore more accurate.

w-x-y-z

Wide area network (WAN)   Connects computer networks together that are not physically close.

Wi-Fi   Data exchange via high radio frequency.

references

Unless otherwise noted, all screenshots come from PrimeSUITE® Software, used with permission of Greenway Medical Technologies, Inc. © 2013 Greenway Medical Technologies, Inc. All rights reserved.

chapter 1

Greenway Medical Solutions. (2013). *Enterprises.* Retrieved from http://www.greenwaymedical.com/enterprises/

Greenway Medical Solutions. (2013). *PrimeSPEECH.* Retrieved from http://www.greenwaymedical.com/solutions/primespeech/

Greenway Medical Technologies. (2013). *Solutions.* Retrieved from http://www.greenwaymedical.com/solutions/

PrimeSuite. (2011–2012). *Greenway PrimeSUITE Clinical Workbook.* Atlanta, GA: Greenway Medical Technologies.

PrimeSuite: *The Power of One.* (2011). Retrieved from http://www.greenwaymedical.com/dynamicData/pdf/products/2011/Greenway_PrimeSUITE.pdf

chapter 2

Chapter opener photo: Getty Images

Figure 2.3: From DS Systems, Inc. PACS.

Figure 2.8: U.S. Department of Health and Human Services. (n.d.). *HITECH Act Enforcement Interim Final Rule.* Retrieved from http://www.hhs.gov/ocr/privacy/hipaa/administrative/enforcementrule/hitechenforcementifr.html

Berry, Kate. (2013, March). HIE Quality Check. *Journal of AHIMA, 84*(3): 28–32.

Certification Commission for Health Information Technology. (2013). *About the Certification Commission for Health Information Technology.* Retrieved from http://www.cchit.org/about.

Department of Health and Human Services, Centers for Medicare and Medicaid Services. (2013). *HIPAA Privacy and Security Standards.* Retrieved from http://www.cms.gov/Regulations-and-Guidance/HIPAA-Administrative-Simplification/HIPAAGenInfo/PrivacyandSecurityStandards.html

Department of Health and Human Services, Centers for Medicare and Medicaid Services. Medicare Learning Network. (2012). *The National Provider Identifier (NPI): What You Need to Know.* Retrieved from http://www.cms.gov/MLNProducts/downloads/NPIBooklet.pdf

Garets, D., and Davis, M. (2005, October). Electronic Patient Records: EMRs and EHRs. *Healthcare Informatics.* Retrieved from http://www.providersedge.com/ehdocs/ehr_articles/Electronic_Patient_Records-EMRs_and_EHRs.pdf

Health Care Administrator. (2004). Retrieved from Health Careers Center website: http://www.mshealthcareers.com/careers/healthcareadmin.htm.

HealthIT.gov. Interoperability Portfolio: Nationwide Health Information Network. Retrieved from http://www.healthit.gov/policy-researchers-implementers/nationwide-health-information-network-nwhin

Information Management. The Problem with Unstructured Data. Retrieved from http://www.information-management.com/issues/20030201/6287-1.html

Institute of Medicine. (2012). *About the Institute of Medicine.* Retrieved from http://iom.edu/About-IOM.aspx

Institute of Medicine. (2013). *Key Capabilities of an Electronic Health Record System.* Retrieved from http://www.iom.edu/Reports/2003/Key-Capabilities-of-an-Electronic-Health-Record-System.aspx

National eHealth Collaborative. About National eHealth Collaborative. Retrieved from http://www.nationalehealth.org/about-national-ehealth-collaborative

Newby, Cynthia. (2009). *HIPAA for Allied Health Careers.* New York: McGraw-Hill Companies.

U.S. Department of Health and Human Services, Office of the National Coordinator for Health Information Technology. (2011). *National Health Information Network: Overview.* Retrieved from http://www.healthit.gov/policy-researchers-implementers/nationwide-health-information-network-nwhin

U.S. Department of Health and Human Services, Office of the National Coordinator for Health Information Technology. Retrieved from http://www.healthit.gov/newsroom/about-onc

U.S. Department of Health and Human Services, Office of the National Coordinator for Health Information Technology. *HITECH and Funding Opportunities.* Retrieved from http://www.healthit.gov/policy-researchers-implementers/hitech-programs-advisory-committees

U.S. Department of Health and Human Services. *HHS Region Map.* Retrieved from http://www.hhs.gov/about/regionmap.html

chapter 3

American Health Information Management Association (AHIMA). (2009, April 24). A Standard for Quality Reporting. *Journal of AHIMA.* Retrieved from http://journal.ahima.org/2009/04/24/a-standard-for-quality-reporting/

American Health Information Management Association (AHIMA). (2010, September). Fundamentals for Building a Master Patient Index/Enterprise Master Patient Index. *Journal of AHIMA.*

Commonwell Health Alliance. Retrieved from http://www.commonwellalliance.org/

Dolin, R.H., Alschuler, L., Beebe, C., et al. (2001, November-December). The HL7 Clinical Document Architecture. *Journal of the American Medical Informatics Association, 8*(6): 552–569.

EHR Incentive Program. *Eligible Professional Meaningful Use Table of Contents Core and Menu Set Measures.* Retrieved from http://www.cms.gov/EHRIncentivePrograms/Downloads/EP-MU-TOC.pdf

Mertz, Jon. (2010). HL7 Standards. HL7 Quality Reporting Document Architecture (QRDA) Defined. Retrieved from http://www.hl7standards.com/blog/2010/01/28/hl7-quality-reporting-document-architecture-qrda-defined/

National Committee on Vital and Health Statistics. (1996). *Core Health Data Elements: Report of the National Committee on Vital and Health Statistics.* Retrieved from http://ncvhs.hhs.gov/ncvhsr1.htm

Newby, Cynthia. (2010). *From Patient to Payment: Insurance Procedures for the Medical Office* (6th ed.). New York: McGraw-Hill Companies.

SearchHealthIT. Continuity of Care Document (CCD). Retrieved from http://searchhealthit.techtarget.com/definition/Continuity-of-Care-Document-CCD

Washington, Lydia. (2013, March 1). ACO Summit Highlights. *Journal of AHIMA.* Retrieved from http://journal.ahima.org/2013/03/01/aco-summit-highlights/

chapter 4

Chapter opener photo: Jose Luis Pelaez Inc/Blend Images LLC

Booth, K.A., Whicker, L.G., Wyman, Terri D., and Moany Wright, Sandra. (2011). *Administrative Procedures for Medical Assisting* (4th ed.). New York: McGraw-Hill Companies.

Green, M.A., and Bowie, M.J. (2011). *Essentials of Health Information Management: Principles and Practices* (2nd ed.). Clifton Park, NY: Delmar, Cengage Learning.

Newby, C. (2010). *From Patient to Payment: Insurance Procedures for the Medical Office* (6th ed.). New York: McGraw-Hill Companies.

Chapter 5

Chapter opener photo: Comstock/Punchstock RF

American Health Information Management Association (AHIMA). (2012, November). Using Medical Scribes in a Physician Practice. *Journal of AHIMA, 83*(11): 64–69 [expanded online version].

Greenway Medical Technologies. (2011). *ePrescribing*. Retrieved from http://www.greenwaymedical.com/solutions/eprescribing/

Recording History: The History of Recording Technology. Retrieved from http://www.recording-history.org/HTML/dicta_tech5.php

Recording History: The History of Recording Technology. The 1970s and the Decline of Dictation. Retrieved from http://www.recording-history.org/HTML/dicta_biz7.php

Recording History: *Edison and Columbia Establish the Business*. Retrieved from http://www.recording-history.org/HTML/dicta_biz2.php

Wiedemann, Lou Ann. (2010, October). CPOE Lessons Learned. *Journal of AHIMA, 81*(10): 54–55.

Chapter 6

Figure 6.2: Sanderson, Susan M. (2013). *Computers in the Medical Office* (8th ed.). New York: McGraw-Hill Companies.

Figure 6.9: Booth, K.A., Whicker, L.G., Wyman, Terri D., and Moany Wright, Sandra. (2011). *Medical Assisting* (4th ed.). New York: McGraw-Hill Companies.

Figure 6.10: Sanderson, Susan M. (2011). *Computers in the Medical Office* (7th ed.). New York: McGraw-Hill Companies.

Booth, K.A., Whicker, L.G., Wyman, Terri D., and Moany Wright, Sandra. (2011). *Administrative Procedures for Medical Assisting* (4th ed.). New York: McGraw-Hill Companies.

Centers for Medicare and Medicaid Services (CMS). *Accountable Care Organizations*. Retrieved from http://www.cms.gov/Medicare/Medicare-Fee-for-Service-Payment/ACO/index.html?redirect=/aco/

Current Procedural Terminology. (2013). Chicago: American Medical Association.

Examples of CPT codes based on CPT 2012.

Examples of HCPCS codes based on HCPCS 2012.

Examples of ICD-9-CM codes based on ICD-9-CM 2013.

Greenway Medical Technologies. (2011). *Prime RCM*. Retrieved from http://www.greenwaymedical.com/dynamicData/pdf/products/2011/Greenway_PrimeRCM.pdf

ICD-10-CM/PCS codes based on Draft ICD-10-CM/PCS codes 2013.

ICD-10-CM Codebook. (2012). Salt Lake City, UT: Contexo Media.

ICD-9-CM Volumes I, II, & III. (2013). Ingenix. Salt Lake City, UT

Newby, C. (2010). *From Patient to Payment: Insurance Procedures for the Medical Office* (6th ed.). New York: McGraw-Hill Companies.

The Qui Tam Online Network. *Common Types of Qui Tam Fraud*. Retrieved from http://www.quitamonline.com/fraud.html

White, S. et al. (2011, June). An ACO Primer. *Journal of AHIMA, 82*(6): 48–50.

World Health Organization. (2013). International Classification of Diseases. Retrieved from http://www.who.int/classifications/icd/en/

Chapter 7

Abdelhak, M., Grostick, S., Hanken, M.A., and Jacobs, E. (2007). *Health Information: Management of a Strategic Resource* (3rd ed.). Philadelphia: Elsevier.

American Medical Association. (1995–2013). *HIPAA Violations and Enforcement*. Retrieved from http://www.ama-assn.org//ama/pub/physician-resources/solutions-managing-your-practice/coding-billing-insurance/hipaahealth-insurance-portability-accountability-act/hipaa-violations-enforcement.page

Centers for Medicare and Medicaid Services, Office for Civil Rights. *Collection Use and Disclosure Limitation. The HIPAA Privacy Rule in Electronic Health Information Exchange in a Networked Environment*. Retrieved from www.hhs.gov/ocr/privacy/hipaa/understanding/special/healthit/collectionusedisclosure.pdf

Certification Commission for Health Information Technology. (2011). Retrieved from http://www.cchit.org/

CNN.com Entertainment. 27 Suspended for Clooney File Peek. Retrieved from http://www.cnn.com/2007/SHOWBIZ/10/10/clooney.records/

Department of Health and Human Services. (2010, March 10). Proposed Establishment of Certification Programs for Health Information Technology; Proposed Rule. *Federal Register, 75*(46): 11327–11373. Retrieved from http://edocket.access.gpo.gov/2010/2010-4991.htm

Department of Health and Human Services. Office of the National Coordinator for Health Information Technology. (2011). *Health IT Home*. Retrieved from http://healthit.hhs.gov/portal/server.pt/community/healthit_hhs_gov__home/1204

Department of Health and Human Services. *Health Information Privacy*. Retrieved from http://www.hhs.gov/ocr/privacy/hipaa/understanding/index.html

Dimick, Chris. (2010, February). Empowered Patient: Preparing for a New Patient Interaction. *Journal of AHIMA, 81*(2): 26–31.

Hamilton, Byron R. (2011). *Electronic Health Records* (2nd ed.). New York: McGraw-Hill Companies.

Heubusch, Kevin. (2011, July). Access Report: OCR Tries Subtraction through Addition in Accounting of Disclosure Rule. *Journal of AHIMA, 82*(7): 38–39.

HIMSS. (2012-2013). *About HIMSS*. Retrieved from http://www.himss.org/ASP/aboutHimssHome.asp

McGuireWoods. (2013). *HIPAA Final Omnibus Rule Implements Tiered Penalty Structure for HIPAA Violations*. Retrieved from http://www.mcguirewoods.com/Client-Resources/Alerts/2013/2/HIPAA-Omnibus-Final-Rule-Implements-Tiered-Penalty-Structure-HIPAA-Violations.aspx

Miaoulis, William M. (2010, March). Access, Use, and Disclosure: HITECH's Impact on the HIPAA Touchstones. *Journal of AHIMA, 81*(3): 38–39, 64.

National Alliance for Health Information Technology. (2008, April 28). *Defining Key Health Information Technology Terms*. Retrieved from http://www.nacua.org/documents/HealthInfoTechTerms.pdf

Table 7.1: Centers for Medicare and Medicaid Services, Office for Civil Rights. *Collection Use and Disclosure Limitation. The HIPAA Privacy Rule in Electronic Health Information Exchange in a Networked Environment*. Retrieved from www.hhs.gov/ocr/privacy/hipaa/understanding/special/healthit/collectionusedisclosure.pdf

Williams, B.K., and Sawyer, S.C. (2010). *Using Information Technology: A Practical Introduction to Computers & Communications* (9th ed.). New York: McGraw-Hill Companies.

Chapter 8

Chapter opener photo: Ryan McVay/Getty Images

Greenway Medical Technologies. (2011). *PrimeSuite® The Power of One™ Ambulatory Solution™* Instruction Manual: PrimeSuite 2011.

Williams, B.K., and Sawyer, S.C. (2011). *Using Information Technology: A Practical Introduction to Computers & Communications* (9th ed.). New York: McGraw-Hill Companies.

Chapter 9

Capsite: *2012 Ambulatory EHR & PM Study*. (2012, September). Retrieved from http://capsite.com/assets/Uploads/2012-Ambulatory-EHR-PM-StudyTOC.pdf

Capsite: *2012 Health Information Exchange Study*. (2012, September). Retrieved from http://capsite.com/assets/Uploads/2012-Health-Information-Exchange-StudyTOC2.pdf

Capsite: *Fifth Annual Ambulatory PM and EHR Study*. (2013, June). Retrieved from http://capsite.com/assets/Uploads/2013-Ambulatory-EHR-Study-TOC6.pdf

Centers for Medicare and Medicaid Services. (2012, August). *Stage 1 vs. Stage 2 Comparison Table for Eligible Hospitals and CAHs*. Retrieved from http://www.cms.gov/Regulations-and-Guidance/Legislation/EHRIncentivePrograms/Downloads/Stage1vsStage2CompTablesforHospitals.pdf

HIMSS. (2012–2013). *Clinical Decision Support*. Retrieved from http://www.himss.org/ASP/topics_clinicalDecision.asp

PrimeSUITE 2011 Users' Manual. (2011). *PrimeSUITE 2011 EHR: Introducing Meaningful Use*.

Table 9.1: Centers for Medicare and Medicaid Services. Medicare & Medicaid EHR Incentive Program: Meaningful Use Stage 1 Requirements. Retrieved from https://www.cms.gov/EHRIncentivePrograms/Downloads/MU_Stage1_ReqOverview.pdf

Table 9.2: Centers for Medicare and Medicaid Services. Medicare & Medicaid EHR Incentive Program: Meaningful Use Stage 1 Requirements. Retrieved from https://www.cms.gov/EHRIncentivePrograms/Downloads/MU_Stage1_ReqOverview.pdf

Tables 9.3 and 9.4: Centers for Medicare and Medicaid Services. (2012, August). *Stage 1 vs. Stage 2 Comparison Table for Eligible Professionals*. Retrieved from http://www.cms.gov/Regulations-and-Guidance/Legislation/EHRIncentivePrograms/Downloads/Stage1vsStage2CompTablesforEP.pdf

U.S. Department of Health and Human Services. (2011). *The DataBank*. Retrieved from http://www.npdb-hipdb.hrsa.gov/

Chapter 10

Chapter opener photo: McGraw Hill Education

Figure 10.1: Williams, B.K., and Sawyer, S.C. (2011). *Using Information Technology: A Practical Introduction to Computers & Communications* (9th ed.). New York: McGraw-Hill Companies.

Figure 10.2: Holcombe, J., and C. (2012). *Survey of Operating Systems* (3rd ed.). New York: McGraw-Hill Companies.

Abdelhak, M., Grostick, S., Hanken, M.A., and Jacobs, E. (2007). *Health Information: Management of a Strategic Resource*. Philadelphia: Saunders.

American Health Information Management Association (AHIMA). (2003). Body of Knowledge, A Vision of the e-HIM Future: A Report from the AHIMA e-HIM Task Force. Supplement to the *Journal of AHIMA*.

American Telemedicine Association. Telemedicine Defined. Retrieved from www.americantelemed.org/i4a/pages/index.cfm?pageid=3333

Association for Medical Ethics. (2011). *History of Evidence-Based Medicine*. Retrieved from http://www.ethicaldoctor.org/History.html

Cantrell, S. (2010). Reference and Information Services in the 21st Century: An Introduction, 2nd ed. *Journal of the Medical Library Association, 98*(3): 264–265. doi: 10.3163/1536-5050.98.3.019

FDA Office of Women's Health. (2011). *Mammograms*. Retrieved from http://www.fda.gov/downloads/ForeConsumers/ByAudience/ForWomen/UCM121896.pdf

Institute of Medicine. (1996). *Telemedicine: A Guide to Assessing Telecommunications for Health Care*. Retrieved from http://www.nap.edu/openbook.php?record_id=5296&page=R1

LaTour, K.M., and Eichenwald-Maki, S. (2010). *Health Information Management: Concepts, Principles and Practice* (3rd ed.). Chicago: AHIMA.

Menachemi, N., Powers, T.L., and Brooks, R.G. (2011). Physician and Practice Characteristics Associated with Longitudinal Increases in Electronic Health Records Adoption. *Journal of Healthcare Management, 56*(3): 183–197. Retrieved from EBSCO*host*.

Shi, L., and Sing, D.A. (2010). *Essentials of the U.S. Health Care System* (2nd ed.). Sudbury, MA: Jones and Bartlett Publishers.

index

CHFM (Certified Health Care Facility Manager), 22
Chief complaint, 57, 74, 89
Children's Hospital, Boston, 163–164
CHPS (Certified in Healthcare Privacy and Security), 21
CIRCC® (Certified Interventional Radiology Cardiovascular Coder), 21
Claims management, 110–112
Clearinghouse, 3, 33
Clinical alerts, 199–202
Clinical Decision Support (CDS), 199–202
  data and information used in, 199–202
  defined, 25
  indexes for, 208–209
  standard reports for, 204
Clinical Documentation Architecture (CDA), 47
Clinical staff/care provider flowchart, 10
Clinical Visit Summary, 192, 193
Clinician/Practitioner Consultant, 21
Clooney, George, 156
Cloud computing, 226
CMA (Certified Medical Assistant), 22
CMS (Centers for Medicare and Medicaid Services), 190, 210
CMS-1500, 3, 46
  administrative uses of, 48–50
  Superbill information on, 112
CNP (Certified Nurse Practitioner), 22
Code Set Rule (HIPAA), 33
Codes
  CPT, 3, 50, 112–113, 120–122, 127
  diagnosis, 50
  Electronic Healthcare Transactions, Code Sets, and National Identifiers Rules, 32–33
  Evaluation & Management, 127–128
  ICD-9-CM, 117–120
  ICD-10-CM, 50
  on Superbills, 112–113
Coding; *see also specific coding systems; specific topics*
  abuse or fraud in, 130
  diagnosis, 117–120
  and documentation, 121–122
  Medicare and Medicaid rules for, 113
  procedure, 118–120
  for Superbills, 112–114
Coding professionals, 21
Columbia Graphaphone Company, 95

Communication management; *see* Managing information and communication
Compliance, 130–131, 144–146
Compliance plans, 130–131, 164–165
Compliance support
  registries for, 209–211
  using dashboard for, 190–199
Computer viruses, 143
Computer-based health information media, 25–27
Computerized physician order entry (CPOE), 98
Confidentiality, 141–142
  breach of, 161
  defined, 141
  and restricted access, 155
Continuity of care, exchange of information for, 163
Continuity of Care Documents (CCD), 47
Co-payment (co-pay), 111, 115–116
Core Objectives, 190–191
Covered entities, 140, 141
CPC (Certified Professional Coder), 21
CPC-H (Certified Professional Coder-Hospital), 21
CPOE (computerized physician order entry), 98
CPT codes; *see* Current Procedural Terminology codes
Credentialing, 211
Critical access hospitals (CAHs), 193
CRNM (Certified Registered Nurse Midwife), 22
Current medications list, 77
Current Procedural Terminology (CPT) codes, 3, 50
  for face-to-face time with patients, 127
  locating, 121–122
  in physicians' offices, 120
  on Superbill, 112–113
Custom reports, 205–208
Customizing displays, 180–181

d

Dashboard, 199
Data
  backing up, 166
  in decision support, 199–202
  encryption of, 166
  entering, 27
  information vs., 24
  from previous health records, 29
  structured vs. unstructured, 24

Data collection, 29–30
  forms as tools for, 72–75
  screen-based tools for, 27–28
Data dictionaries, 48
Data integrity, 158–160
Data security; *see* Security
Davis, M., 29, 239
Death registries, 209
Decision support; *see* Clinical Decision Support (CDS)
Decryption (VPNs), 225
Deductibles, 111
Default values, 59, 180
Demographic data, 3, 4
  defined, 46
  editing, 58–59
Department of Health and Human Services (HHS), 33, 190
Department of Veterans Affairs, 222
Desktop, customizing, 181
Detail reports, 204–205
Diagnosis codes, ICD-10-CM, 50
Diagnosis coding, 117–120
Diagnosis Index, 208
Diagnosis problem list, 100–102
Dictaphone, 95
Dictation, 95–96
Dimick, Chris, 240
Directory information, 141
Disaster Recovery Plan, 166
Discharge registries, 209
Discharge summary (note), 89
Disclosure of information; *see* Information disclosures
Disease indexes, 208–209
Displays, customizing, 180–181
Doctor of Medicine (MD), 22
Doctor of Osteopathy (DO), 22
Documentation, coding and, 121–122
Dolin, R. H., 239
Drug allergies, 78
Drug formularies, 192
Drummond Group, Inc., 147

e

Ediphone, 95
Editing demographic data, 58–59
EHR; *see* Electronic Health (Medical) Record
EHR Incentive Programs, 36
Eichenwald-Maki, S., 241
Electronic claims submission, 3
Electronic encounter form (Superbill), 112–114

index

H&P report (History and Physical report), 89
HPI (history of present illness), 74, 89–90

i

ICD (*International Classification of Diseases*), 117–118
ICD-9-CM, 117–120
ICD-10-CM, 3, 50
    codes on Superbills, 112
    locating codes from, 121–122
    Procedure Coding System, 118–120
ICSA Labs, 147
Imaging technology, 222
Immunization registries, 210
Implementation Manager, 21
Implementation Support specialist, 21
Importing documents, 177–178
Inconsistent information (in patient's history), 79–80
Indexes, 208–209
InfoGrad, 147
Information; *see also* Health information
    data vs., 24
    in decision support, 199–202
    exchange of, 163–164
    inconsistent or unclear, 78–79
    managing; *see* Managing information and communication
Information disclosures
    accounting of, 144, 162
    in exchanges of information, 163–164
    policies and procedures for, 160–162
Information exchange, 163–164
Information systems, 36–38
Information Technology (IT), 147
In-network status, 208
Institute of Medicine (IOM), 31, 222
Insurance claims
    claims management, 110–112
    looking up status of, 116–117
    sending, 3
Insurance fraud, 121
Insurance information, capturing, 60–61
Insurance payments
    posting, 128–129
    submitting, 123–125
Insurance plans, 126
    alerts based on, 115
    patient portal options in, 221
    types of, 130

Insurance verification, 111
Integrity
    in chart amendment, 158
    data, 158–160
Interface with PrimeSUITE, 98
Internal communications, 175–176
International Classification of Diseases (ICD), 117–118
International Classification of Diseases, 9th edition, Clinical Modification; see ICD-9-CM
International Classification of Diseases, 10th revision, Clinical Modification; see ICD-10-CM
Internet, 175
Interoperability, 5
Intranet, 175
IOM (Institute of Medicine), 31, 222
IT (Information Technology), 147

j

Jacobs, E., 240, 241

k

Known drug allergies, 78

l

LAN (local area network), 224
LaTour, K. M., 241
Legal requirements, 32–36; *see also specific laws*
    compliance, 130–131, 144–146
    knowledge of, 219
Libraries
    building, 126–127
    in PrimeSUITE, 48
Licensed Practical Nurse (LPN), 22
Live (real-time use), 179
Local area network (LAN), 224

m

MA (medical assistant), 22
Malware, 143
Managed care plans, 111, 115, 208
Managers, user rights for, 152
Managing information and communication, 174–185
    customizing displays, 180–181
    importing documents to the EHR, 177–178
    internal communications, 175–176
    master files, 179–180

    organizing work-task lists, 182–183
    reminders, 183–184
    templates, 179
MAR (medication administration record), 197
Master files, 179–180
Master Patient (Person) Index (MPI)/Patient list, 2, 37, 51–52, 209
MD (Doctor of Medicine), 22
Meaningful use (MU), 24, 33
    of administrative data, 50
    compliance with, 165
    ePrescribing, 96
    for evidence-based medicine, 223
    meeting standards of, 190–199
    problem list of diagnoses, 100
    in sharing health information, 160
    stages of, 33
Medicaid
    and adoption of EHR, 192
    coding rules of, 113
    EHR Incentive Programs, 36
    fraud, 121
Medical assistant (MA), 22
Medical dictation and transcription, 95
Medical history, 72–77
Medical necessity, 113
Medical record number, 51
Medically necessary tests/procedures, 121
Medicare
    ACO models from, 123
    coding rules of, 113
    Core Objectives, 190–191
    EHR Incentive Programs, 36
    fraud, 121, 130
    Menu Objectives, 191–192
    physician credentialing for, 211
Medicare Shared Savings program, 123
Medication administration record (MAR), 197
Medication list, 77
MedsFile.com, 222
Menachemi, N., 241
Menu Objectives, 191–192
Mertz, Jon, 239
Miaoulis, William M., 240
Microsoft Health Vault, 222
Minimum necessary information, 141
Moany Wright, Sandra, 239, 240
MPI; *see* Master Patient (Person) Index (MPI)/Patient list
MU; *see* Meaningful use

index